Leadership and Negotiation in the European Union

Jonas Tallberg offers a novel perspective on some of the most fundamental questions about international cooperation and European Union
politics. In the first systematic theoretical and empirical exploration of
the influence wielded by chairmen of multilateral negotiations, Tallberg
develops a rationalist theory of formal leadership and demonstrates its
explanatory power through carefully selected case studies of EU negotiations. He shows that the rotating Presidency of the EU constitutes a
power platform that grants governments unique opportunities to shape
the outcomes of negotiations. His provocative analysis establishes that
Presidents, while performing vital functions for the EU, simultaneously
exploit their privileged political position to favor national interests.
Extending the scope of the analysis to international negotiations on
trade, security, and the environment, Tallberg further demonstrates
that the influence of the EU Presidency is not an isolated occurrence
but the expression of a general phenomenon in world politics – the
power of the chair.

JONAS TALLBERG is an Associate Professor in the Department of
Political Science, Stockholm University and a Research Fellow at the
Swedish Institute of International Affairs. He has published numerous
articles on international cooperation and EU politics, and is the author
of *European Governance and Supranational Institutions: Making States
Comply* (2003).

Themes in European Governance

Series Editor

Andreas Føllesdal

Editorial Board

Stefano Bartolini
Beate Kohler-Koch
Percy Lehning
Andrew Moravcsik
Ulrich Preuss
Thomas Risse
Fritz W. Scharpf
Philip Schlesinger
Helen Wallace
Albert Weale
J. H. H. Weiler

The evolving European systems of governance, in particular the European Union, challenge and transform the state, the most important locus of governance and political identity and loyalty over the past 200 years. The series *Themes in European Governance* aims to publish the best theoretical and analytical scholarship on the impact of European governance on the core institutions, policies and identities of nation states. It focuses upon the implications for issues such as citizenship, welfare, political decision-making and economic, monetary and fiscal policies. An initiative of Cambridge University Press and the Programme on Advanced Research on the Europeanisation of the Nation-State (ARENA), Norway, the series includes contributions in the social sciences, humanities and law. The series aims to provide theoretically informed studies analysing key issues at the European level and within European states. Volumes in the series will be of interest to scholars and students of Europe both within Europe and worldwide. They will be of particular relevance to those interested in the development of sovereignty and governance of European states and in the issues raised by multi-level governance and multi-national integration throughout the world.

Other books in the series:
Paulette Kurzer *Markets and Moral Regulation: Cultural Change in the European Union*

Leadership and Negotiation in the European Union

Jonas Tallberg

CAMBRIDGE
UNIVERSITY PRESS

CAMBRIDGE UNIVERSITY PRESS
Cambridge, New York, Melbourne, Madrid, Cape Town, Singapore, São Paulo

CAMBRIDGE UNIVERSITY PRESS
The Edinburgh Building, Cambridge CB2 2RU, UK

Published in the United States of America by Cambridge University Press,
New York

www.cambridge.org
Information on this title: www.cambridge.org/9780521683036

First published 2006

Printed in the United Kingdom at the University Press, Cambridge

A catalogue record for this book is available from the British Library

ISBN-13 978-0-521-86452-7 hardback
ISBN-10 0-521-86452-6 hardback
ISBN-13 978-0-521-68303-6 paperback
ISBN-10 0-521-68303-3 paperback

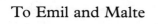
To Emil and Malte

Contents

Illustrations

Acknowledgments

One of the classic contributions to bargaining theory speaks of the *art* and *science* of negotiation. Better than ever before, I now understand that these are two entirely different things. While sharpening my ideas about international bargaining, the five years of work on this book have helped little in honing my negotiating skills. If intellectual stimulus and institutional support had to be won through guile and strategizing, rather than offered by generous colleagues and departments, then this project would not have reached the end.

This book originates from a collaborative research project at Lund University on the Presidency of the European Union. My most heartfelt thanks go to project colleagues Bo Bjurulf, Ole Elgström, Rikard Bengtsson, and Matilda Broman, whose contributions to my work and well-being over these five years have gone far beyond the intellectual. Next to this group, a large number of people have offered incisive comments and helpful suggestions of tremendous value. I especially want to acknowledge Karen Alter, Derek Beach, Simon Bulmer, Nicola Catellani, Elisabeth Corell, Kjell Goldmann, Gunnel Gustavsson, Kenneth Hanf, Adrienne Héritier, Madelaine Hosli, Christer Jönsson, Andrew Moravcsik, Ulrika Mörth, John Odell, Hanna Ojanen, Johan P. Olsen, Craig Parsons, Adriaan Schout, Philippa Sherrington, Gunnar Sjöstedt, Eric Stern, Maria Strömvik, Ulf Sverdrup, Helen Wallace, Oran Young, and the anonymous reviewers for Cambridge University Press.

I benefited greatly from presentations and discussions of this project at ARENA of the University of Oslo, Birkbeck College of the University of London, the Danish Institute of International Affairs, Lund University, McGill University, the Robert Schuman Centre of the European University Institute, Stockholm University, the Swedish Institute of International Affairs, Syracuse University, as well as conferences arranged by the ECPR Standing Group on International Relations, the International Studies Association, the Spanish Political Science Association, and the Swedish Political Science Association. Earlier versions of parts of the current manuscript appeared in a number of publications. I am grateful to Blackwell and Routledge for permission to draw on those texts here, as well as to the anonymous reviewers who offered constructive comments on those articles.

I am highly grateful to the Department of Political Science at Lund University for allowing me to spend an undue amount of time in Stockholm, and to the Swedish Institute of International Affairs for generously hosting me in Stockholm. Moreover, I wish to acknowledge the generous financial support of the Bank of Sweden Tercentenary Foundation, as well as the logistical support of the Department of Political Science at Stockholm University at the final stage of completing the book.

Finally, and on a personal note, I would like to thank my family for love, encouragement, and perspective. Your importance for my work – and all other aspects of my life – cannot be exaggerated. I dedicate this book to my sons Emil and Malte, both of whom were born during the work on the book – and both of whom already show a disconcerting willingness to exploit their father's shortcomings in the negotiations of everyday life.

Abbreviations

ACEA	European Automobile Manufacturers Association
APEC	Asia-Pacific Economic Cooperation
ASEAN	Association of South East Asian Nations
AU	African Union
BATNA	best alternative to a negotiated agreement
BEAR	Barents Euro-Arctic Regional Council
CAP	Common Agricultural Policy
CBSS	Council of Baltic Sea States
CFCs	chlorofluorocarbons
CFSP	common foreign and security policy
CiO	Chairman-in-Office
Coreper	Committee of Permanent Representatives
CSCE	Conference on Security and Cooperation in Europe
EC	European Community
ECSC	European Coal and Steel Community
EEC	European Economic Community
EFTA	European Free Trade Association
EGARA	European Group of Automotive Recycling Associations
EMU	Economic and Monetary Union
EPC	European political cooperation
EU	European Union
FCMA Treaty	Friendship, Cooperation and Mutual Assistance Treaty
G8	Group of Eight
GATT	General Agreement on Tariffs and Trade
IAEA	International Atomic Energy Agency
IGC	intergovernmental conference
IMF	International Monetary Fund
INC	Intergovernmental Negotiating Committee
JHA	justice and home affairs
LOS	law of the sea

NATO	North Atlantic Treaty Organization
NGO	non-governmental organization
NNA	neutral and non-aligned Countries
OECD	Organisation for Economic Cooperation and Development
OEEC	Organisation for European Economic Cooperation
OSCE	Organization for Security and Cooperation in Europe
QMV	qualified majority voting
SEA	Single European Act
TEU	Treaty on European Union
TNC	Trade Negotiations Committee
UK	United Kingdom
UN	United Nations
UNCLOS	United Nations Conference on the Law of the Sea
UNEP	United Nations Environmental Programme
UNFCCC	United Nations Framework Convention on Climate Change
US	United States
WTO	World Trade Organization

1 Introduction

Multilateral negotiations today constitute the most prominent method by which states address joint problems, resolve disagreements, and formulate common norms in world politics. Yet international relations (IR) scholars still grapple with the most fundamental questions raised by this practice, pertaining to issues of efficiency and distribution in international cooperation. Why do some negotiations lead to agreements that exploit all possible joint gains, whereas others collapse or produce sub-optimal bargains? Why are some states more successful than others in securing benefits from multilateral agreements?

This book is about the influence wielded by the formal leaders of multilateral negotiations – those state or supranational representatives that chair and direct negotiations in the major decision bodies of international organizations and conferences. The book offers a systematic theoretical and empirical exploration of formal leadership in multilateral bargaining. It conceives of the chairmanship as a power platform in international politics, and argues that actors in control of this office enjoy unique opportunities to shape the outcomes of multilateral negotiations. Formal leaders fulfill functions that make it more likely for negotiations to succeed and possess privileged resources that make it possible to steer negotiations toward the agreements they most prefer.

In the book, I present and test a theory of formal leadership that synthesizes elements of rational choice institutionalism and general bargaining theory. The theory develops a coherent argument for the origin of the chairmanship as an institutional form in decision-making, for the power resources of negotiation chairs, and for the effects of formal leadership on the outcomes of multilateral bargaining. It positions negotiation chairs in the strategic context of multilateral negotiations, where politics is shaped by interests, information, and institutions. The theory generates predictions about when, why, and how negotiation chairs wield influence over the efficiency and distributional outcomes of multilateral negotiations.

I assess the explanatory power of this theory through an in-depth study of negotiations in the European Union (EU), as well as a review of comparative evidence from regime negotiations on security, trade, and the environment. In the EU, the Presidency office has rotated between the member states of the organization for nearly five decades. I show that the powers of the Presidency historically have evolved in response to functional pressures in EU cooperation and a continuous search by European governments for efficient forms of intergovernmental decision-making. On the basis of six carefully selected case studies, I further demonstrate that the Presidency constitutes a power platform in EU bargaining, permitting governments at the helm to raise the efficiency of negotiations and steer outcomes in their own favor.

The question of whether the European experience is unique or can be generalized to other areas of international cooperation is confronted through a review of negotiations in three institutional settings that vary in the organizational design of the chairmanship: the Conference on Security and Cooperation in Europe (CSCE) and its successor, the Organization for Security and Cooperation in Europe (OSCE); the General Agreement on Tariffs and Trade (GATT) and its successor, the World Trade Organization (WTO); and United Nations (UN) conferences on the law of the sea, the ozone layer, and climate change. The comparative record suggests that the influence of the Presidency in EU negotiations is not an isolated occurrence, but an expression of a general phenomenon in world politics – the power of the chair.

For most policy-makers and everyday negotiators, the argument that "the chair matters" is uncontroversial. Regardless of whether they themselves have directed international negotiations, or experienced the effects of other actors' access to this power platform, they tend to recognize the political implications of the chairmanship. In fact, most people who have ever served as chairmen would probably admit that this position is accompanied by a capacity to affect decision-making through resources that other participants do not enjoy.

However, political scientists have been slow to acknowledge the power of the chair and so far are unable to provide a theoretically grounded explanation of when, why, and how formal leadership matters. The main explanation is the widespread and convenient assumption in most bargaining analysis that the parties are functionally and formally equivalent – a product of this sub-field's heritage from game theory. Negotiation is seen as a process between actors that enjoy the same formal status, but differ in terms of power capabilities, preferences, information, ideas, and alternatives to negotiated agreements.[1] Where existing

---

[1] For overviews of the literature on international negotiation, see Zartman 1994b; Hampson with Hart 1995, ch. 1; Hopmann 1996; Starkey, Boyer, and Wilkenfeld 1999; Jönsson 2002; Kremenyuk 2002.

literature stresses the importance of political leadership or entrepreneurship, this is typically conceptualized as informal influence, anchored in structural power, entrepreneurial capacity, or intellectual capital – not in formal power positions.[2] Yet, as I demonstrate in this book, what distinguishes negotiation chairs from other actors in multilateral bargaining is the formal control over the nature of the game, which offers unique opportunities for influence over the outcomes of negotiations.

The argument in this book carries implications for ongoing debates in political science on negotiation and decision-making. At a general theoretical level, it challenges accounts that depict negotiations as a naturally efficient process, explains why chairmen frequently emerge as driving political forces, calls for a revised understanding of bargaining power, and offers a theory of formal leadership that can be extended to political decision-making in general. At the specific level of EU politics, it explains how the Presidency enables national governments to reach efficient agreements without recourse to mediation by supranational institutions, why EU accords often are tilted toward the interests of the state currently at the helm, and why the rotating Presidency has been subject to a reform debate in recent years.

The theory: formal leadership in multilateral negotiations

In a nutshell, the theory presented in this book suggests that multilateral bargaining is subject to collective-action problems that lead states to delegate functions of agenda management, brokerage, and representation to the chairmanship of international organizations and multilateral conferences. With these functions follow a set of power resources: asymmetrical access to information and asymmetrical control over procedure. By executing the functions they have been delegated, and by wielding these resources to collective benefit, formal leaders help states negotiate more efficiently. Yet the very same informational and procedural advantages may be exploited for private gain as well. While constrained by formal institutional rules, opportunistic chairs seek to promote the negotiation outcomes most conformant with their own interests, with implications for the distribution of gains in international cooperation.

This logic of this theory, developed at length in Chapter 2, can be conveniently summarized as two straightforward arguments about

---

[2] Sandholtz and Zysman 1989; O. Young 1991, 1999a; Underdal 1994; Hampson with Hart 1995; Malnes 1995; Moravcsik 1999a; Sjöstedt 1999. For a recent contribution that shares this book's ambition to theorize the influence of formal leaders, see Odell 2005.

the demand for, and supply of, formal leadership. The core of the first argument is a functionalist claim about the origin of the chairmanship as an institutional form. At the most general level, it purports to explain why the chairmanship today is a standard feature in political decision-making bodies, whether local, national, or international. In the international context, it seeks to explain why national governments, sensitive to challenges of their sovereign authority, agree to create and empower formal institutions of process control in multilateral decision bodies. The theory provides a functionalist answer to this puzzle, suggesting that the rationale of the chairmanship as an institutional form is its capacity to mitigate collective-action problems in decentralized bargaining.

More specifically, this argument points to three forms of collective-action problems that risk preventing efficient exchange. Agenda failure refers to the absence of progress in negotiations because of shifting, overcrowded, or underdeveloped agendas. Negotiation failure refers to deadlocks and breakdowns in bargaining that are caused by the parties' inability to identify the underlying zone of agreement, because of stratagems that conceal or distort their true preferences. Finally, representation failure refers to restrictions in cooperation that arise from the absence of a formula for how the group of negotiating states should be represented *vis-à-vis* third parties.

The theory further posits that states, in order to escape or reduce these collective-action problems, delegate powers of process control to the chairmanship of international organizations and multilateral conferences. These process powers comprise functions of agenda management, brokerage, and representation, which answer directly to the functional demands in decentralized bargaining. As agenda manager, the chair is expected to delimit and structure the agenda, thus making it negotiable. As broker, the chair is expected to facilitate agreement by engineering compromise proposals around which bargaining can converge. As representative, the chair is expected to act as the external agent of the collective negotiation group, ensuring convergence on common positions *vis-à-vis* third parties.

The second argument speaks to the effects of empowering chairmanship offices in international cooperation. It seeks to explain why the chairmanship, once vested with powers of process control, becomes a political platform with implications for the efficiency and distribution of gains in multilateral bargaining. The theory specifies the informational and procedural resources of negotiation chairs, as well as the formal constraints under which they operate. Furthermore, it explains why and how the particular design of the chairmanship affects possibilities, constraints, and dynamics in the supply of formal leadership.

The theory suggests that the influence of negotiation chairs is derived from informational and procedural power resources integral to the office and the functions they have been delegated. By virtue of their position, formal leaders obtain private information about the parties' resistance points, acquire an unusual expertise in the dossiers under negotiation, and develop a superior command of formal negotiation procedure. Furthermore, negotiation chairs enjoy asymmetrical control over the procedural parameters of multilateral negotiations, ranging from general decisions on the sequence, frequency, and method of negotiation, to specific decisions on the agenda, conduct, and results of individual negotiation sessions.

By drawing on these power resources, negotiation chairs can help states overcome bargaining impediments that prevent the realization of collective gains. Privileged access to information enables formal leaders to construct viable compromises. Privileged control over procedure permits formal leaders to structure the negotiation process and individual sessions in ways favorable to agreement. But the very same power resources may be exploited to pursue private gains as well. The theory posits that opportunistic chairs will seek to exploit this exclusive preference information and procedural control to promote agreements whose distributional implications they privately favor. The influence of negotiation chairs over bargaining outcomes therefore comprises both efficiency and distribution.

However, formal leaders are not free to impose their will on other parties in multilateral negotiations. The theory conceives of the formal institutional environment as an intervening factor that conditions when, where, and how negotiation chairs exert influence over outcomes. Agenda-setting rules influence the capacity of negotiation chairs to promote or block proposals. Decision rules shape the ease with which formal leaders can favor proposals that satisfy the requirements of an efficient agreement and meet the partisan interests of the chair. The institutional design of the chairmanship – rotation between states, election of one state's representative, or appointment of a supranational official – shapes the control mechanisms states put in place and the resultant room for maneuver of negotiation chairs.

To summarize: this theory offers testable propositions about the demand for, and supply of, formal leadership in multilateral negotiations. Privileging interests, information, and institutions as explanatory variables, it generates specific hypotheses about the conditions under which states are likely to delegate powers to formal leaders, and the conditions under which formal leaders are likely to influence outcomes in multilateral bargaining.

The evidence: negotiations in the European Union and beyond

The empirical heartland of this book is negotiations in the European Union. Since the late 1950s, the Presidency of the EU has rotated between the member states on a six-month basis. The government which holds the Presidency is responsible for the chairmanship of the working groups, committees, and ministerial meetings in the Council of Ministers – the EU's central decision forum – as well as the summits of heads of state and government in the European Council.[3]

The research design

The influence of the Presidency in EU negotiations is the subject of a limited body of literature that is predominantly atheoretical and descriptive in orientation, and rarely attempts to communicate with general theoretical debates on negotiation and decision-making.[4] Slightly simplified, studies of the Presidency split into three major categories. The first category consists of descriptions of the functioning of the Presidency, often in the context of general accounts of the Council and EU decision-making.[5] The second consists of studies of individual Presidencies, where the main ambition is to evaluate the performance of a member state during its period at the helm.[6] The third category

---

[3] For overviews of the structure and functioning of the Council, see Wallace 2002; Westlake and Galloway with Digneffe 2004; Hayes-Renshaw and Wallace 2006. For a full listing of Presidencies since 1958, see Appendix. The EU Constitutional Treaty of 2004 foresees changes to the organization of the chairmanship in select intergovernmental bodies. At present, it appears unlikely that this treaty will be ratified by all member states. However, in the concluding chapter, I explain how the theory advanced in this book sheds important light on the sources and potential effects of the proposed reforms.

[4] The substantive literature on intergovernmental and inter-institutional bargaining in the EU tends to draw on general theories of negotiation and decision-making, but typically makes few attempts to integrate the Presidency into these theoretical models. For a similar assessment, see Schmidt 2001. On intergovernmental bargaining at constitutional conferences, see Laursen and Vanhoonacker 1992; Edwards and Pijpers 1997; Moravcsik 1998; Moravcsik and Nicolaïdis 1999; Laursen 2002; Beach 2005. On inter-institutional legislative bargaining, see Mesquita and Stokman 1994; Steunenberg 1994; Crombez 1996; Golub 1999; Tsebelis and Garrett 2000; Thomson, Stokman, Achen, and König 2006.

[5] Edwards and Wallace 1977; Wallace 1985; Bassompierre 1988; Kirchner 1992; Wurzel 1996; Schout 1998; Sherrington 2000, 41–44, 172–175; Westlake and Galloway with Digneffe 2004, ch. 18; Hayes-Renshaw and Wallace 2006, ch. 5.

[6] E.g., O Nuallain 1985; Kirchner and Tsagkari 1993; Ludlow 1998; Martikainen and Tiilikainen 2000; Maurer 2000; Lequesne 2001; Tallberg 2001; *Cooperation and Conflict* 2003.

is composed of the limited number of works that draw on general political science theories of agenda setting, negotiation, and mediation, in order to explain the role and influence of the Presidency in EU decision-making.[7]

With few exceptions, this literature is highly skeptical about Presidencies' capacity to steer outcomes in their own favor. This perspective is frequently summarized in a statement by Jean-Louis Dewost, former head of the Council's Legal Service, who describes the Presidency as a "*responsabilité sans pouvoir*" – a responsibility without power.[8] If we disaggregate this influential position into substantive claims about influence, three arguments are particularly prominent: (1) the chairmanship has not been conferred any formal powers of initiative and Presidencies therefore cannot set the EU's policy agenda; (2) Presidencies are constrained by existing policy agendas and by external or unexpected events that require their attention; and (3) the influential norm of the neutral Presidency forces governments at the helm to eschew the pursuit of national interests.

The research design of this book breaks with that of existing research on the EU Presidency. Instead of general descriptions of the office or impressionistic evaluations of governments' performance in the chair, I provide a detailed historical tracing of the development of the Presidency, as well as six case studies of Presidency influence in EU negotiations. The empirical examination is specifically designed to test the theory of formal leadership, and does not attempt to explain, for instance, variation between states in the conduct of the Presidency.[9] The case study approach allows for detailed process tracing, involving a reconstruction of the negotiations, a tracking of causal mechanisms, and an evaluation of the influence of the Presidency.[10] Demonstrating influence requires more than observing that a Presidency government was active and negotiations eventually were successful – process tracing makes such a qualified evaluation possible. Furthermore, I engage in counterfactual analysis in order to assess whether a particular Presidency's contribution was original or redundant.[11] In all cases,

---

[7] Metcalfe 1998; Svensson 2000; Elgström 2003a; Kollman 2003; Tallberg 2003a, 2004; Bengtsson, Elgström, and Tallberg 2004.

[8] Dewost 1984, 31.

[9] This is a common theme in existing literature, which traditionally has emphasized national political traits, such as economic and administrative capabilities, attitude toward European integration, and domestic political context. For a recent comparative exploration of EU Presidencies, see Elgström 2003b.

[10] George and McKeown 1985; King, Keohane, and Verba 1994; George and Bennett 2005.

[11] Fearon 1991; Tetlock and Belkin 1996.

Table 1.1. *The cases*

Agenda management	Brokerage	Representation
German Presidency and car recycling directive	German Presidency and Agenda 2000 reforms	Swedish Presidency and EU transparency rules
Finnish Presidency and Northern Dimension initiative	French Presidency and IGC 2000 reforms	Danish Presidency and EU enlargement talks

I evaluate the likelihood that the negotiations would have resulted in the same outcome, had another member state, with different preferences, been in control of the Presidency. The empirical evidence presented in the study is based on primary documents, secondary sources, and interviews with representatives of EU governments and institutions.

The cases, summarized in Table 1.1, are drawn from the German, Finnish, French, Swedish, and Danish Presidencies in the time period 1999–2002, and cover the issue areas of enlargement, institutional reform, environmental policy, budgetary policy, and foreign policy. The selection is based on three considerations. First, I have systematically selected cases where the Presidency government holds preferences at one end of the spectrum, which makes it relatively easier to empirically trace and demonstrate influence over distributional outcomes, compared to cases where Presidencies hold central preferences.[12] Moreover, it is relatively more difficult for Presidencies with extreme preferences to achieve their most preferred outcome, which grants the cases I have selected least-likely qualities. Naturally, this selection criterion also means that the cases chosen exclusively involve dossiers where the Presidencies in question possess distinct and known preferences, rather than diffuse, unknown, or even non-existing preferences. Second, I have chosen cases to ensure variation in formal agenda-setting and decision rules, identified as important intervening variables in the theory of

---

[12] In cases where Presidencies hold central preferences, their favored agreement is not likely to differ substantially from the expected equilibrium agreement. Whereas Presidencies might mobilize their privileged resources to make sure that the outcome stays close to the expected equilibrium, these efforts will appear as consensus building around the median preference. Where Presidencies, by contrast, hold extreme preferences, we would expect to see active exploitation of the chair's informational and procedural resources for purposes of shifting outcomes away from the expected equilibrium and toward their own ideal point, that is, from the center and toward the end of the spectrum of preferences.

formal leadership. Third, I have selected cases from a broad range of issue areas, including both high- and low-profile dossiers, as well as multiple Presidencies, involving both large and small member states, in order to control for political salience and state capability, which existing literature frequently points to as determinants of Presidency influence. The implications of these selection criteria for the capacity to generalize the findings are discussed in the concluding chapter of the book.

The findings

The central empirical findings of the book can be summarized in three arguments about the historical development of the Presidency office, the influence of Presidency governments in EU negotiations, and the patterns of formal leadership in international bargaining at large.

First, the historical evidence presented in Chapter 4 strongly suggests that the Presidency office has evolved in response to functional demands in EU negotiations, stemming from experienced or anticipated problems of agenda failure, negotiation failure, and representation failure. When first established in 1957, the Presidency possessed only weak procedural responsibilities. Its subsequent evolution into an office with substantial functions in agenda management, brokerage, and representation has gone hand in hand with developments in the EU's internal decision-making environment and external political ambitions. EU governments have continuously adjusted and extended the functions of the Presidency in search of more efficient methods of intergovernmental cooperation.

The office of the Presidency was delegated agenda-management functions in response to a decreasing capacity of the European Commission to dictate the European Community's (EC) substantive agenda, and a growing fragmentation in Council decision-making that made agendas increasingly unwieldy and uncoordinated. Next to the creation of the European Council in 1974, the strengthening of the Presidency constituted member states' primary solution for ensuring coordination of the political agenda across decision-making bodies. One central component of this strategy was the introduction in the 1980s of the Presidency program, whereby governments at the helm assign priority to the issues on the political agenda and structure meeting agendas to this end.

The engagement of the Presidency as broker was the product of a growing complexity in EC decision-making that rendered it more difficult to identify potential agreements, and of institutional reforms that created a demand for more active mediation. Whereas the Commission had taken on brokerage responsibilities in the early years of European integration, the Presidency developed into member governments' preferred architect of compromise from the late 1960s and onwards. To facilitate brokerage, the Presidency was equipped with specific mediation instruments, notably, the practice of bilateral confessionals, through which member states offer the Presidency privileged information about national bottom lines.

Yet nowhere are the functional pressures behind the development of the Presidency's powers as prominent as in the area of representation. The Presidency's function as an internal representative in interinstitutional legislative negotiations developed in direct response to the need for a Council negotiator *vis-à-vis* the European Parliament. By the same token, the Presidency constituted member governments' preferred choice as external representative when the EC, from the early 1970s and onwards, sought to present a unified foreign policy front *vis-à-vis* the rest of the world.

The second important finding is comprehensive empirical evidence in favor of the Presidency office as a platform for political influence in European cooperation. The six case studies in Chapters 4 to 6 demonstrate that Presidency governments raise the efficiency of EU bargaining, while simultaneously steering negotiations in their own favor. The functions performed by the Presidency enable member states to negotiate on the basis of delimited agendas, uncover underlying zones of agreement, and present coordinated positions *vis-à-vis* third parties. Yet, regardless of structural power capabilities, EU governments simultaneously exploit the chairmanship for national political purposes, wielding its privileged power resources for private gain.

The management of the agenda permits Presidencies to assign priority to competing political concerns. The cases drawn from the Finnish and German Presidencies in 1999 demonstrate that Presidencies' influence over the agenda both takes the shape of traditional agenda setting and includes forms of non-decision-making. Presidencies call attention to prioritized concerns by including them in the official Presidency program, scheduling informal meetings devoted to these issues, and placing proposals on the formal agenda, directly or indirectly. Presidencies downplay nationally sensitive issues by refusing to recognize their political salience, assigning limited negotiation time, or even dropping dossiers from formal decision agendas.

The engineering of intergovernmental bargains permits Presidencies to select among multiple potential agreements and steer negotiations toward outcomes they privately prefer. The cases drawn from the German and French Presidencies in 1999 and 2000 illustrate that the institutional practices specifically developed to aid the Presidency serve double purposes. Presidencies use privileged information obtained through bilateral consultations to extract concessions from adversaries, and single negotiating texts to keep desired components on the negotiation table and unwelcome options away from it. Furthermore, Presidencies speed up negotiations and improve the chances of agreement on nationally prioritized issues through decisions on the frequency and format of bargaining sessions.

The representative function in internal and external bargaining grants Presidencies the opportunity to influence the terms of agreements negotiated with third parties. The cases drawn from the Swedish and Danish Presidencies in 2001 and 2002 suggest that the engagement of the Presidency as representative presents EU governments with a classic principal–agent problem, involving divergent preferences, incomplete control, and agent discretion. Privileged by informational and procedural asymmetries, Presidencies attempt to steer negotiations with third parties toward their own ideal outcome. More specifically, Presidencies exploit the position at the interface between two nested bargaining arenas to play off recalcitrant parties against each other, initiate informal negotiations beyond the control of government principals, and negotiate *fait accompli* agreements.

These findings support a perspective on the Presidency office as a negotiation institution that allows EU governments to overcome bargaining impediments, and whose distributional implications are made acceptable to the member states through the system of rotation. The alternation of the Presidency avoids the concentration of chairmanship power in one member state or supranational institution, by granting each government, in turn, a privileged opportunity to shape EU policymaking. Slightly simplified, governments accept the exploitation of the Presidency in the present, because they will get their chance in the future. As a high-ranking European Commission official pointedly expressed it in one of the interviews conducted for this book: "When you are not the Presidency, you are swallowing bitter pills every day, only because you know that you will have the Presidency one day and the others will have to swallow their bitter pills. You suffer for six years and in the seventh you get to bash the others. The Presidencies are always overstepping the limits of neutral behavior. What you want is a Presidency that is skillfully violating you so that it is not publicly visible."[13]

The third important finding of the book pertains to the capacity to generalize these results. While lending support to the theory of formal

---

[13] Interview, 9 February 2001.

leadership, the evidence from EU negotiations simultaneously raises questions about the explanatory reach of the theory. Is the phenomenon of negotiation chairs who wield power and influence outcomes isolated to the EU, or is it a general feature of international cooperation? To address this question, Chapter 7 places the European experience in a comparative perspective and considers evidence from the CSCE/OSCE, the GATT/WTO, and the UN conferences on the law of the sea, the ozone layer, and climate change. Each negotiation context conforms to one of the alternative ways of organizing the chairmanship, which allows us to test the hypothesis that institutional design shapes the discretion and influence of negotiation chairs. The comparison suggests that the European experience is far from exceptional. In all contexts, formal leaders have been delegated central functions in the negotiations and influenced outcomes. Yet the kind of powers the chairmanship office has been equipped with and the form of influence formal leaders have exerted vary across the three settings.

The comparative evidence endorses the claim that functional demands drive the delegation of tasks and responsibilities to the chairmanship. States empower formal leaders to address collective-action problems whose removal makes it easier to negotiate efficient agreements. The cases reveal how the powers conferred on formal leaders vary with the particular pattern of functional needs in a negotiation setting, as well as the presence of alternative leaders performing similar functional tasks. Whereas East–West dialog in the CSCE mainly gave rise to a strong demand for third-party brokerage, the expansion of the OSCE's operational activities during the 1990s led governments to delegate substantial powers of agenda management and representation. In the GATT/WTO, the high level of issue conflict and the demanding consensus rule have produced a strong demand for brokerage, whereas the practice of US–EU pre-negotiations over trade priorities has limited the demand for agenda management. The UN-sponsored environmental negotiations all illustrate how broad conference mandates and equal agenda-setting rights easily produce overcrowded negotiation agendas, leading the parties to endow the conference chairmanships with important agenda-management and brokerage powers, especially the power to formulate single negotiating texts. Neither global trade rounds nor multilateral environmental conferences have produced a demand for representation by formal leaders.

The comparative record further underscores the argument that formal leaders in international cooperation possess informational and procedural resources that enable them to influence outcomes, but are constrained by formal institutional rules. These international negotiations offer several illustrations of formal leaders who have facilitated interstate agreement, particularly as brokers engaging in bilateral consultations, extracting concessions, and developing single negotiating texts. The evidence on distributional influence is less clear-cut. In trade and environmental negotiations, as well as in the CSCE during the Cold War, the combination of highly divergent preferences and demanding decision rules greatly restricted the capacity of negotiation chairs to shape distributional outcomes. In the OSCE, however, independent executive powers grant the governments at the helm discretion in agenda management and representation, with implications for the relative priority assigned to competing political concerns. The empirical evidence points to the institutional design of the chairmanship as a powerful explanation. Where states institute rotating chairmanships, they are less concerned with issues of control and grant more extensive discretion to negotiation chairs, than in cases where they elect a chairman from one of the parties or delegate this task to a supranational official.

The implications: leadership, efficiency, and distribution

The argument in this book carries important implications for the study of EU politics and international cooperation, developed at length in Chapter 8. More specifically, it forces us to reconsider three aspects of negotiation and decision-making in Europe and beyond.

First, this book helps to explain why intergovernmental negotiations in the EU often lead to efficient agreements, and why interventions by supranational actors tend to be redundant. The empirical argument about the Presidency thus speaks to the ongoing debate in EU studies on the influence of supranational institutions versus national governments. Contributions highlighting supranational entrepreneurship typically emphasize scarcities of information and ideas in EU negotiations, and suggest that the Commission helps governments to overcome these bottlenecks. By contrast, intergovernmentalist analyses typically present EU bargaining as a process where the member states themselves are fully capable of removing whatever collective-action problems impede efficient exchange.

This book lends support to the intergovernmentalist claim by specifying perhaps the most important institutional mechanism that enables governments to reach efficient bargains. Through the rotating Presidency, governments take turns in providing the efficiency-enhancing functions of agenda management, brokerage, and representation, leaving limited demand for supranational entrepreneurship. The performance of these tasks by Presidencies has been made possible by a gradual conferral of process powers to the chairmanship, in response to collective-action problems in EU cooperation. In this search for a more efficient institutional framework for intergovernmental cooperation, the Commission has often constituted an alternative solution. Yet, increasingly aware of the Commission's political agenda, EU governments have in most cases eschewed the services of the supranational executive and instead strengthened the authority of the rotating Presidency, thus retaining control over outcomes among themselves.

Second, this book challenges the dominant perspective on negotiation efficiency and political leadership in game-theoretical bargaining analysis. This literature typically conceives of decentralized negotiations as naturally efficient, involving no, or low, transaction costs. Bargaining and decision-making take place on a frictionless "spot market." The central dilemma for negotiators is the tension between cooperative and competitive moves, not impediments in the process of bargaining. States possess sufficient information about each other's preferences to identify mutually beneficial agreements, and face no shortage of ideas or focal points around which specific agreements can be constructed. This perspective on negotiation efficiency translates into a skeptical position on the potential contribution of leaders and entrepreneurs in multilateral bargaining. If transaction costs are low or non-existent, there will be little demand for political leadership, which will prove either redundant or futile.

This book grants support to a competing perspective, where bargaining impediments and transaction costs are normal and ever-present ingredients of the negotiation process and political leadership is in demand. It suggests that the very existence of the chairmanship as an institutional form is a direct effect of those very bargaining impediments that many game-theoretical models assume do not exist. It claims that we cannot understand the delegation of agenda management, brokerage, and representation functions to chairmanship institutions, unless we recognize the collective-action problems that motivate states to empower formal leaders. It supports this theoretical argument with extensive empirical material, demonstrating how states in the EU and elsewhere turn to formal leaders for help when confronted with overloaded agendas, deadlocked negotiations, or an absence of institutional formulas for representation *vis-à-vis* third parties.

Third, this book suggests that traditional conceptions of bargaining power must be revised if they are to properly explain the outcomes of multilateral negotiations. The dominant perspective on bargaining power in the literature states that the distribution of gains will reflect the parties' best alternatives to a negotiated agreement. The better this alternative is, the greater a party's bargaining power will be. This proposition has also been formulated in terms of preference intensity and asymmetrical interdependence. The party with the most to gain from an agreement will be most eager to conclude a deal and therefore most willing to offer concessions. Conversely, a party with an attractive back-up alternative will be less eager to conclude an agreement at any cost and therefore less willing to offer concessions.

This book does not offer an alternative comprehensive theory of bargaining power. But it demonstrates why the conventional wisdom must be supplemented with an understanding of the power wielded by formal leaders. More specifically, the book identifies the informational and procedural power resources of negotiation chairs, and explains when, why, and how these privileged resources permit formal leaders to shift outcomes away from the equilibria predicted by traditional bargaining theory. International agreements with distributional conditions unusually conformant with the interests of formal leaders should not present a puzzle.

The plan of the book

This introduction is followed by seven chapters. Chapter 2 presents the theory of formal leadership. I describe the functional logic behind the delegation of agenda-management, brokerage, and representation functions to the chairmanship office, identify information and procedural control as the primary power resources of negotiation chairs, and present hypotheses about when, how, and why formal leaders influence the efficiency and distributional outcomes of multilateral negotiations. Furthermore, I outline briefly what an alternative theoretical perspective, grounded in sociological institutionalism, would present as the sources, resources, and effects of formal leadership in multilateral negotiations.

Chapter 3 traces the historical development of the office of the EU Presidency, from its inception in 1957 to today. The analysis covers the evolution of each of the three key functions – agenda management, brokerage, and representation. The examination of each function is further subdivided into assessments of the Presidency's evolving role in multiple areas of EU activity, effectively raising the number of empirical observations. The chapter's central argument is that EU governments have delegated political responsibilities to the Presidency in response to experienced or anticipated collective-action problems. The evolution of the Presidency office reflects a continuous search on the part of EU governments for more effective forms of negotiation and decision-making.

Chapters 4 to 6 explore the Presidency's capacity to influence the outcomes of EU negotiations within the functions of agenda management, brokerage, and representation. In each chapter, I first identify the key parameters of the strategic context in which the Presidency executes its particular function, and then present the case studies. The general argument in these chapters is that the Presidency office presents the incumbent with opportunities to favor its own national interests, in the process of raising the overall efficiency of the negotiations. Chapter 4 covers the efforts of the German Presidency in 1999 to prevent the adoption of a domestically problematic EU directive on car recycling, and the Finnish Presidency's campaign that same year to anchor the proposal for a northern dimension in EU foreign policy on the political agenda. Chapter 5 examines the German Presidency's brokering of a compromise on the so-called Agenda 2000 reform package, as well as the French Presidency's engineering of an agreement on the Nice Treaty in 2000. Chapter 6 explores the Swedish Presidency's negotiations with the European Parliament in 2001 on a European freedom of information act, and the Danish Presidency's negotiations with ten prospective EU members over the terms of their accession agreements.

Chapter 7 puts the European experience in a comparative, international perspective, examining evidence on formal leadership in security, trade, and environmental negotiations. I conclude that the pattern of delegation to the various chairmanship institutions reflects varying functional demands in the three negotiation settings. The chapter further identifies the institutional design of the chairmanship as a central explanation for the varying extent to which rotating, elected, and supranational negotiation chairs are capable of influencing the distributional dimension of multilateral agreements.

Chapter 8 concludes the book, summarizing its findings and outlining its implications for the study of negotiation and decision-making in EU studies and IR theory. I explain how the book's argument about the Presidency challenges prevailing conceptions of efficiency and distribution in EU negotiations, and sheds important light on the sources and potential effects of proposals to reform this office. Expanding beyond the European context, I discuss the book's findings for international cooperation at large, and identify its challenges to existing notions of negotiation efficiency, bargaining power, and leadership in IR theory.

2 Formal leadership: a rational institutionalist theory

The central argument of this book is that the empowerment of chairmanship institutions in international cooperation reflects a rational response by states to collective-action problems in decentralized bargaining, and enables formal leaders both to raise the likelihood of negotiation success and to favor their own preferred outcome. This chapter presents in greater detail the logic of this theoretical argument, summarized in Figure 2.1.

The theory of formal leadership draws on rational choice institutionalism, originally developed in the study of American politics and subsequently imported into IR theory: a view of politics as a series of contracting dilemmas that may prevent or inhibit mutually advantageous exchange; a functionalist approach to institutional choice and development; a conception of states as rational actors that behave instrumentally in the pursuit of their preferences; a recognition of the agency problems inherent in the processes of delegation; and a perspective on formal rules as enabling and constraining factors.[1] Simultaneously, this theory integrates core elements of rationalist bargaining theory: a recognition of the collective-action problems involved in complex multilateral negotiations; an emphasis on the tension between cooperative and competitive negotiation moves; an appreciation of information as a bargaining asset; a perspective on leaders and entrepreneurs as strategic actors; and an analysis of negotiated outcomes in terms of efficiency and distribution.[2] The epistemological affinity between the two literatures is substantial, and the scope for synergies in theory development significant and important.[3]

---

[1] For overviews, see Hall and Taylor 1996; Peters 1999; Schneider and Aspinwall 2001; Weingast 2002.
[2] For overviews, see H. Young 1991; Hopmann 1996.
[3] For a discussion of the value of combining negotiation analysis and rational choice institutionalism, especially principal–agent theory, see Nicolaïdis 1999.

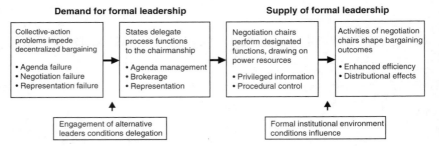

Figure 2.1. Formal leadership: a rational institutionalist theory

The theory of formal leadership is causal, conditional, and can be generalized. It generates testable cause-and-effect propositions about the delegation of process powers to the chairmanship, and about the influence of negotiation chairs on political outcomes. The theory is conditional, in that it isolates sources of variation in the demand for and supply of formal leadership, and should not be misunderstood as an argument that negotiation chairs are always powerful and influential in international cooperation. It is deliberately formulated in general theoretical terms, since the logic is extendable to decision-making at other levels of political organization. The formulation of causal, conditional, and generalizable propositions distinguishes this theory from previous attempts in the literature to explore the role of chairmen, and answers to calls for systematic theorizing about the conditions under which negotiation chairs matter in multilateral cooperation.[4]

The chapter is divided into three parts. The first part explains why decentralized bargaining gives rise to a number of collective-action problems, and why the delegation of agenda-management, brokerage, and representational powers to the chairmanship constitutes a functional solution to these problems. The second part explains why the office of the chairmanship, once vested with powers of process control, becomes a political platform with implications for the efficiency and distribution of gains in multilateral negotiation. I isolate the informational and procedural resources of the chairmanship, identify the formal institutional factors that shape the provision of formal leadership, and explain how the actions of negotiation chairs affect outcomes in world politics. The third part of the chapter describes briefly what an alternative theoretical

---

[4] Lang 1989; Antrim and Sebenius 1992; Underdal 1994.

perspective, drawn from sociological institutionalism, would present as the sources, resources, and effects of formal leadership in multilateral negotiations.

The demand for formal leadership

Why do national governments, highly sensitive to challenges of their decision-making authority, agree to vest powers of process control in a specific office: the chairmanship? More generally, why is the institution of the chairmanship a standard feature in political decision-making organs? The theory of formal leadership provides a distinctly functionalist answer to this puzzle: the rationale of the chairmanship as an institutional form is its capacity to solve or mitigate collective-action problems that arise in decentralized bargaining.

A functionalist explanation of institutional design

Functionalist explanations account for causes in terms of their effects, and constitute the preferred approach of rational choice theorists for dealing with questions of institutional creation and design. In the study of international cooperation, for instance, theorists have explained the demand for international institutions in general, and the delegation of powers to supranational institutions in particular, with the functional benefits to states of such arrangements.[5] A similar functionalist explanation has been advanced to account for the organization of legislative–executive relations in American politics, and the delegation of powers to regulatory agencies, constitutional courts, and central banks.[6] In sum: "Institutions, in the rational choice perspective, are designed to overcome identifiable shortcomings in the market or the political system as means of producing collectively desirable outcomes."[7]

The functionalist argument about institutional design should not be misunderstood as a claim that a certain institution is the only, or even at all times the most efficient, solution to a problem. It only suggests that a particular institution was established in the anticipation that it would generate certain desirable functional benefits for its creators: "Fortunately, functional analysis does not have to show that a given set of institutions was uniquely well adapted to the environment in order to

---

[5] E.g., Keohane 1984; Martin and Simmons 1998; Tallberg 2002; Pollack 2003.
[6] E.g., Shepsle 1979; Weingast and Marshall 1988; Epstein and O'Halloran 1999; *West European Politics* 2002.
[7] Peters 1999, 59.

make a causal argument. . . . But a sound functional argument does have to provide good reasons to believe in a causal connection between the functions that an institution performs on the one hand and its existence on the other."[8]

My central claim is that the chairmanship as an institution in political decision-making should be understood as a functional response to collective-action problems in decentralized bargaining. When designing international negotiation bodies, states create the office of the chairmanship and delegate powers of process control to this office, in the expectation that it will mitigate problems of agenda failure, negotiation failure, and representation failure. Agenda failure refers to the absence of progress in negotiations because of shifting, overcrowded, or underdeveloped agendas. Negotiation failure refers to deadlocks and breakdowns in bargaining that are caused by the parties' inability to identify the underlying zone of agreement, because of stratagems that conceal or distort their true preferences. Representation failure, finally, refers to restrictions in cooperation that arise from the absence of a formula for how the group of negotiating parties should be represented *vis-à-vis* third parties.

The functions that states confer on the chairmanship – agenda management, brokerage, and representation – answer directly to these collective-action problems. As agenda manager, the chair is expected to delimit and structure the agenda, thus making it negotiable. As broker, the chair is expected to facilitate agreement by sounding out state concerns, formulating single negotiating texts, and constructing compromises. As representative, the chair is expected to act as the external agent of the collective negotiation group, ensuring convergence on joint positions *vis-à-vis* third parties. Whether states equip the chairmanship with one or several of these responsibilities is a function of the pattern of collective-action problems in each empirical case. If this theory correctly captures the sources of demand for formal leadership, we would expect the powers delegated to the chairmanship in various multilateral contexts to vary with the pattern of experienced or anticipated collective-action problems identified by states.

The creation and empowerment of the chairmanship is rarely a one-time decision, taken in full anticipation of collective-action problems that are likely to arise in future interaction. Rather, this argument is open to a dynamic adaptation of the design of the chairmanship, in response to new or intensified collective-action problems. The theory of formal leadership shares this dynamic perspective on institutional design with

[8] Keohane 1984, 81.

other rationalist accounts, in economics as well as political science. Oliver Williamson, for instance, emphasizes how economic organizations are subject to dynamic processes of institutional learning and revision: "Once the unanticipated consequences are understood, those effects will thereafter be anticipated and the ramifications can be folded back into the organizational design. Unwanted costs will then be mitigated and unanticipated benefits will be enhanced. Better . . . performance will ordinarily result."[9]

The chairmanship is not the only institution that can fulfill the functions of agenda management, brokerage, and representation, even if it probably is the most prevalent. A cursory glance at the organization and practice of international cooperation is sufficient to establish that other actors than formal leaders are sometimes engaged to perform these functions. In some international settings, supranational secretariats enjoy formal prerogatives in agenda setting and external representation. In others, states – individually or in coalition – have gained privileged informal positions in the shaping of the agenda and the brokering of compromises. The existence of alternative institutional solutions to agenda failure, negotiation failure, and representation failure suggests that these collective-action problems constitute necessary, but not sufficient, reasons for the delegation of process powers to the chairmanship. Empirical evaluations of the theory of formal leadership must therefore be sensitive to the political context in which a particular chairmanship institution is embedded, especially the existence of competing institutional solutions to the three forms of collective-action problems.

Below, I explain in detail why agenda failure, negotiation failure, and representation failure are likely problems in decentralized bargaining, and why the delegation of agenda management, brokerage, and representational powers to the chairmanship is undertaken in the expectation that formal leaders can help states overcome these problems.

The demand for agenda management

When agendas are unstable, overcrowded, or underdeveloped, states' capacity to negotiate and conclude efficient agreements is seriously reduced. This proposition is well anchored in modern negotiation analysis, as well as in the rationalist literature on legislative decision-making. At its most basic, agenda failure is an effect of the complexity

[9] Williamson 1995, 216.

of multilateral negotiations, involving a large number of parties, preferences, and proposals. At its most advanced, it is a consequence of multidimensional issues or multi-peaked preferences in majority-rule systems. The theory of formal leadership suggests that the delegation of powers of agenda management to the institution of the chairmanship offers a functional solution to this problem.

Negotiation analysts commonly stress that complexity increases manifold as we move from bilateral to multilateral settings. "There's a world of difference between two-party and many-party negotiations," notes Howard Raiffa.[10] Similarly, William Zartman emphasizes: "The overarching characteristic of multilateral negotiation is its complexity along all conceivable dimensions."[11] Multilateral negotiations of today are not only multi-party, but also multi-issue and multi-level. Negotiations seldom deal with one individual issue, but constitute systems of bargaining over a broad range of more or less related dossiers, and often consist of multiple negotiation forums at multiple levels of organization. To some extent, the inclusion of multiple issues can facilitate agreement in multilateral negotiation, by allowing for cross-cutting compromises and the construction of package deals that leave everyone better off.[12] Yet there are limitations to this rule, as Richard Walton and Robert McKersie note in their seminal contribution to negotiation analysis: "The parties would want to avoid having an overwhelming number – so that the negotiators are not overloaded and do not need to devote too much time sorting through items to the detriment of genuine exploitation of particular items."[13] Conflicts over the format of the agenda and the priority of the items can force states to devote scarce time and resources to pre-negotiation talks and preparations whose sole purpose is to arrive at a negotiable agenda.[14]

The complexity of modern multilateral negotiations, suggests Gilbert Winham, has brought about a shift in the challenges facing international negotiators: "The principal problem for most contemporary negotiators is not to outwit their adversaries, but rather to create a structure out of a large mass of information wherein it is possible to apply human wit. The classical diplomat's technique of the management of people through guile has given way to the management of people through the creation

---

[10] Raiffa 1982, 251.
[11] Zartman 1994a, 3. See also Touval 1989; Hampson with Hart 1995, ch. 2; Hopmann 1996, ch. 13.
[12] Walton and McKersie 1965, 145–146; Sebenius 1983.
[13] Walton and McKersie 1965, 146.
[14] Saunders 1985; Stein 1989.

of system and structure."[15] The bottom line of the negotiation literature is that the agenda risks becoming either underdeveloped or
overcrowded, in the absence of some form of agenda management.

The fear of agenda failure is shared by rational choice theorists in the
study of legislative politics. As discovered already by the Marquis de
Condorcet, and later developed by Richard McKelvey, William Riker,
and others, decision systems that grant equal agenda-setting opportunities to all actors are liable to issue cycling and will be unable to secure
stable majorities for the proposals advanced.[16] The heart of the problem
is the multidimensionality of political issues. An issue is multidimensional when it involves more than one dimension on which the parties
disagree, for instance, left/right next to environmentalist/industrialist.
This is a defining characteristic of most issues in politics. According to
the rationalist analysis of legislative politics, the effect of multidimensionality is a constant shifting of coalitions depending on what aspect of
the issue is being considered. Each proposal can be beaten by another
proposal, and therefore no proposal constitutes an equilibrium that the
parties can agree on. The agenda is cyclically unstable.

The argument originally was developed in relation to national legislatures, but it also sheds light on the challenges of arriving at stable
outcomes in multilateral negotiations.[17] The issues that are up for
negotiation in international politics can seldom be reduced to one dimension. Instead, negotiations on regional integration, trade liberalization,
security management, and environmental protection tend to be multidimensional, and it is common that coalition patterns shift depending on
what dimension of an issue is being considered.

The primary functional solution to the problem of agenda failure is the
institutionalization of procedures for agenda control. Negotiation theorists point to procedures and practices for dealing with complexity, such
as issue sequencing and subtraction, coalition building, and single negotiating texts.[18] Rational choice theorists, for their part, speak of how
institutional arrangements in legislative politics, such as agenda-setting
power, gate-keeping authority, and sequential choice, can prevent the
manifestation of agenda instability.[19]

---

[15] Winham 1977, 88–89.
[16] Condorcet 1785; McKelvey 1976; Riker 1980. For good discussions, see Fiorina and
    Shepsle 1989; Mesquita 1990; Shepsle and Weingast 1995; Scharpf 1997, 156–161.
[17] Mesquita 1990.
[18] Raiffa 1982, ch. 17; Sebenius 1983, 1996; Dupont 1994; Hampson with Hart 1995,
    ch. 2.
[19] Shepsle 1979; Shepsle and Weingast 1984; Fiorina and Shepsle 1989; Baron 1994.

The theory of formal leadership suggests that the delegation of agenda-management powers to the chairmanship constitutes a prominent strategy for dealing with the risk of agenda failure in multilateral bargaining. Just as national politicians design legislative institutions in order to avoid issue cycling, states delegate agenda-management tasks to the chairmanship of multilateral negotiation bodies for purposes of avoiding agenda failure. The responsibilities conferred on the chairmanship typically comprise the solutions prescribed by negotiation theory and legislative studies for dealing with overcrowded, underdeveloped, or unstable agendas. The chairmanship generally possesses the authority to take general decisions on the sequence, frequency, and method of negotiation, as well as specific decisions on the structure of meetings, the format of the meeting agenda, the right to speak, the voting procedure, and the summary of results. By executing these powers, negotiation chairs can keep the agenda to manageable proportions, assign priority to issues on the agenda, and structure the negotiations. Expressed in a more pedestrian way, agenda management makes it possible for states with competing interests and contrasting views to debate, negotiate, and decide in an orderly way.

Agenda management involves the execution of three forms of influence – agenda setting, agenda structuring, and agenda exclusion.[20] Agenda setting refers to the introduction of new issues on the policy agenda, and involves efforts to raise the awareness of a problem and to develop innovative proposals.[21] Agenda structuring refers to the emphasizing or de-emphasizing of issues already on the policy agenda, through decisions on the sequence and priority of issues under negotiation. Agenda exclusion, finally, refers to the removal or barring of issues from the policy agenda through the execution of the chairman's gate-keeping function, essentially a form of non-decision-making.[22] In sum, formal leaders may be described as the gardeners of the political agenda, who cut and prune, remove the weeds, sow new seeds, and add the extra nourishment that allows some plants to grow into their full potential.

The demand for brokerage

In multilateral bargaining, states have tactical reasons to withhold information about their true preferences. Yet this stratagem simultaneously risks undermining the possibility of reaching an accord, by concealing

---

[20] Tallberg 2003a.
[21] Schelling 1960; Kingdon 1984.
[22] Bachrach and Baratz 1962, 1963.

the underlying zone of agreement. Despite preferences that offer possibilities for agreement, negotiations may break down. The theory of formal leadership suggests that the engagement of negotiation chairs as brokers constitutes a functional response to this problem.

What I term negotiation failure is one of the classic bargaining problems.[23] Rationalist bargaining theory suggests that negotiations can break down for two reasons: either because the parties, once they have exchanged information about each other's preferences, discover that negotiations cannot yield a better outcome than existing alternatives; or because parties with joint interests in an agreement conceal information about their actual preferences, to the effect that existing alternatives appear more attractive than a negotiated outcome. As opposed to the first situation, the second constitutes a true bargaining tragedy, since the parties walk away from the negotiations despite a sufficient zone of agreement, sometimes also denoted "settlement range," "bargaining zone," or "contract zone." Duncan Luce and Howard Raiffa describe this tension between cooperative gain and informational strategizing as "the real bargaining problem," whereas David Lax and James Sebenius label it "the negotiator's dilemma."[24]

The essence of the dilemma is preference information. For purposes of finding an agreement that satisfies all participants – a Pareto-improving bargain – states must signal what they can and cannot accept. Yet revealing information about one's true preferences is both risky and non-tactical. It is risky because it exposes a party to exploitation and the misfortune of not receiving any gains in return for its sacrifices. It is non-tactical because it deprives a party of the weapon of concessions that can be used to extract favors from others. Instead, states have incentives to be cagey, secretive, or even dishonest about their true preferences, for instance, by exaggerating the value of their own concessions and downplaying the benefit of others' concessions. The result is a distorted picture of preferences that either reduces the perceived zone of agreement, with the effect that "gains are left on the table," or eliminates it altogether, with the effect that negotiations break down.

The logic of this bargaining problem is strong in bilateral negotiations – its standard representation. Yet it is compounded in the multilateral setting, with its particular difficulties of communicating preferences and exchanging information among a large number of

---

[23] E.g., Luce and Raiffa 1957; Walton and McKersie 1965; Lax and Sebenius 1986, ch. 2; O. Young 1991.

[24] Luce and Raiffa 1957, 134; Lax and Sebenius 1986, ch. 2.

participants.[25] As Fen Osler Hampson notes: "The chief obstacles to multilateral negotiations are complexity and uncertainty: complexity created by the large number of parties to the negotiation and issues on the table, uncertainty heightened by the difficulties of communicating preferences and exchanging information among a large number of participants."[26] Whether the number of participating states is 15, 50, or 150, it constitutes a challenge for the parties to identify each other's true preferences and jointly construct an agreement that captures the zone of agreement that might – but need not – exist.

The theory of formal leadership suggests that delegation of brokerage responsibilities to the chairmanship of multilateral conferences and international organizations constitutes a common way for states to deal with the risk of negotiation failure. This act of delegation seldom involves the conferral of formal powers. Instead, it takes the shape of a practice among states to share information about their private preferences with negotiation chairs, and a mandate for negotiation chairs to formulate single negotiating texts around which bargaining can converge. Through bilateral encounters with the bargaining parties, negotiation chairs are provided with privileged information about state preferences. This information permits them to identify any underlying zone of agreement and construct compromises that can capture this zone. The authority to formulate a single negotiating text facilitates this process and allows negotiation chairs to cut through the complexity of competing and overlapping state proposals.

This argument is a variant of the frequent claim in the negotiation literature that brokers or mediators can help states to agreements that they are unable to reach on their own.[27] Lax and Sebenius emphasize that the use of a broker can reduce the tension in the negotiator's dilemma: "A mediator or third party who enjoys the trust of the parties can enhance the flow of information by only passing on information that, in his judgement, will not hurt the other party. By acting as a selective conduit of information, a third party can reduce the expected or feared cost of disclosing information."[28] Thomas Schelling integrates the mediator into game-theoretical models of bargaining: "A mediator, whether

---

[25] Winham 1977; Sebenius 1983; Touval 1989; Zartman 1994a; Hampson with Hart 1995, ch. 2.

[26] Hampson with Hart 1995, 23.

[27] On multilateral negotiations, see, especially, Winham 1979; O. Young 1991; Underdal 1994. See also the specific literature on mediation in bilateral conflicts: Young 1967; Stenelo 1972; Touval and Zartman 1985; Bercovitch and Rubin 1992; Bercovitch 1996; Kleiboer 1998.

[28] Lax and Sebenius 1986, 172.

imposed on the game by its original rules or adopted by the players to facilitate an efficient outcome, is probably best viewed as an element in the communication arrangements or as a third player with a payoff structure of his own who is given an influential role through his control over communication."[29] Raiffa underlines the sacrifice involved in conferring brokerage responsibilities to a third party: "It's my belief that in a great number of such cases, joint gains could be realized if only the contending parties were willing to yield up enough sovereignty to allow a mediator to help them devise creative alternatives and to help them analyze their joint problem."[30]

The demand for representation

In the conventional view of multilateral negotiations, the process of interstate bargaining is seen as relatively self-contained: states engage in negotiations with each other in search of an agreement which permits them to reconcile their differences and reach joint gains. Yet, in many actual cases of cooperation in world politics, multilateral bargaining in one area or body is nested within broader processes of negotiation and may even be dependent on agreements with external actors. In such cases, the negotiating states must find a formula for their collective representation *vis-à-vis* third parties. The theory of formal leadership suggests that the delegation of representational authority to the chairmanship of multilateral conferences or international institutions constitutes a response to this demand.

Multilateral negotiations seldom take place in a vacuum, though this simplifying assumption has served bargaining analysis well. More often, negotiations are intertwined with external political processes. The shape of interdependencies and interactions between negotiation forums and their external environments varies greatly. Slightly simplified, three forms seem particularly prominent. First, international institutions and rule systems are today increasingly interdependent, since activities in one issue area often impact on activities in another field. Regime theorists have labeled this interdependence "institutional interplay" and frequently point to the relationships between trade regimes, environmental regimes, and social regulation regimes.[31] One of the implications of

---

[29] Schelling 1960, 144.
[30] Raiffa 1982, 219.
[31] See, e.g., Young 1999b, ch. 7, 2002; Oberthür and Gehring 2001; Stokke 2001a, 2001b.

institutional interplay is the need for states to manage relations between international negotiation and decision-making forums.

Second, international organizations or multilateral conferences seldom encompass all potential members and negotiating parties. The membership of regional associations is by definition limited, and not even global regimes and institutions incorporate all sovereign states. Restricted membership creates a demand for procedures to handle relations with non-members. Furthermore, the membership of international regimes and institutions is seldom constant, but tends to grow over time, as additional states sign on. In many cases, the expansion of the membership requires negotiations between existing and prospective members over the terms of accession and the implementation of regime rules.

Third, the outcomes of multilateral bargaining may be directly dependent on the outcome of collective negotiations with third parties. Negotiation theorists have conceptualized the phenomenon of interdependent bargaining in a number of ways. Walton and McKersie analyze labor negotiations in terms of inter- and intra-organizational negotiations.[32] Robert Putnam and others speak of two-level games – intertwined inter- and intrastate negotiations in world politics.[33] Fritz Scharpf uses the term joint-decision system to describe interdependent negotiations at multiple levels.[34] George Tsebelis refers to nested games where the outcomes in one game are dependent on the outcomes in another game.[35] Lax and Sebenius conceptualize these interdependencies as a challenge for the manager in the middle, forced to balance internal and external negotiations.[36] This form of interdependent decision-making creates a demand for external negotiation agents.

The theory of formal leadership suggests that the delegation of authority to the chairmanship constitutes a functional solution to the representation problem. Whereas an individual can negotiate on its own behalf, a composite actor cannot engage in negotiations as is, but must delegate the power of representation to an agent. Just like states cannot be represented by all citizens in multilateral negotiations, international organizations cannot be represented by all constituent member states in their external relations. Hence, where international organizations and conferences are involved in interdependent decision-making, this requires that states agree on an institutional arrangement for representation and

---

[32] Walton and McKersie 1965.
[33] Putnam 1988; Evans *et al.* 1993.
[34] Scharpf 1988, 1997, ch. 6.
[35] Tsebelis 1990.
[36] Lax and Sebenius 1986.

negotiation. States' decision to empower the chairmanship, by allowing the incumbent to speak on behalf of the collective, constitutes a subset of the general phenomenon of representation powers being delegated to negotiating agents.[37]

In sum, the theory of formal leadership predicts that the powers conferred on the chairmanship of international negotiation bodies will reflect particular functional demands in cooperation, and be concentrated in the areas of agenda management, brokerage, and representation. Empirical data lend support to this core hypothesis when providing evidence of a causal link between experienced or anticipated collective-action problems and specific acts of delegation in these three areas. By contrast, empirical data challenge this proposition if the conferral of authority to the chairmanship is random, or systematically addresses other problems than agenda failure, negotiation failure, and representation failure.

The supply of formal leadership

What are the consequences of empowering chairmanship institutions in international cooperation? The theory of formal leadership suggests that the office of the chairmanship, once vested with powers of process control, becomes a political platform with implications for the outcomes of multilateral negotiations. In this section, I specify the power resources of formal leaders, explain how opportunistic negotiation chairs may exploit their privileged position for private gain, identify enabling and constraining factors in the institutional environment, and describe the potential impact on the outcomes of multilateral negotiations.

Power resources: privileged information and procedural control

The office of the chairmanship offers the incumbent a set of power resources that may be used to pursue both collective interests and private concerns. These power resources are integral to the office and the three functions commonly delegated to the chairmanship. Analytically, they split into two forms: asymmetrical access to information, and asymmetrical control over negotiation procedure.

By virtue of their position, negotiation chairs enjoy privileged access to information that otherwise is unavailable or costly to acquire. In principal–agent theory, the information asymmetries that negotiation

---

[37] Mnookin and Susskind 1999.

chairs benefit from are labeled hidden information and hidden action.[38] Hidden information refers to a situation where the agent possesses or acquires information through its activities that the principals do not possess and cannot obtain. Hidden action refers to a situation where the behavior of an agent is not fully observable and transparent to the principals. In multilateral bargaining, these forms of information asymmetry are expressed in at least four ways.

First, formal leaders tend to gain a better picture of the intensity and distribution of state preferences than the negotiating parties. The practice of bilateral encounters, at which states offer negotiation chairs privileged information about national resistance points provides formal leaders with significant informational advantages.

Second, negotiation chairs tend to acquire an unusual technical knowledge of the subject matter, sometimes referred to as content expertise in the negotiation literature.[39] This information is not unavailable to the negotiating parties – indeed, this is the stuff of the actual bargaining – but it is often relatively more costly for them to obtain. Typically, formal leaders can draw on the content expertise built up over time in the secretariats of international organizations and multilateral conferences. These bodies are specialized in the subject matter of the particular regime, and traditionally constitute a resource at the chairman's special disposal.[40]

Third, negotiation chairs tend to develop an unusual command of the formal negotiation procedure, sometimes referred to as process expertise in the literature.[41] Just like content expertise, process expertise is not unobtainable to the negotiating parties, even if the collection of this information requires that states commit scarce resources to the task. Again, negotiation chairs generally benefit from the legal and procedural advice that international secretariats can offer.[42] In many cases, these secretariats contain entire departments exclusively devoted to procedural and legal matters.

Fourth, formal leaders tend to know more about their own influence over outcomes than the negotiating parties. This logic comes to its clearest expression in the function of representation, where informational asymmetries can prevent states from isolating the contribution of

---

[38] See Holmström 1979; Arrow 1985; Kiewiet and McCubbins 1991, ch. 2; Miller 1992, chs. 6–7.
[39] Wall and Lynn 1993; Metcalfe 1998.
[40] Hamlet 2002; Beach 2004.
[41] Wall and Lynn 1993; Metcalfe 1998.
[42] Hamlet 2002; Beach 2004.

their own agent from that of the external counterpart. Principals typically abstain from instituting strong mechanisms of control in the area of representation, because of the negative effects on the agent's capacity to conclude deals with third parties. As Sophie Meunier explains in the context of executive fast-track delegation in US trade policy:

> A more extensive delegation of negotiating competence has one immediate effect on the process of bargaining with third countries: it improves the chances of concluding an international agreement. When the negotiators have been delegated more extensive flexibility, autonomy, and authority by the principals, they have more institutional latitude to find creative bargaining solutions. They can successfully negotiate an international agreement, knowing that their principals will not be allowed to bicker on the details of the deal.[43]

The second major power resource of negotiation chairs is the asymmetrical control over negotiation procedure, owing to formal powers vested in the office of the chairmanship. Simplifying slightly, this control consists of two parts: control over the general negotiation process, and control over specific negotiation sessions. As process manager, the chair enjoys privileged control over decisions on the sequence of negotiations (from pre-negotiation phase to negotiation phase and agreement phase), the frequency of negotiating sessions (and associated time for internal deliberations and bilateral interaction), the format of negotiations (multilateral, minilateral, or bilateral), and the method of negotiation (competing proposals or single negotiating text). As manager of individual negotiation sessions, the chair opens and concludes meetings, structures the meeting agenda, allots the right to speak, directs voting procedures, and summarizes the results obtained. Expressed in more political terms, the chair tends to enjoy asymmetrical control over who gets to say what, when, how, and to what effect. This control is probably what most people associate with the chair of any decision-making organ.

Opportunism and influence: exploiting the chairmanship for private gain

By drawing on these power resources negotiation chairs can help parties overcome bargaining impediments that prevent the realization of collective gains. Yet the very same power resources can be exploited to pursue private preferences as well. The theory conceives of formal leaders as opportunistic actors who will seek to take advantage of the chairmanship in order to favor their own interests in the bargaining process.

---

[43] Meunier 2000, 118. See also Nicolaïdis 1999.

Whereas the creation and empowerment of the chairmanship may be necessary to address harmful collective-action problems and reach efficient bargaining outcomes, it simultaneously grants the actor in control of this office an opportunity to shift the distribution of gains to its own advantage. Information about preferences, proposals, and procedures is political hard currency, as is the power to control the process and format of the negotiations. The asymmetrical distribution of these assets to the advantage of formal leaders opens up possibilities for political exploitation that negotiation chairs will not be hard pressed to make use of. This conception of formal leaders as opportunistic actors with private interests resonates with the principal–agent literature on delegation, as well as the bargaining literature on mediation and leadership.

Principal–agent theory posits that opportunism is an ever-present problem when decision power is delegated from one actor to another. As Roderick Kiewiet and Mathew McCubbins emphasize: "There is almost always some conflict between the interests of those who delegate authority (principals) and the agents to whom they delegate it. Agents behave opportunistically, pursuing their own interests subject only to the constraints imposed by their relationship with the principal. The opportunism that generates agency losses is a ubiquitous feature of the human experience."[44] In the same vein, Terry Moe explains why the creation of new political agents, in this case an agency, produces interest conflict and opportunistic action:

Once an agency is created, the political world becomes a different place. Agency bureaucrats are now political actors in their own right: they have career and institutional interests that may not be entirely congruent with their formal missions, and they have powerful resources – expertise and delegated authority – that might be employed toward these "selfish" ends. They are new players whose interests and resources alter the political game.[45]

The bargaining literature similarly recognizes that leaders, entrepreneurs, and mediators are players in their own right, with their own interests in the negotiation process. Oran Young stresses that "entrepreneurial leaders are self-interested: they are motivated or driven to exercise leadership to further their own values or goals rather than to fulfill some sense of ethical responsibility to the community."[46] In the same way, it is a typical addendum in the literature on third-party intervention that mediators have interests too. Raiffa notes: "The intervenor has

---

[44] Kiewiet and McCubbins 1991, 5.
[45] Moe 1990, 143.
[46] O. Young 1991, 296. See also Frohlich, Oppenheimer, and Young 1971, 58; Fiorina and Shepsle 1989. For a diverging opinion, see Malnes 1995.

aspirations, ideals, values, judgments, and constraints of his own. Thus, he can be thought of as another player in the game – albeit a special type of player." Similarly, Schelling describes a mediator as "a third player with a payoff structure of his own who is given an influential role through his control over communication."[47]

Consider, on this basis, how the delegation of agenda-management, brokerage, and representation functions to the chairmanship simultaneously opens up possibilities for opportunistic action. As agenda manager, negotiation chairs are endowed with formal procedural instruments that permit the organization of a negotiable agenda; yet the structuring of the agenda is not a neutral exercise, since it involves prioritizing some issues at the expense of others. As broker, negotiation chairs are granted privileged access to information about the parties' true preferences in their pursuit of viable compromise proposals; yet this exclusive preference information may be used to promote agreements with certain distributional outcomes rather than others. As representative, negotiation chairs enjoy the power to bargain on behalf of the group; yet the interaction with third parties offers possibilities to present positions and strike bargains that diverge from the group's median preference. In sum, the same asymmetrical advantages in information and procedural control that can be used to help negotiating parties overcome collective-action problems, can also be used to influence distributive outcomes in favor of the chair.

The formal institutional environment: enabling and constraining factors

The extent to which negotiation chairs succeed in shifting distributional outcomes in their own favor is conditioned by the institutional environment in which they operate. The institutional environment consists of formal rules and procedures that enable and constrain negotiation chairs in the execution of agenda management, brokerage, and representation. The theory of formal leadership suggests that two factors are of particular importance in shaping the chair's distributional influence: the formal institutional rules governing agenda setting and decision-making, and the institutional design of the chairmanship. These institutional factors affect outcomes by opening, facilitating, discouraging, or obstructing certain courses of action by negotiation chairs.

[47] Raiffa 1982, 24; Schelling 1960, 144. See also Stenelo 1972, 29; Lax and Sebenius 1986, 173–176; Hampson with Hart 1995, 18; Carnevale and Arad 1996.

Formal institutional rules   Agenda-setting and decision rules set the formal parameters of multilateral negotiations. Agenda-setting rules regulate which actors are allowed to table proposals in a particular decision-making forum. These rules shape the ease with which the chair can favor the introduction of proposals it wants to promote or, alternatively, block the introduction of proposals it wants to keep from collective consideration. Simplifying slightly, we can speak of two ideal types of agenda-setting rules, each of which carries specific implications for the capacity of negotiation chairs to shape distributional outcomes.

In the first kind of arrangement, agenda-setting power is vested in one specific actor that enjoys the exclusive privilege of formulating proposals for the agenda. Unless this happens to be the chairmanship, this model is associated with limitations on the discretion of formal leaders. Negotiation chairs will be unable to present formal proposals on their own initiative, but must convince the agenda setter to table them as its own. The agenda setter effectively constitutes a veto player whose support must be secured if formal leaders are to wield influence over the proposals put on the agenda. At the same time, we should remember that negotiation chairs enjoy means of influencing decision agendas that extend beyond formal agenda setting. Even when dependent on privileged agenda setters for the tabling of proposals, formal leaders retain the capacity to emphasize or de-emphasize proposals on the agenda.

In the second kind of arrangement, the parties possess equal agenda-setting powers. Where this model is used, negotiation chairs will find it relatively easier to influence the formal agenda. Where the chairmanship is organized on a governmental basis, negotiation chairs can introduce formal proposals through the states they simultaneously represent. Where the chairmanship is organized on a supranational basis, negotiation chairs do not enjoy an agenda-setting channel of their own, but need to convince one of the parties to present their proposals as its own. Yet equal agenda-setting rights benefit formal leaders indirectly as well. By permitting all parties to present proposals, this arrangement raises the risk of overcrowded negotiation agendas and the likelihood of agenda-management powers being delegated to the chairmanship, notably, the authority to formulate single negotiating texts that replace the multitude of competing proposals.

Decision rules shape the ease with which the chair can promote proposals that satisfy the requirements of an efficient bargain and meet the partisan interests of the chair. The distinction between unanimity and majority voting is the most fundamental, and well illustrates the implications of variation in decision rules.[48]

Where unanimity or consensus is prescribed as the method of decision, formal leaders must take the interests of all parties into consideration, and will find it difficult to steer negotiations toward their own ideal point. Finding an efficient agreement will in itself constitute a major challenge. Given a certain distribution of preferences, the requirement of unanimity leads to a more limited zone of agreement compared to more generous decision rules. The number of possible agreements that make all states better off is simply lower than under any other decision rule. This effectively reduces the capacity of negotiation chairs to promote their most preferred outcome.

Where decisions may be taken through majority voting, it is relatively easier for states to reach an efficient outcome and for negotiation chairs to influence the distributional dimension of this outcome. Majority voting makes it easier to mobilize the support necessary for an agreement to be concluded, since not all parties must be brought on board. In addition, this decision rule makes it possible to extract concessions from parties with extreme preferences, which otherwise risk being marginalized and excluded. This expands the range of alternative efficient agreements and makes it relatively easier for formal leaders to steer negotiations toward their own preferred solutions.

The effects of agenda setting and decision rules are conditioned by the distribution of actor preferences in any given empirical context. Three aspects merit particular attention. First, the impact of alternative agenda-setting arrangements will depend on the preferences of formal agenda setters – exclusive or multiple – relative to those of negotiation chairs. Second, regardless of decision rule, negotiation chairs with central preferences will find it relatively easier than chairs with extreme preferences to promote agreements that also satisfy their distributional interests. Third, where formal leaders with outlier interests function as representatives in negotiations with external parties, the preferences of the external counterpart may both improve and worsen the chair's chances of obtaining its preferred outcome. The external party expands the chair's room for maneuver if it holds preferences that are more radical, whereas it reduces the chair's room for maneuver if its

---

[48] On the implications of decision rules for bargaining patterns and outcomes, see Hopmann 1996, ch. 13; Scharpf 1997; Meunier 2000; Tsebelis 2002.

interests instead are positioned closer to the median preference in the internal negotiation group.

Institutional design of the chairmanship   The world of multi-lateral bargaining offers three alternative institutional models for the chairmanship office: (1) rotation of the chairmanship between the participating states, (2) election of a chairman from one of the participating states, and (3) appointment of a supranational official as chairman.[49] The theory of formal leadership suggests that the institutional design carries important consequences by shaping the room for maneuver of negotiation chairs.

Rotation of the chairmanship is likely to create dynamics of diffuse reciprocity between the participating states that work to the advantage of formal leaders. This model effectively entails a sharing over time of the gains that states can derive from the chairmanship. The system of rotation makes the distributional implications of the office acceptable to states. Instead of investing time and resources in costly control mechanisms, we would expect states to offer each other latitude in the execution of the chairmanship, as all parties eventually get their privileged opportunity to direct the negotiations. Moreover, rotation in itself constitutes a form of control, by putting a time limit on each state's exploitation of the office. The risk of discontinuity in the execution of agenda management, brokerage, and representation is likely to be the most prominent concern in the rotation model.

When states elect a chairman from one of the parties, the question of control becomes a central concern and discontinuity a non-issue. Unless states wish to grant one of the parties extraordinary means of securing national interests, they will establish means of control. The election process itself offers an instrument of *ex ante* control.[50] By electing chairs from states with central and/or weak preferences in the issues under negotiation, the parties can effectively reduce the likelihood that negotiation chairs will shift distributional outcomes from the expected equilibrium. In addition, states can limit the room for maneuver through *ex post* oversight procedures.[51] For instance, the participating states can institute time limits, re-election restrictions, or a system of co-chairmen with incentives to monitor each other.

---

[49] See Fiorina and Shepsle 1989 for a general discussion of alternative ways of selecting privileged agenda setters, with distinct parallels to these models.

[50] On *ex ante* control mechanisms generally, see McCubbins, Noll, and Weingast 1987; Fiorina and Shepsle 1989.

[51] On *ex post* control mechanisms generally, see McCubbins and Schwartz 1984.

When states adopt a supranational design for the chairmanship, control remains an issue, even if the risk is lower that outcomes will be systematically structured to the advantage or disadvantage of any particular government. Supranational secretariats hold preferences of their own, normally the furthering of the political ideals embodied in the international organization or conference they serve. The supranational promotion of these ideals typically consists of efforts to facilitate the process of cooperation and tends to serve the collective good of the regime. While favoring the most ambitious parties on each individual dossier, the aggregated effect on state interests is likely to be diffuse, given variation between the parties in the relative weight attributed to alternative issues.

Impact on outcomes: efficiency and distribution

The final stage of the theory of formal leadership consists of the impact of the chair's activities on bargaining outcomes. This impact is conceptualized through the dimensions of efficiency and distribution.[52] Any observable effect on outcomes along any of these two dimensions is evidence of the independent input of negotiation chairs in multilateral bargaining. This impact is the product of the previous stages of the theory: the delegation of agenda management, brokerage, and representation functions to the chairmanship; the wielding of informational and procedural power resources for collective and private gain; and the enabling and constraining effect of the formal institutional environment.

Figure 2.2 conveys the potential influence of formal leaders along these two dimensions. In this simplified two-party negotiation, the welfare of A is measured on the vertical axis and the welfare of B on the horizontal axis. For pedagogical reasons, it is convenient to illustrate the contribution of formal leaders to outcomes as two sequential steps, even if this is a simplification, since real-world chairmen tend to affect the efficiency and distributional dimensions simultaneously.

At the first stage, the chair facilitates decision-making through the execution of agenda management, brokerage, and representation, thus raising the efficiency of the negotiations. In the figure, this effect is signified by the arrow that moves the welfare frontier outwards. The ultimate agreement is one that is Pareto-efficient, that is, when negotiations have reached a point – the Pareto frontier – where no other

---

[52] This is a common distinction in the literature. See, e.g., Schelling 1960; Walton and McKersie 1965; Raiffa 1982; Lax and Sebenius 1986; Krasner 1991; P. Young 1991; Scharpf 1997; Moravcsik 1998.

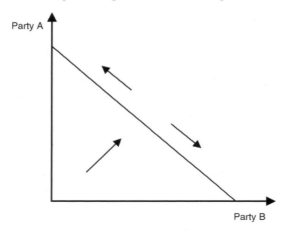

Figure 2.2. Influence of formal leaders over outcomes

agreement exists that could improve general welfare. The negotiation literature frequently refers to this improvement in efficiency as a movement away from outcomes that "leave gains on the table" to outcomes that exploit the full potential for agreement.

At the second stage, the chair affects the distribution of gains among the bargaining parties by promoting the one agreement – among a range of efficient outcomes – that is closest to its own preferred position. In the figure, this effect is signified by the two arrows along the new welfare frontier, which indicate movement toward alternative outcomes with varying distibutional implications for A and B. Exploiting its asymmetrical advantages in information and procedural control, the chair selects the equilibrium closest to its own ideal point.

In the end, it is an empirical question whether negotiation chairs exert influence over decision-making outcomes. Whereas some scholars claim that leadership and entrepreneurship are necessary conditions for agreement, this is not the implication of the theory of formal leadership.[53] Instead, this theory suggests that the power of the chair in multilateral bargaining is conditional and subject to variation, depending on identifiable factors in the negotiation setting. Empirical data lend support to the theory's central hypotheses if the influence of negotiation chairs can be linked to informational and procedural power resources, and varies as predicted with formal constraints in the institutional environment. By

[53] E.g., O. Young 1991, 302.

contrast, empirical data that give evidence of random patterns of influence, or systematically speak to alternative power resources and behavioral constraints, challenge the same propositions.

An alternative approach: sociological institutionalism

The theory put forward above presents a coherent rationalist argument about the demand for, and supply of, formal leadership. Rather than offering an eclectic framework of factors drawn from competing theoretical approaches based on alternative epistemological and ontological foundations, the theory consistently builds on rationalist assumptions and privileges rationalist explanatory variables. Yet rational choice institutionalism does not constitute the only possible theoretical take on the questions raised in this book. In this section, I proceed to formulate an alternative approach, drawn from sociological institutionalism.

While posing similar questions about institutional creation, change, and consequences, rational choice institutionalism and sociological institutionalism offer widely divergent responses.[54] The differences between the two approaches have been eloquently captured in the distinction between two alternative logics of action: the logic of consequentiality and the logic of appropriateness.[55] In the political world of consequentialism, actors are driven by strategic calculations on how to maximize expected utility, given fixed and exogenously given preferences. Political outcomes are the result of strategic interaction, where "human actors choose among alternatives by evaluating their likely consequences for personal or collective objectives, conscious that other actors are doing likewise."[56] In the political world of appropriateness, by contrast, actors are driven by a wish to do the right thing in a certain institutional context, where identities, expectations, norms, and roles define what constitutes appropriate behavior. "Human actors are imagined to follow rules that associate particular identities to particular situations, approaching individual opportunities for action by assessing similarities between current identities and choice dilemmas and more general concepts of self and situations."[57]

Although no coherent sociological account of formal leadership comparable to the rationalist theory I advance so far has been presented, this

---

[54] For comparisons of the various forms of institutionalism, see Hall and Taylor 1996; Immergut 1996; Peters 1998; Aspinwall and Schneider 2000.
[55] March and Olsen 1989, 1998.
[56] March and Olsen 1998, 949.
[57] March and Olsen 1998, 951.

Table 2.1. *Competing perspectives on formal leadership*

	Rational choice institutionalism	Sociological institutionalism
Institutional development	Efficient; designed to address specific functional demands; adjusted when functional needs change	Inefficient; designed to fit legitimate institutional model; slow adaptation to changing environmental demands
Power resources	Asymmetric access to information and asymmetric control over negotiation procedure	Legitimacy of claim to authority, and capacity to persuade through good arguments
Constraints on behavior	Formal rules and actor preferences strategic calculation of costs and benefits	Informal norms about appropriate behavior: socialization and internalization

approach generates expectations that can be formulated as competing hypotheses. Disaggregating general theoretical positions into specified causal claims, I suggest that sociological institutionalism offers alternative hypotheses on three of the central components of the rationalist theory of formal leadership. These two competing perspectives are summarized in Table 2.1.

First, sociological institutionalism challenges the rationalist claim that institutions are created in response to specific functional needs, and subsequently adapt efficiently to changing demands in the environment. Instead, sociological institutionalists perceive of institutional creation and development as processes where low priority is given to concerns of efficiency, relative to concerns of legitimacy.[58] States adopt certain institutional solutions because these are widely accepted as legitimate and appropriate – not because they necessarily are the most efficient. This is seen as explaining the phenomenon of isomorphism – the spread of organizational models across functional domains through processes of emulation and diffusion. Furthermore, sociological institutionalism emphasizes the slow pace of institutional adaptation to changing demands in the political environment.[59] Political actors seldom enjoy the capacity to instantaneously adjust institutions to unexpected consequences and changing functional pressures. The match between political institutions

---

[58] DiMaggio and Powell 1983; Powell and DiMaggio 1991; Scott and Meyer 1994. For a good illustration of this argument in the context of European cooperation, see McNamara 2002.

[59] March and Olsen 1998; Pierson 2000. For a good illustration of this argument in the context of European cooperation, see Pierson 1996.

and environmental demands is therefore less automatic, less continuous, and less precise than rational choice institutionalists assume. If sociological institutionalists are right, we would expect legitimacy to play a more prominent role than efficiency in the creation and empowerment of chairmanship offices, institutional emulation to be a stronger determinant than functional pressure in the design of chairmanship offices, and stickiness rather than adaptation to characterize the development of chairmanship offices over time.

Second, sociological institutionalism challenges the rationalist conception of informational advantages and formal powers as central political resources. Instead, sociological institutionalists stress the legitimacy of an actor's claim to authority, and persuasion through good and normatively appropriate arguments.[60] Actors' perceptions of interests, alternatives, problems, and solutions are seen as malleable – not fixed. Informal authority and the ability to convince others through the power of the argument therefore become important means for influencing political outcomes. Leadership and authority rest less on formal power and hierarchy than on trust, legitimacy, and social acceptance. This sociological perspective resonates well with claims in the negotiation literature about the importance of legitimacy for successful brokerage and mediation.[61] The chairmanship is seen as a source of legitimacy in itself, which negotiation chairs can draw on in their efforts to influence the parties. At the same time, negotiation chairs can easily ruin this legitimacy, the trust of the parties, and the chances to win support for their arguments, if they violate widely held principles of appropriate behavior, notably, the notion that chairmen should be impartial. If this approach correctly captures the power resources of formal leaders, we would expect to see negotiation chairs influence agreements, not when they mobilize informational and procedural resources, but when they evoke the legitimacy of the office to persuade the parties of their interest in a particular outcome.

Third and finally, sociological institutionalism conceives of informal norms of appropriate behavior as the primary constraint on actor behavior, and challenges the rationalist emphasis on formal rules and cost-benefit calculations.[62] According to this perspective, states operate in a universe of prescriptive and proscriptive norms that specify appropriate behavior. Norms spread and become internalized through processes of socialization, thus changing the way actors conceive of their interests.

---

[60] Kingdon 1984; March and Olsen 1989; Hall 1997; Risse 2000.
[61] Lang 1989; Bercovitch 1992; Hopmann 1996, ch. 12; Metcalfe 1998.
[62] March and Olsen 1989, 1998; Finnemore and Sikkink 1998; Checkel 2001.

Actors conform to these norms, not on the basis of cost-benefit calculations, but because they wish to do the right thing in a given situation. Following this logic, sociological institutionalists would expect negotiation chairs to be guided by widely held conceptions of appropriate behavior, rather than strategic gains calculations. We know from the negotiation literature that the expectation of neutral and impartial behavior constitutes one such norm.[63] Hence, instead of opportunistic chairs that exploit the office within the bounds set by formal rules, we would expect to see negotiation chairs that strive to meet the norm of neutrality with limited regard to private interests.

In sum, sociological institutionalism generates competing expectations on the sources, resources, and effects of formal leadership, thus offering a theoretical alternative to the rationalist approach presented in this chapter. Whereas the empirical tests in this study mainly are designed to evaluate the rationalist theory of formal leadership, they provide unstructured indications on the explanatory power of the sociological alternative as well. In the concluding chapter, I will revisit the sociological challenge and consider the evidence generated in the empirical part. The next chapter begins the empirical exploration of formal leadership in European and international negotiations, by examining the institutional development of the EU Presidency.

[63] Lang 1989; Carnevale and Arad 1996; Metcalfe 1998; Elgström 2003a.

3 The institutional development of the EU Presidency: a search for efficient cooperation

The Presidency has traveled far in half a century of European integration. When the office was first established in the 1950s, it possessed almost no political powers. Today, Presidencies perform functions of agenda management, brokerage, and representation that put them at the center of European cooperation. How can this remarkable transformation of the EU chairmanship be explained? Existing literature tends to present the historical evolution of the Presidency as an accidental and unanticipated process. Helen Wallace concludes: "The Presidency. . . represents a combination of reactions to events, the follower not the creator of fashion and convention."[1] In the same vein, Emil Kirchner argues: "The Council Presidency can be described as a body that has grown in status more by default than by design."[2]

This chapter argues in favor of a functionalist interpretation of the Presidency's development from an insignificant administrative office into a powerful political platform. It suggests that the primary sources behind this evolution are developments in the EU's internal decision-making and external political ambitions that have given rise to real or anticipated problems of agenda failure, negotiation failure, and representation failure. Member governments have responded to these collective-action problems by delegating new and more far-reaching responsibilities to the Presidency. The search for efficient modes of negotiation and decision-making has been the *leitmotif* of this process, which has taken place through continuous and incremental adjustment of the Presidency's tasks. Where other institutional solutions than the conferral of authority on the Presidency have been available, these alternatives have been duly considered and discarded. Where the rotation design of the Presidency has given rise to predictable problems of discontinuity, EU governments have sought to address this through the

---

[1] Wallace 1985, 2.
[2] Kirchner 1992, 71.

creation and strengthening of mechanisms of continuity, such as the Council Secretariat and means of cooperation between Presidencies.

Critics of functionalist explanations typically criticize rational choice institutionalists for drawing conclusions about the causes of an institution from the functions it performs, and for paying insufficient attention to processes of institutional development over time.[3] The account in this chapter seeks to avoid both weaknesses. First, it does not stop at the establishment of a match between the functions performed by the Presidency and the collective-action problems specified in the theory of formal leadership, but maps the reasons behind these institutional choices as revealed through historical documents and analyses. Second, it explicitly looks at institutional design as a dynamic process that unfolds over time, and carefully traces the key junctures in the empowerment of the EU chairmanship.

Properly speaking, the EU Presidency historically has not constituted one office, but several chairmanship institutions, of which three are particularly prominent. When European integration was first launched in the 1950s within the framework of the EC, the member states created the rotating office of Presidency within the Council of Ministers, the sole intergovernmental decision body at the time. When member governments in the early 1970s proceeded to establish European political co-operation (EPC) outside the formal framework of the EC, they created a second Presidency office, which subsequently was kept on when foreign policy coordination was upgraded through the establishment of the EU's common foreign and security policy (CFSP) in the early 1990s. Similarly, the founding in 1974 of the European Council as a body for summit meetings brought about a third Presidency institution. Since the member state that has held the EC Presidency has performed the same function in the EPC and the European Council as well, the three Presidencies have often been conceived of as one. Yet, in terms of historical development, they have followed different trajectories and are therefore treated as three separate cases in this chapter. This approach serves the methodological purpose of expanding the number of observations, thus strengthening the reliability of the results.

While clearly the most central institutional settings, the EC, the EPC/CFSP, and the European Council are no longer the only arenas of EU policy-making where the Presidency chairs meetings and manages the decision process. The expansion of EU cooperation has led to the creation of additional institutional frameworks that are formally distinct from

---

[3] For a particularly well-developed criticism, see Pierson 2004, ch. 4.

those that have been dominant in a historical perspective. Since the early 1990s, EU governments are engaged in police cooperation and judicial cooperation within the so-called "third pillar" of justice and home affairs (JHA). Furthermore, since the late 1990s, the member states coordinate national policy in select domains, such as employment and education, through the so-called open method of coordination. While non-negligible components of EU cooperation today, these institutional frameworks are of a more recent origin and still less comprehensive in scope. This chapter therefore centers exclusively on the evolution of the office of the Presidency within the EC, the EPC/CFSP, and the European Council.

The chapter, which draws on a combination of primary documents and secondary accounts, is divided into four sections. The first three sections map the process through which the Presidency offices in the three intergovernmental arenas gained increasing responsibilities of agenda management, brokerage, and representation. The fourth section explains how EU governments over the years have evaluated and discarded proposals for alternative chairmanship arrangements, attempting instead to compensate for the weaknesses of the rotation design.

The evolution of agenda management

The Presidency's function as agenda manager has grown from limited procedural responsibilities in the 1950s into a political function in the 2000s. This evolution is the product of a gradual process of institutional adaptation on the part of EU governments, in response to functional pressures in EU decision-making. The development of agenda management has followed the same logic in the three areas of intergovernmental negotiation, but all have had slightly different trajectories. Whereas the Presidency's agenda-management role developed in competition with the European Commission in the EC, this office held exclusive responsibilities of coordination, initiation, and execution in the EPC and the European Council.

Agenda management in the European Community

In the original design of the EC, the Presidency was entrusted with a set of procedural tasks: chairing Council sessions, preparing the agenda, taking minutes, signing documents on behalf of the Council, notifying decisions, and representing the Council *vis-à-vis* the Common Assembly, the precursor to the European Parliament.[4] However, it was the

---

[4] Council of Ministers of the European Economic Community 1958.

European Commission which enjoyed exclusive authority to set the Community's substantive agenda. Neither member governments individually, nor the Council collectively, enjoyed any formal right to present proposals for new EC rules. In the late 1950s and the first half of the 1960s, the Commission's agenda setting was focused on the ambition of the European Economic Community (EEC) Treaty to establish a customs union by the end of 1969. This treaty commitment also shaped the agenda of the Council, which was largely pre-determined.[5] The Commission's active use of its formal agendasetting powers, and the Treaty's constraining effect on the direction of the Community's early policy development, ensured that the Council's decision agenda was neither overcrowded nor underdeveloped. The decision-making environment placed no other demands on the Presidency than to conduct administrative and procedural tasks.

The second half of the 1960s witnessed the initiation of two political processes with important implications for the Presidency office. First, the Commission's capacity to control the EC agenda was reduced as a result of the so-called empty-chair crisis in 1965–1966.[6] The sources of the conflict were France's refusal to shift to more supranational modes of decision-making in the Council, and its rejection of a Commission proposal for new financing arrangements in the EC's agricultural policy. The French government led by Charles de Gaulle decided to boycott Council decision-making, and this crisis only came to an end with the so-called Luxembourg compromise in 1966. This postponed the introduction of majority voting and required the Commission to consult national governments before putting proposals on the agenda of the Council. The crisis, the compromise, and de Gaulle's continued antagonism dealt a hard blow to the Commission. While retaining its formal monopoly on policy initiation, the institution was stripped of its informal authority as the principal motor of European integration. The Commission of the 1970s and early 1980s is commonly described as a reactive and restrained body, lacking the political standing to provide leadership in European cooperation.[7]

The second important development was the growing fragmentation of Council decision-making. The scope and intensity of the Council's activities had increased during the 1960s, and the completion of the

---

[5] Wallace 1985, 3; Westlake 1999, 36.

[6] For discussions, see Lindberg and Scheingold 1970, 96–97; Moravcsik 1998, 227–230; Stirk and Weigall 1999, ch. 5.

[7] See, e.g., Kirchner 1992, 72; Cockfield 1994, 111; Grant 1994, 61–65; Nugent 1995, 121–122; Ross 1995, 23–25.

customs union in 1968 further fueled this development, by opening up the decision agenda to other policy concerns. The expansion of the EC's policy interests led to the creation of new ministerial configurations, committees, and working groups in the Council. Decision-making became increasingly compartmentalized. Describing the workings of the Council in the 1970s, Simon Bulmer and Wolfgang Wessels note: "[T]he Council of Ministers became progressively more unable to co-ordinate policy developments across the whole spectrum of EC activity."[8] Similarly, Martin Westlake observes: "Council agendas were over-crowded and badly organized . . . and the Council's authority had become weakened by the growing autonomy of sectoral Councils and their preparatory bodies."[9]

The effect of these two parallel processes was an increasing demand for agenda management. The decline of the Commission created a political vacuum, and the fragmentation of Council business called for means of coordinating the EC's political agenda. The delegation of additional agenda-management powers to the Presidency constituted member governments' primary solution, in addition to the creation of the European Council in 1974. The effect was to "ascribe to the Presidency burdens, functions and opportunities for leverage which were not explicitly part of the initial institutional design."[10]

From the late 1960s onwards, EC governments formalized and extended the Presidency's agenda-management responsibilities. In an updated version of the Council's rules of procedure, the member states formally confirmed the Presidency's procedural responsibilities.[11] In 1974, member governments adopted a package of reforms, formalizing the Presidency's responsibilities for internal coordination. That same year, the newly created European Council entrusted the Belgian prime minister, Leo Tindemans, with the task of drawing up a report on insti-tutional reform.[12] The Tindemans report underlined the need to strengthen coordination in the Council, and suggested that the role of the Presidency be reinforced.

In December 1978, the European Council initiated yet another as-sessment of the EC institutions, when setting up the committee of the "Three Wise Men." Reporting back in December 1979, the committee's

---

[8] Bulmer and Wessels 1987, 19.
[9] Westlake 1999, 40.
[10] Wallace 1985, 3.
[11] Council of the European Community 1979. The rules of procedure were formulated after the Merger Treaty of 1965, but not formally adopted until 1979.
[12] Tindemans 1976. For a detailed account, see Vandamme 1987.

primary conclusion on the Council pertained to the necessity of strengthening the Presidency's agenda-management function:

> In improving the Council's performance, the first priority is to strengthen the Presidency in its dual role of organizational control and political impetus. It is no accident that the functions of the Presidency have been both expanded and more widely recognized in recent years. The strong central management which it can provide offers the most natural means of compensating for the centrifugal tendencies within the Council. It bears the prime responsibility for tackling the spread of specialized business, the ramifying inter-institutional relations, the differing interests and behaviour of the Member States. . . . [I]f the Presidency does not do this job, there is no longer anyone else who can fill the breach.[13]

The Three Wise Men further emphasized the need to recognize that "the State holding the Chair has certain *fixed responsibilities* for the management of Council business and the good working of the Community as a whole."[14] The heads of state and government responded to this call in December the following year: "The prime role of the Presidency, assisted at all levels by the General Secretariat, involves in particular organizing work, preparing Council agendas, monitoring progress in discussions within working groups and coordinating the work done with a view to ensuring the consistency of Council decisions."[15] In 1983, member governments introduced an element of accountability for the Presidency, in recognition of the political dimension of its agenda-management responsibilities, when requiring each Presidency to present its work program to the European Parliament at the beginning of its term, and report on progress achieved at the end of the term.[16]

The strengthening of the Presidency's agenda-management function in the late 1960s, 1970s, and early 1980s was accomplished without changing the formal prerogatives laid down in the Treaty. Through consecutive reform packages and continuous changes in Council practice, governments expanded the role of the Presidency in stabilizing and shaping the EC's political agenda. By the mid-1980s, the Presidency had become the central managing force in the Council, coordinating the agendas of the various Councils, committees, and working groups. Despite the absence of a formal mandate, the Presidency had also gained an actual role in setting the agenda, at the expense of the Commission. As the Belgian diplomat Philippe de Schoutheete concluded in the mid-1980s:

---

[13] Three Wise Men 1979, 35.
[14] Three Wise Men 1979, 35. Emphasis in original.
[15] Quoted in Wallace 1985, 6.
[16] European Council 1983.

The Presidency, compensating for, or profiting from, the gradual weakening of the role and prestige of the Commission following the crisis of 1966, now exercises certain competences that the authors of the Treaty of Rome recognized as belonging to the Commission such as management, initiative, the search for compromise. It is the weakening of the Commission which has led to, and partly justified, the increased role of the Presidency in the working of the Treaty of Rome.[17]

The Presidency's rise to prominence had knock-on effects in other parts of the EU's decision-making system, most notably for the standing of the General Secretariat of the Council. Member governments recognized that the rotation of the Presidency from one state to another every six months, while efficient as a power-sharing arrangement, caused certain discontinuities in the operational work of the Council. The Council Secretariat, established in 1958, held the solution to this problem.[18] For a long time the Council Secretariat was restricted in size and resource, reflecting the initial decision in favor of the Commission as the independent supranational "secretariat" in the EC. When the Presidency was forced into a more pronounced agenda-management role, the demand for the support services of the Council Secretariat increased in parallel. Between 1959 and 1975, the number of officials rose from 264 to 1,475.[19] The early 1980s marked the beginning of a new period of reinforcement, when the Council Secretariat, led by Niels Ersbøll, gained a more pronounced advisory role. As one observer noted: "Interestingly, the Council Secretariat, while preserving its collective loyalty to the Council as a whole, has, in effect, become largely a Presidency Secretariat in a much more explicit sense than was previously the case."[20]

The 1980s and the 1990s were decades of constitutional reform in Europe. The original EEC Treaty was revised through the Single European Act (SEA, 1986), the Treaty on European Union (TEU, 1991), the Amsterdam Treaty (1997), and the Nice Treaty (2000). Neither of these treaties brought any fundamental change to the Presidency's agenda-management function within the EC. Rather, the Presidency continued to develop in an incremental fashion and in response to demands for initiative and coordination in the Council.

From the mid-1980s onwards, the task of agenda management became increasingly geared toward executive, political functions. In 1985, EU governments decided to complete the EC's internal market

---

[17] Schoutheete 1988, 74–75.
[18] On the Council Secretariat, see Hayes-Renshaw and Wallace 1997, ch. 4; Westlake 1999, ch. 13; Sherrington 2000, 49–53; Hamlet 2002; Beach 2004.
[19] Westlake 1999, 320.
[20] Wallace 1985, 12.

before the end of 1992 through a large-scale legislative program.[21] Simultaneously, the SEA and the TEU moved EC cooperation into new issue areas, such as the environment and regional policy. The escalation in Council activity is reflected in the number of ministerial meetings, which rose from 60 in 1980 to 94 in 1993 – an increase of more than 50 percent.[22] Member governments responded to the growing pressure on the Council machinery by conferring on the Presidency an explicit authority to prioritize among competing policy concerns. As Fiona Hayes-Renshaw and Helen Wallace explain: "[T]he sheer volume of work of the Council quite simply meant that it required more active management."[23] In 1988, it was decided that each Presidency should present a comprehensive work program for its six-month period at the helm, and in 1993, this procedure was formally integrated into the Council's rules of procedure.[24] The new work program consisted of three parts: a political declaration of intent, setting out the policy priorities of the incoming Presidency; a schedule over all meetings during the six-month period; and indicative agendas for all Council meetings at the ministerial level, specifying subjects for debate and decision. The agenda-management function was further strengthened by the formal conferral in 1993 of a right for the Presidency to propose issues for general policy debates, and the steadily growing use of informal meetings in the Presidency country with agendas dictated by the host government.

The most significant development during the remaining part of the 1990s and the early 2000s pertained to the mechanisms of continuity instituted by member governments. The enlargement of the EU from twelve to fifteen member states in 1995, and the prospect of another enlargement to include countries in Central and Eastern Europe with more limited administrative capacities, highlighted the question of discontinuity in the management of the EU agenda. Proposals to strengthen the Council Secretariat's support function and to establish means of cooperation between consecutive Presidencies were forwarded and put into practice.[25] Whereas legislative programs stretching over several years had been a reality since the internal market initiative, the member states went one step further in 2002, when introducing a multi-annual strategic program drawn up by consecutive Presidencies in

---

[21] For an analysis of the implementation of this program and its pressure on the EC decision-making machinery, see Tallberg 2003b, ch. 3.
[22] Westlake 1999, 60.
[23] Hayes-Renshaw and Wallace 1997, 135.
[24] Council of the European Union 1993. See also Council Secretariat 1997, 10.
[25] Council Secretariat 1999, 2002; Council of the European Union 1999e, 2002a, 2002b.

cooperation.[26] The effect of these measures was to mitigate the discontinuity inherent in the rotation of the office. As two close observers conclude:

[T]he presidency under the first pillar has become so institutionalised and so hedged in by operating constraints that it can withstand quite striking variations in performance by individual governments in office and, even, the extraordinary pressure of a major election in the country that provides the chair . . . Thus the presidency helps to make the Council tick over more smoothly and more quickly, but the Council is not dependent on the hazards of performance by particular presidencies.[27]

Agenda management in the EPC/CFSP

When EC governments decided to initiate cooperation in foreign policy in the 1970s, through the establishment of the EPC, this policy regime was placed outside the conventional Community framework. The purpose was to encourage consultation and coordination on foreign policy, not to harmonize policy through supranational decision-making and binding rules.[28] These intentions were reflected in the institutional design of the EPC, which did not leave any place for the Commission in the initiation of policy. Instead, member governments conferred prerogatives of coordination and initiative on the Presidency.

In the founding document of the EPC, the Luxembourg report of 1970, the member states laid down a set of procedural arrangements that included a specification of the role and mandate of the Presidency.[29] Meetings were to take place at the initiative of the Presidency and in the Presidency's country. It was the responsibility of the Presidency to determine whether and how the member states should consult with each other when responding to international crises. The Presidency should function as chairman, both in ministerial meetings and in meetings of the Political Committee, comprising the heads of the political departments in the foreign affairs ministries. In formal terms, all member states shared the same right to propose subjects for political consultation. In practice, the Presidency, as first among equals, gained the primary responsibility to set and structure the foreign policy agenda. "[W]hilst the intergovernmental method could effectively sideline the Commission in EC decision-making, it required a replacement for

---

[26] European Council 2002a.
[27] Hayes-Renshaw and Wallace 1997, 154.
[28] Smith 2004, 71–77.
[29] Foreign Ministers of the European Community 1970.

the Commission's role. The Council Presidency became this replacement and the sole forum through which Council of Ministers' activities were initiated, co-ordinated and represented."[30]

In July 1973, the member governments met in Copenhagen to assess the first years of cooperation. The Copenhagen report became the second constitutional document of the EPC and further developed the Presidency's responsibilities in terms of coordination and execution.[31] The Presidency was charged with the tasks of managing the communications system set up to facilitate consultation among the foreign ministries, of organizing consultations among the embassies of the member states, and of handling policy linkages between the EPC and the EC. Furthermore, it was made explicit that the Presidency had a special responsibility for initiating foreign policy consultations and for ensuring the proper implementation of EPC conclusions.

The next revision of the EPC framework took place through the issuing of the London report in 1981.[32] With few exceptions, the Presidency's agenda-management function remained untouched. The degree to which agenda setting had devolved upon the Presidency was reflected in a reminder in the report that other states could submit proposals for action as well. Furthermore, the report specified the role of the Presidency in preparing the agenda and summarizing the discussions of informal, so-called Gymnich meetings, between the foreign ministers. The most important institutional innovation with implications for agenda management was the creation of a small secretariat for the EPC.[33] During the late 1970s, it had gradually become more apparent that the light organizational structure posed a challenge to the efficiency of the EPC. The expanding foreign policy agenda increased the administrative burden of the Presidency, and the rotation of the office constituted a source of discontinuity. The member governments decided that the Presidency should be assisted by a small team of officials seconded from preceding and succeeding Presidencies – effectively constituting a small EPC secretariat. In the 1983 Stuttgart solemn declaration, national governments confirmed the dual strategy of simultaneously strengthening the Presidency's powers of initiative and the means of operational support.[34]

---

[30] Kirchner 1992, 73. See also Wallace 1985, 8; Bonvicini 1988, 59.
[31] Foreign Ministers of the European Community 1973. For discussions, see Schoutheete 1988, 71; Nuttall 1992, 75.
[32] Foreign Ministers of the European Community 1981.
[33] Wallace 1985; Schoutheete 1988; Sanches da Costa Pereira 1988.
[34] European Council 1983.

In the mid-1980s, observers of the EPC unanimously underlined the central role of the Presidency in supplying agenda management. Wallace emphasized: "The strengthening of the Presidency-based infrastructure . . . reflects a high degree of satisfaction and mutual congratulation at the successful performance of the Presidency as an institution in its own right."[35] Similarly, de Schoutheete concluded: "The growth in the scope and effectiveness of political cooperation was made possible only by the constantly increasing authority vested in the Presidency."[36] Etienne Davignon, who presided at the birth of the EPC, explicitly linked the demand for the Presidency to the complexity of multilateral cooperation: "In multilateral diplomacy, decisions are difficult to take and in a Community of twelve the task of reconciling different positions remains complex. A common policy will only be possible if two conditions are met: the political will to make the voice of Europe heard; the delegation of a guiding role to the Presidency."[37]

The Presidency maintained its central position in the management of the EPC agenda throughout the 1980s and 1990s, despite rounds of institutional change in foreign policy cooperation. The SEA brought the EPC within the EC treaties, the TEU entailed a qualitative leap by establishing procedures for a common foreign and security policy, and the Amsterdam Treaty strengthened these arrangements. These treaty revisions anchored in formal terms what had been political practice for some time. Explains one Council insider: "The Presidency is in most cases the driving force behind the pace and policy content of initiatives in the CFSP field. While other Member States and the Commission are also entitled to initiate proposals, the Presidency, because of its authority and because this role is generally expected of it, is in a stronger position to take such initiatives."[38]

Furthermore, the treaty changes in the late 1980s and 1990s brought a reinforcement of operational support through the secretariat. The SEA established a permanent EPC secretariat in Brussels, whereas the TEU brought the EPC Secretariat within the confines of the General Secretariat of the Council. The Amsterdam Treaty, finally, sharpened the Council Secretariat's foreign policy profile, by granting its secretary general the title of high representative for the CFSP and equipping this office with a small policy-planning unit. The strengthening of the secretariat off-loaded some of the Presidency's administrative burdens and

---

[35] Wallace 1985, 9.
[36] Schoutheete 1988, 82.
[37] Davignon 1986, 5.
[38] Galloway 1999b, 222.

ensured greater continuity in the operative structures of the EU's common foreign policy.

Agenda management in the European Council

When EC governments in 1974 founded the European Council as an institutionalized form of summitry outside the Community framework, they chose an intergovernmental design for agenda management, similar to the one created for the EPC four years earlier. The Commission, whose weak political leadership had constituted a prominent reason for creating the European Council, was not endowed with any prerogatives in the preparation of the agenda.[39] Instead, the Presidency *de facto* gained the main responsibility for the agenda.

The so-called Paris communiqué establishing the European Council stated that the heads of state and government were to meet three times a year, accompanied by their foreign ministers.[40] The responsibility for the preparation of the European Council agenda was endowed to all member states collectively, through their foreign ministers. Furthermore, the communiqué provided for an administrative secretariat, set to organize the summits. It is notable that the Paris communiqué contained few explicit references to the Presidency of this body, which was to be held by the prime minister or president of the member state currently functioning as the Presidency in the EC.

However, as soon as the European Council became operational, the responsibility for the administrative and political preparation and execution of summits devolved upon the Presidency. "Its whole construction, as something apart from the regular institutional framework, created a vacuum which the presidency filled, taking on some of the functions performed by the Commission and the Council Secretariat under the more orthodox Community procedures."[41] It became established practice that two out of three yearly meetings were held in the Presidency country, and the remaining meeting in one of the "EC capitals" – Brussels, Strasbourg, and Luxembourg. Notwithstanding the provisions for an administrative secretariat in the Paris communiqué, the member governments refrained from creating one, for fear of setting up another independent body.[42] Instead, the Presidency would have to rely on its

---

[39] On the origin of the European Council, see Bulmer and Wessels 1987, ch. 2; Werts 1992, ch. 1; Taulègne 1993, chs. 1–2.

[40] European Council 1974.

[41] Hayes-Renshaw and Wallace 1997, 134.

[42] France insisted on a permanent secretariat in Paris, but the Benelux countries feared that such a body would challenge the role of the Commission. See Bulmer and Wessels 1987, 51; Westlake 1999, 23.

own organizational resources. Similarly, the political preparations of summits were entrusted to the Presidency. Even if the foreign ministers engaged in preparatory discussions, this group did not constitute a functional forum for the formulation of a delimited and manageable agenda.

The late 1970s and the early 1980s witnessed a number of initiatives aimed at boosting the organizational framework of the European Council.[43] In 1977, French president Valéry Giscard d'Estaing initiated a discussion about the organizational deficit of the European Council. One of Giscard d'Estaing's central suggestions was to strengthen the Presidency. At the summit in London that same year, the heads of state and government adopted a declaration on the organizational rules of the European Council.[44] The London declaration explicitly granted the Presidency a role in the advance preparation of the agenda, and assigned the Presidency the task of providing the only record of conclusions.

By the mid-1980s, the Presidency's special responsibility for the agenda of European Council meetings had become institutionalized. Only through cutting and pruning by the Presidency did the agenda reach proportions amenable to bargaining. As Simon Bulmer and Wolfgang Wessels concluded in 1987: "The presidency-in-office has a clear discretionary role in narrowing down the agenda from the rather large set of topics that emerges initially."[45] The methods of political preparation had reached the format that essentially would remain in place until 2002. For purposes of sounding out concerns and anchoring priorities, the chairman of the European Council would undertake a trip to all capitals, a *tour des capitales*, where he or she met bilaterally with the other heads of state and government. Shortly before the summit, the foreign ministers in the General Affairs Council would conduct an exchange on the agenda items, and then the Presidency would circulate the final agenda a week before the summit.

The SEA and the TEU incorporated the European Council into the formal treaties. Whereas the shift in formal standing altered little in the functioning of the European Council, it coincided with more substantive changes in practice. The Irish Presidency in 1990 was the first to host two European Council meetings, whereas none was held in the EC capitals.[46] This marked the beginning of the custom for each Presidency government to hold two meetings in the home country – one informal summit in the middle of the six-month period, and one formal summit at

---

[43] For a discussion, see Werts 1992, 326–327.
[44] European Council 1977.
[45] Bulmer and Wessels 1987, 52. See also Werts 1992, 78.
[46] With the exception of Belgium, Luxembourg, and France, of course, which often had hosted two summits in their capacity as home countries of the EC capitals.

the end of the period. This change carried political implications. Each Presidency now enjoyed two opportunities to shape and structure the agenda of the European Council. Furthermore, the substantive agenda of the informal meeting truly constituted the exclusive domain of the Presidency, which was at liberty to decide the theme for these summits.

The late 1990s and early 2000s witnessed changes in the working methods of the European Council with effects on the Presidency's role in defining the agenda. First, as part of a reform package adopted in Seville in 2002, the preparation of the agenda and the associated conclusions became more institutionalized.[47] Whereas the Presidency's role in the pre-summit phase previously had consisted of informal bilateral consultations with other governments over the agenda, it now became one of managing regular pre-negotiations between the member states on the central issues on the agenda. Second, the Presidency's capacity to set the agenda of informal summits was reduced by the increasing habit of the European Council to pre-program its own agenda, in an effort to achieve greater continuity in policy development. It became standard practice for the informal spring summit of the European Council to address cooperation on employment, competitiveness, and sustainable development, whereas the fall meeting took on cooperation on asylum, immigration, and cross-border crime.

Agenda management: assessing the institutional development

The evolution of the Presidency's agenda-management powers reflects a process of gradual and continuous institutional adaptation in response to functional demands in EU decision-making. When real or anticipated problems of agenda failure have become more prominent, EU governments have conferred new powers of agenda management on the Presidency and expanded its arsenal of weapons. When EU governments have established new arenas of intergovernmental cooperation, they have evaluated alternative institutional solutions and settled on the Presidency as the preferred agenda manager.

Even if the development of the Presidency's agenda-management function followed different trajectories in the EC, the EPC, and the European Council, these processes point to the same logic of institutional evolution. In the EC, the Presidency's role as agenda manager evolved from limited, procedural responsibilities in the original template

---

[47] European Council 2002a; Ludlow 2002, 38–55; interviews, Swedish government official, 24 September 2004; Council Secretariat official, 3 November 2004.

of institutions, into a central role in the political shaping of the agenda from the 1980s and onwards. The driving forces in this development were the decline of the Commission in the formulation of the EC's substantive agenda, and the growing fragmentation of Council decision-making. From the late 1960s and onwards, consecutive rounds of adaptation in institutional practices reinforced the Presidency's function as agenda manager. One central component was the introduction in the late 1980s of the Presidency program, whereby governments-in-office assign priority to the issues on the EC agenda and structure concrete meeting agendas to this end. Interestingly, this transformation took place through incremental changes in political practices over more than forty years, rather than formal treaty revisions at historical turning points.

The institutional development of the Presidency's agenda-management function in the EPC and the European Council followed a different trajectory. When these arenas of intergovernmental cooperation were set up in the first half of the 1970s, member governments chose not to transfer the established institutional model of the EC. Intent on keeping the supranational Commission outside, and content with the growing agenda-management role of the Presidency in the EC, member governments placed the Presidency in the driving seat already at the creation of the EPC and the European Council. Even if all governments formally held the same power of initiative, it became standard practice for the Presidency to present most proposals. Where the member governments attempted to provide agenda management collectively, these attempts generally failed and triggered the conferral of responsibilities on the Presidency. In the EPC, the Presidency quickly emerged as the primary source of political initiatives, assisted by an increasingly well-developed secretariat, instituted to provide continuity and operational support. In the European Council, the administrative and political preparation and execution of summits devolved upon the Presidency, which gained a discretionary role in defining and delimiting the agenda. When member governments subsequently sought to develop the EPC and boost the political clout of the European Council, the strengthening of the Presidency constituted an important component.

The evolution of brokerage

Unlike the Presidency's agenda-management and representation functions, its role as broker in EU negotiations has never been anchored in formal treaty texts and rules of procedure. Instead, it is the product of political practices that have evolved over time, in response to growing state demands for mediation, single negotiating texts, and coalition building. Whereas the Commission originally took on important broker-age tasks in the EC, the Presidency developed into the principal archi-tect of compromise from the late 1960s onwards. In the EPC and the European Council, the Presidency did not face competition from the Commission and constituted member governments' preferred broker from the beginning. To facilitate mediation by the Presidency, the member states have equipped this office with a specific set of brokerage instruments.

Brokerage in the European Community

In the original design of the EC, the Commission's function as agenda setter went hand in hand with the responsibility to broker compromises between the member states in the Council. Not being one of the bargain-ing parties, the Commission was expected to be detached from the special interests of member governments, and was therefore able to function as an impartial and credible mediator. This was the dominant pattern in the late 1950s and the first half of the 1960s. For instance, Leon Lindberg and Stuart Scheingold note in their seminal study of the EEC that brokerage and consensus building was one of the Commission's central sources of influence.[48]

The late 1960s and the early 1970s brought a number of develop-ments that worked against the Commission and in favor of the Presi-dency as the member governments' preferred mediator. The empty chair crisis affected not only the Commission's position as agenda manager, but its role as broker as well. Distrusted for its supranational intentions, the Commission was increasingly excluded from the central bargaining processes. For the member governments, the Luxembourg compromise posed a double challenge, prolonging the use of unanimity as decision rule and reducing the credibility of the Commission as broker. "Whilst the Commission took a battering from the impact of the Luxembourg compromise and, for a long time, played a subservient role to the Council of Ministers, the latter, in turn, found itself confronted with a seemingly unsolvable task of working out compromises among EC members."[49]

The Presidency met the demand for a mediator capable of brokering compromises among the member states. "A change of emphasis for the main mediating role took place, from the Commission – originally

---

[48] Lindberg and Scheingold 1970, 93–95.
[49] Kirchner 1992, 72.

the principal architect of the compromises – to the Presidency."[50] This shift was reinforced by later political and institutional developments. In the mid-1980s, Wallace observed: "The Commission has acquired more of its own vested interests with the passage of time. As the 'eleventh Member State' it is less well placed to behave impartially. With the Commission less able and perhaps less willing to act as the package-broker, something of a vacuum has been created. The increased role of the Presidency thus in part represents an adaptive response from within the Council."[51] Similarly, Philippa Sherrington notes at the end of the 1990s: "[T]he President is often viewed as the preferred mediator by member states meeting in the Council."[52]

Nowadays, it is common to speak of the so-called Presidency compromise.[53] The existence of a specific term for compromises proposed by the chair reflects the Commission's original role as mediator and the Presidency's subsequent development into the preferred broker. In EC negotiations, where the Commission formulates all legislative initiatives, the Presidency compromise typically consists of a draft agreement that attempts to take the negotiating parties' positions into consideration, without being bound by the Commission's original proposal. In strictly intergovernmental negotiations, where the member states formulate the proposals, the Presidency's document automatically gains the status of single negotiating text, around which bargaining is planned to converge.

The demand for the Presidency as broker can partly be seen as a product of the increasing complexity of the EC decision-making environment. The expansion of Council business, and the associated growth in ministerial councils, committees, and working groups, created a pressure and a potential for package deals engineered by the Presidency. Furthermore, the number of bargaining parties increased over time, as a result of "successive waves of enlargement, each wave making consensus in the Council more difficult to achieve."[54] More actors do not necessarily aggravate decision-making, but if they expand the spectrum of preferences, then agreement becomes more difficult to achieve. In the EC, the accession of the UK in 1973 had such an effect on decision-making.[55]

That said, the expanding policy agenda simultaneously offered new opportunities for cross-cutting package agreements, involving

---

[50] Werts 1992, 95.
[51] Wallace 1985, 7.
[52] Sherrington 1998, 4.
[53] See, e.g., Hayes-Renshaw and Wallace 1997, 146–147; Nicoll 1998, 5–6; Westlake 1999, 308.
[54] Westlake 1999, 38. See also Sherrington 2000, 44.
[55] Golub 1999, 752.

concessions and trade-offs in multiple issue domains. The Presidency's position as the link between the different bargaining arenas in the Council offered unique possibilities for channeling information and identifying possible deals. The expectations attached to the Presidency's ability to deliver agreement in this complex decision-making environment were reflected already in the 1979 report of the Three Wise Men: "The Presidency's basic duty in this process is simply to get results. . . . It must urge the debate towards conclusions by using the most appropriate combination of weapons at its disposal (pressure, mediation, compromise proposals, time-limits, voting)."[56]

Another important development with implications for the Presidency's brokerage function was the string of institutional reforms from the mid-1980s until 2000. These treaty revisions gradually replaced unanimity with qualified majority voting (QMV) as the decision rule in the Council, and gave the European Parliament a more prominent position in the legislative process. The SEA provided for qualified majority voting in a number of domains, most notably, the internal market. The TEU extended this decision rule, as did the Amsterdam and Nice Treaties. The possibility of adopting legislation through majority voting led to changes in the brokerage role of the Presidency. Rather than seeking broad solutions that reflected the lowest common denominator among governments, the Presidency was set with the task of identifying viable coalitions and rallying support for proposals that could gather a sufficient majority. The adoption in 1987 of new rules of procedure for the Council provided the Presidency with additional weapons for these purposes, notably, the formal authority to call votes. The most important implication of this prerogative was not the actual calling of votes, which remained a rare occurrence, but the reinforcement of the Presidency's capacity to steer the negotiation process. It became common practice for the Presidency to work toward a minimum agreement, supported by the requisite number of member states, and then invite outliers to join the majority, under the threat of voting.

The SEA strengthened the position of the Parliament in EC decision-making through the introduction of the cooperation procedure, which made it possible for the European Parliament to make legislation it disliked difficult for the Council to adopt. The TEU extended the Parliament's powers by broadening the use of the cooperation procedure, and by introducing the co-decision procedure, which granted the Parliament the same status as the Council in the adoption of legislation. The

---

[56] Three Wise Men 1979, 36.

Amsterdam and Nice Treaties expanded the areas of co-decision. These reforms carried important consequences for the Presidency as broker. The obligation for the Commission to take the Parliament's positions into consideration when amending its proposals between readings further reduced its capacity to function as a brokering force within the Council.[57] Moreover, the Presidency's task of representing the Council in legislative negotiations with the Parliament (discussed in the next section) put the Presidency in the position of having to engineer an early agreement in the Council, or else it would have little to present to the Parliament.

Brokerage in the EPC/CFSP

The ambition to present a united front in international affairs made brokerage a central part of the EPC. The combination of competing foreign policy interests and the requirement of unanimous agreement created a strong demand for mediation and consensus building. From the moment the EPC was established, it was the Presidency that met this demand for brokerage.[58] Member governments' decision to leave the Commission outside the EPC left the Presidency without a competitor, and the formal responsibilities in agenda management and representation made the Presidency the natural candidate for the role as informal broker in the EPC. Yet the challenges of foreign policy coordination proved formidable, and member states' activities in this area since the 1970s have often been presented as an uphill battle, characterized by diverging national interests and insufficient institutional mechanisms.[59] The proposal to strengthen the Presidency has been a recurring element in the discussion of potential solutions.

In the mid-1980s, the Presidency's brokerage function was described in the following way: "The Presidency plays a fundamental role in this process of permanent conciliation. Through the contacts made, the confidences received, the precise knowledge of facts, the Presidency-in-Office must, at each level, endeavour to know the precise limits of possible concessions of each partner and their priority objectives. It must trace the path that leads to agreement, and to a common success."[60]

Developments in European cooperation made certain that the demand for Presidency brokerage remained high. Enlargement of the EC to include new member states with divergent foreign policy interests reduced

---

[57] Nicoll 1998, 5.
[58] Schoutheete 1988, 75.
[59] See, e.g., Peterson and Sjursen 1998; Zielonka 1998; Smith 2001.
[60] Schoutheete 1988, 79. See also Bassompierre 1988, 62–63.

the zone of agreement and made common positions more difficult to arrive at. One example is the accession of Greece in 1981, which posed new challenges to the unity of the organization, because of its outlier position on issues pertaining to the Balkans and Turkey.[61] Similarly, the accession in 1995 of three non-aligned states – Austria, Finland, and Sweden – brought countries into the EU with particular views on the organization's association with the North Atlantic Treaty Organization (NATO).

Another explanation of the continuous demand for brokerage has been the development of the EU's foreign policy ambitions. Whereas the original intention of the EPC was consultation on foreign policy, the member states subsequently formulated more far-reaching and demanding goals. In the TEU, the member states declared their ambition to develop a common foreign and security policy through systematic cooperation and common positions on all central foreign policy issues. The Amsterdam Treaty raised the level of aspiration further by introducing more demanding forms of cooperation, such as joint actions (foreign policy operations) and common strategies (long-term foreign policy strategies *vis-à-vis* regions or problems). The Nice Treaty expanded the planned domain of cooperation into the area of defense, formulating goals on crisis management and conflict prevention. Taken together, the new ambitions have raised the stakes in foreign policy cooperation and have made the Presidency's engineering of consensus increasingly important. For instance, the EU will be unable to act rapidly and forcefully in European and international crises where it now seeks a role, unless member governments are capable of reaching early agreement. The challenges involved were painfully illustrated by the coordination problems experienced in association with the wars in Yugoslavia in 1991, in Kosovo in 1999, and in Iraq in 2003. Even if the late 1990s and the early 2000s have witnessed a more prominent position for the Council Secretariat in the shaping of EU foreign policy, the Presidency has remained the dominant engineer of consensus.

Brokerage in the European Council

The demand for brokerage was strong from the moment the European Council was founded. Part of the rationale for creating this body had been the inability of the Council to reach agreements in a context of unanimity requirements and divergent national interests.[62] The

---

[61] See, e.g., Strömvik 1998; Luif 2003.
[62] See, e.g. Bulmer and Wessels 1987, ch. 2.

European Council could alleviate this problem by functioning as an appellate body, where the heads of state and government made final attempts to strike deals that ministers had been unable to clinch in the Council. In the 1977 London declaration, the member governments defined the task of settling issues outstanding from discussions at lower levels as one of the central functions of the European Council, next to informal exchanges and guidelines for future action.[63] Over the years, this has remained an important function of the European Council, and the agenda of every summit includes one or several issues referred from the Council.

Furthermore, the demand for brokerage has been fueled by the European Council's role in stitching together package agreements on policy reform or institutional reform. Whereas the Council has often been unable to negotiate cross-sectoral package deals because of its policy divisions, the European Council has held the promise of agreement, owing to its horizontal perspective and political authority. The expansion of the EU's policy remit has secured a continuous demand for package agreements engineered in the European Council. Of particular note is the institutionalized practice of grand bargains on the EU's financial perspectives – multi-annual budgets that define the member states' contributions to, and benefits from, the EU's major spending policies over an extended period of time.[64] By the same token, the European Council, as the highest political organ in the EU, has constituted the designated bargaining arena for the final negotiations on new treaties. Each intergovernmental conference (IGC) since the adoption of the SEA in 1986 has been concluded through intense bargaining between the heads of state and government at a European Council summit.

From the outset, the primary responsibility to provide brokerage fell on the Presidency. Research on the European Council's first ten years suggests that the Presidency played a central role in the engineering of major bargains.[65] The Presidency's formal function in agenda management translated into a special responsibility in the brokering of agreements. Since many of the portfolios that reached the European Council were "hard cases," where the member states had been unable to reach agreement at lower levels, the Presidency was confronted with the challenge of identifying an underlying zone of agreement. Over the years, two practices developed specifically for this purpose – the *tour des capitales* and the confessional.

---

[63] European Council 1977.
[64] Laffan 2000.
[65] Werts 1992.

Besides allowing the Presidency to rally support for its agenda before the summit, the *tour des capitales* permitted the Presidency to collect information on state preferences through bilateral encounters. The practice of the Presidency to engage in shuttle diplomacy in preparation for the European Council summits began in the 1970s and reached an early peak during the French Presidency in 1984, when the French president François Mitterrand held no less than thirty meetings with other heads of government.[66] The *tour des capitales* subsequently became standard practice, even if the recent enlargement of the EU to twenty-five member states poses a challenge to this tradition. The format of the bilateral encounter enables prime ministers to share information about their bottom lines with the Presidency, thus improving the chances of summit agreements on contentious issues. The confessional was developed to serve the same purpose during the course of actual meetings, in the European Council as well as the Council. When confronted with a negotiation deadlock, the Presidency would adjourn the plenary proceedings for bilateral and confidential discussions with individual delegations. Wallace and Hayes-Renshaw explain: "The objectives are threefold: first, to encourage individual delegations to be more open and more direct about the 'bottom lines' of their negotiating positions; second, to put pressure more fiercely on individual delegations to make concessions; and, third, sometimes, to offer 'unofficial' inducements to cooperation."[67]

The end product of European Council negotiations are the conclusions that are collectively adopted at the end of the summit. Since the 1977 London declaration, these conclusions have been formally adopted under the authority of the Presidency. In practice, however, the Presidency conclusions have always been subject to intense bargaining, since they are the only record of the decisions taken at the meeting. The development of the drafting process illustrates the problems of decentralized bargaining and the demand for the Presidency as broker.[68] In the 1970s and the early 1980s, European Council conclusions were in practice negotiated by special representatives of the heads of state and government – so-called sherpas. Following conventional summit procedures, the sherpas would establish preliminary agreement where permitted, and then "bracket" outstanding issues, which were left for the executives to handle. Yet this arrangement was far from satisfactory. Reservations were added to reservations, since the sherpas lacked the

---

[66] Bulmer and Wessels 1987, 54.
[67] Hayes-Renshaw and Wallace 1997, 147.
[68] Westlake 1999, 28. See also Werts 1992, 101–104; Bulmer and Wessels 1987, 57–58.

authority to reveal bottom lines, effectively producing unnegotiable draft texts. In 1982, this system was abandoned. Instead, the drafting of conclusions was entrusted to the Presidency, assisted by the Council Secretariat and the Commission. This arrangement has "to everybody's relief and satisfaction, imposed much-needed order on a previously chaotic exercise."[69]

Brokerage: assessing the institutional development

The evolution of the informal practice of brokerage is more difficult to trace than the development of agenda management and representation, which is reflected in formal treaties and rules of procedure. That said, existing primary and secondary evidence suggests that the Presidency has developed into the principal architect of compromise in the EU, often at the expense of the Commission. Single negotiating texts formulated by the Presidency have become the norm in most areas of EU cooperation. Member states' demand for the brokerage services of the Presidency have been driven by a number of developments in the EU's decision-making environment. The accession of new member states has expanded the spectrum of preferences and made agreement more difficult to reach. The increasing number of parties and the growing complexity of EU decision-making has made it more difficult to identify the underlying zone of agreement. The increasing interdependence between multiple negotiation arenas has produced a demand for cross-sectoral package agreements. New decision rules and legislative procedures have called for more active coalition building. In all three areas of cooperation, member governments have responded to these developments by inviting the Presidency to perform an increasingly prominent brokerage role and equipping the office with specific mediation instruments.

Just like the Presidency's agenda-management function, its role as broker in the EC originally developed in relation to the Commission's decline in political standing. Increasingly aware and sceptical of the supranational executive's private agenda, member governments began to rely more heavily on the rotating Presidency as their preferred broker during the 1960s. Even if the Commission continued to function as an occasional mediator, the Presidency gradually evolved into the dominant engineer of agreement. The demand for the Presidency's services subsequently increased, as developments in the EC decision-making environment made efficient agreements more difficult to arrive at. The

---

[69] Westlake 1999, 28.

expansion of Council business created a pressure for package agreements that the Presidency was uniquely well positioned to deliver. Similarly, the gradual shift to majority voting in the Council, and the rise of the Parliament as legislative interlocutor, pushed the Presidency into new practices. The Presidency compromise became a concept in its own right.

In the EPC and the European Council, member governments' decision to eschew the service of the Commission left the Presidency without a contender. In addition, the chairmanship's formal responsibilities in agenda management and representation made the Presidency the natural candidate for the role as informal broker. For partly different reasons, both decision arenas were subject to notable risks of negotiation failure and strong demands for consensus building. The rationale of foreign policy coordination was to present a unified European front in response to events in world politics, and this required that governments reached unanimous agreement on short notice. The accession of states with particular foreign policy interests, as well as the formulation of more far-reaching foreign policy ambitions, ensured a strong demand for Presidency brokerage. Similarly, brokerage was in demand in the European Council, charged with the tasks of negotiating package deals, concluding intergovernmental conferences, and settling controversial issues referred from the Council. For purposes of helping the Presidency in the task of identifying underlying zones of agreement, member governments developed the *tour des capitales* and the confessional as specific brokerage practices. Moreover, the important drafting of European Council conclusions eventually devolved upon the Presidency.

The evolution of representation

Since the early 1970s, the Presidency has, step by step, acquired more encompassing responsibilities as the Council's representative in relation to other EU institutions and third parties in world politics. Member states' original decision to engage the Presidency as spokesperson was motivated by a concrete risk of representation failure: "An obvious reason for the emergence of the Presidency was the fact that the Council, as a composite body, had no other evident means of representing itself *vis-à-vis* the other institutions, the press and media, or the wider world."[70] When EU governments subsequently stepped up their ambitions in international politics and the Parliament gained meaningful

---

[70] Westlake 1999, 37.

legislative powers, the Presidency was delegated the power of negotiating agreements on their behalf.

External representation

The Presidency's function as external representative developed hand in hand with an increasing need for the EU to structure its relations with the rest of the world. "The presidency role in speaking for the EU and for its members has grown exponentially over the past 20 years."[71] This growth in representational responsibilities has been both quantitative and qualitative. On the one hand, the member states have sought to speak with one voice – the Presidency's – in an increasing number of international forums and in relation to an increasing number of states. On the other hand, the Presidency has been granted more far-reaching representational prerogatives over time.

When founding the EEC, member governments delegated the function of external representation to the Commission in the areas covered by the new treaty, such as foreign trade and foreign aid. These powers were not extended when the EPC was established in the early 1970s. Instead, the member states opted for strictly intergovernmental arrangements, and chose the rotating Presidency as their collective representative. The arrangement was not entirely novel, since the Presidency had represented the Council in the negotiations leading to the 1963 Yaoundé convention, establishing forms of cooperation with eighteen African countries, as well as the 1963 association agreement with Turkey.[72]

The 1970 Luxembourg report charged the Presidency with the task of functioning as a liaison between the member states and the four applicant countries at the time – Denmark, Ireland, Norway, and the United Kingdom.[73] In the 1974 Copenhagen report, the foreign ministers of the participating states delegated the general task of external representation to the Presidency, when deciding that the government in office should speak on their behalf in EPC dialog with friendly states.[74] The heads of state and government conferred the same responsibilities of external representation on the Presidency when the European Council was founded later that year.[75] These formal provisions were rapidly

---

[71] Hayes-Renshaw and Wallace 1997, 149.
[72] Westlake 1999, 37.
[73] Foreign Ministers of the European Community 1970.
[74] Foreign Ministers of the European Community 1973.
[75] European Council 1974.

transformed into actual practice. Notably, the Presidency began to speak on behalf of the member states in the UN General Assembly in 1975.[76]

The early 1980s witnessed a reinforcement of the Presidency's function as collective representative in external affairs. These changes took place against the backdrop of increasing EPC action in the second half of the 1970s, involving more intense consultations among the member states, as well as growing demands for contact channels with third parties and expectations on concerted European involvement in the near abroad. The 1981 London report brought two significant innovations to the Presidency's representational function. First, member governments explicitly supplemented the Presidency's power to issue collective declarations with the right to meet with third parties on their behalf:

As European political cooperation intensifies and broadens, the Ten as such will appear as significant interlocutors. Third countries will increasingly express the desire to enter into more or less regular contact with them. It is important that the Ten should be able to respond effectively to these demands, in particular *vis-à-vis* countries of special interest to them, and that they should speak with one voice in dealings with them. The Presidency may meet individual representatives of third countries in order to discuss certain matters of particular interest to the country in question. The Presidency may respond to a request for contacts by a group of ambassadors of Member States of organizations with which the Ten maintain special links.[77]

Second, member governments coupled the delegation of these representational powers with the establishment of the so-called troika as an instrument of continuity.[78] When meeting with the third countries, the government in office would be accompanied by representatives of the preceding and succeeding Presidencies. This arrangement had been in use since the 1977 Belgian Presidency, but was formally confirmed by the London report. It remained in place until the late 1990s, when the composition of the troika was modified. The troika ensured an element of continuity in the EC's external relations, despite the rotation of the Presidency office. Furthermore, it made sure that one of the major member states would always be part of the EPC's international delegations, thus ensuring adequate political clout.

The 1983 Stuttgart solemn declaration underlined member states' commitment to the London reforms, emphasizing the importance of "strengthening the Presidency's powers of initiative, of co-ordination

---

[76] Schoutheete 1988, 72.

[77] Foreign Ministers of the European Community 1981. For a discussion, see Smith 2004, 126–129.

[78] For discussions, see Bonvicini 1988, 53; Westlake 1999, 41.

and of representation in relations with third countries," as well as "appropriately strengthening operational support for successive Presidencies, corresponding to the increasing tasks which they have to perform."[79] By the mid-1980s, the Presidency's function as collective representative in external affairs was well established:

As the external relations of the Community have expanded, so different formulae have been agreed for representing common positions, which have come to impose more and more of this responsibility on the Presidency. Since the establishment of political co-operation, the representational role of the Presidency has taken a quantum leap forward now that the Ten have become actively involved in foreign policy collaboration in various new areas and problems that hitherto were the sole responsibility of individual Member States.[80]

The evolution since the mid-1980s has been characterized by two parallel institutional developments: the conferral of more encompassing powers of representation to the Presidency, and the strengthening of the Council Secretariat's role. Both developments have been driven by events and processes in world politics, which have pushed member governments to seek broader and deeper foreign policy coordination, with implications for external representation.

The delegation of additional representational powers originated with a set of formative experiences in the late 1980s and early 1990s, which pointed to weaknesses in the institutional structure of foreign policy coordination. It was the lack of a unified stance, rather than effective concerted action, that characterized the EC's response to the velvet revolutions in Eastern Europe in 1989–1991, the war in the Gulf in 1991, and the outbreak of civil war in Yugoslavia in 1991. This incapacity was a driving force in member governments' decision at Maastricht to transform the EPC into the CFSP, involving more ambitious policy instruments.

The hostage crisis in Iraq in 1990, when EC governments sent separate envoys to negotiate with the Iraqis, demonstrated the need for a collective, external negotiation capacity.[81] When faced with the crisis in Yugoslavia shortly thereafter, the member governments sent the Presidency as negotiator and diplomatic reaction force. This *ad hoc* arrangement signified an important shift in the function of the Presidency as external representative. It was the first time that EC governments had delegated authority to the Presidency to engage in foreign

---

[79] European Council 1983.
[80] Wallace 1985, 19.
[81] Nuttall 2000, 137–140.

policy negotiations on their behalf, effectively granting the Presidency the same powers enjoyed by the Commission in external trade negotiations.[82]

This *ad hoc* arrangement was introduced at the same time as the bargaining on the new common foreign and security policy was coming to a close at the 1991 intergovernmental conference, and it was not included in the new institutional setup. Instead, the new treaty confirmed the existing position of the Presidency in external representation. When EU governments were given an opportunity to revise the institutional structure of the CFSP at the 1996–1997 IGC, the introduction of an external negotiating mandate for the Presidency was one of the significant innovations.[83] Just as in representation by the Commission in external trade, this negotiation mandate was coupled with the requirement of unanimous support in the Council for the adoption of negotiated agreements.

At the same time, the late 1990s witnessed a broadening of the formula for external representation, to address concerns of discontinuity. The Amsterdam Treaty empowered the secretary general of the Council Secretariat to function as high representative for the CFSP. Simultaneously, the original troika was recast to effectively comprise the Presidency in office, the high representative of the CFSP, and the commissioner in charge of external policy. While providing greater continuity and visibility compared to the previous arrangement, this formula raises questions about the coherence of EU external policy, and is described by CFSP observers as unfinished institutional business.[84]

Internal representation

The growing requirements of interaction between the EU institutions have resulted in an increasingly prominent role for the Presidency as member governments' representative *vis-à-vis* the Parliament and the Commission.

Even if the Presidency had already been granted the authority to represent the Council in its dealings with the Common Assembly in 1958, the actual demand for representation was limited at the time.[85] Decision-making authority was concentrated in the Council and the Assembly enjoyed little political power. The first significant change took place as a result of agreements in 1970 and 1975 to revise the budget

---

[82] Nuttall 2000, 200; Strömvik 2005, 72.
[83] For a discussion, see Whitman 1998.
[84] Smith 2004, 229–230.
[85] Council of Ministers of the European Economic Community 1958.

provisions of the EEC Treaty. The Parliament gained considerable powers in the formulation of the EC budget, effectively transforming the Council and the Parliament into two branches of the Community's budget authority. The requirement of inter-institutional cooperation presented a problem of representation for the Council. As Westlake puts it: "The Council consists of a representative from each Member State. Each has equal and distinct status . . . Who, then, should represent the Council before the Parliament?"[86] The member governments chose to appoint the Presidency as their intermediary in budget negotiations with the Parliament.

From 1970 to 1975, the Presidency's function in the budgetary dialogue consisted of forwarding the Council's collective views on the Commission's draft budget and the Parliament's proposed changes. The mandate did not contain any powers to negotiate agreements on behalf of the Council. This exchange of views proved sterile and inefficient, with the effect that the institutions in 1975 revised the arrangements and introduced the so-called conciliation procedure.[87] The conciliation committee consisted of representatives of the three institutions and was convened to negotiate agreement. On the Council side, the Presidency was the lead representative. These inter-institutional arrangements were further developed in 1982, when the so-called "budget trialogue" was introduced.[88] This was composed of the chairman of the European Parliament's Budget Committee, the Presidency representative in the Budget Council, and the responsible Commissioner. It was primarily convened at the end of the budget procedure, to settle outstanding divisions between the institutions. On occasion, these negotiations were supplemented by an informal practice of one-on-one encounters between the Presidency and the Parliament representative, for the purpose of chiseling out an agreement.

By the mid-1980s, the Presidency had developed into the Council's natural representative *vis-à-vis* the Parliament. "The Council Presidency has . . . become increasingly important in acting as the channel for liaison between the Council and the directly elected European Parliament . . . The sheer increase in the volume of Council work has generated a parallel increase in contacts with the Parliament. As pressure from the Parliament for greater attention has strengthened, so the demands on the Presidency to make regular reports and to answer questions have

---

[86] Westlake 1999, 332.
[87] Nicoll 1999, 184.
[88] Nicoll 1998, 4; 1999, 183–184.

grown."[89] Yet, compared to what would follow, the level of institutional interaction was still limited.

The quantitative and qualitative leap occurred with the conferral of additional legislative powers to the Parliament, first through the SEA, and then through the TEU and the Amsterdam Treaty. Prior to the SEA, the Council had only been required to consult the Parliament, without any obligation to take its views into consideration when adopting legislation. The introduction of the cooperation procedure in 1987 made it possible for the Parliament to make legislation it disliked difficult for the Council to adopt. The rejection of a proposal by the Parliament meant that the Council only could adopt the act if unanimous agreement could be achieved. Thus, the Council was forced to take the Parliament's views seriously and engage in inter-institutional negotiations. The Council's representative in this process was the Presidency, which presented member governments' collective views in the formal and informal bargaining stages of the cooperation procedure. It became established practice for the presidents of the three institutions to meet in a weekly "trialogue" devoted to legislative concerns.[90]

The TEU significantly intensified inter-institutional contacts through the creation of the co-decision procedure, involving three readings and equal legislative status for the two institutions. New EU legislation could only be adopted if the Council and the Parliament agreed. The existence of mutual veto power forced the two legislative institutions into a close relationship of interdependence. An essential innovation of the co-decision procedure was the conciliation committee, modeled on the pre-existing arrangement in the budgetary field. If the Council and the Parliament remained in disagreement after two readings, they could convene a special conciliation committee, composed of fifteen members from each institution. The purpose was to agree on a joint text, which could be referred back to each institution for adoption. In practice, most of the negotiation activity takes place in informal, so-called "trialogue" negotiations between the heads of the two delegations. As Richard Corbett, then vice chairman of the Parliament's committee on institutional affairs, explains:

In practice, negotiations between 15 on each side of the table are impossible and the Presidency is usually dispatched to negotiate with the Chair and Rapporteur of the relevant Parliamentary committee – the full conciliation committee meeting only for an initial discussion and to give formal approval of any deals

---

[89] Wallace 1985, 17.
[90] Westlake 1999, 44–45.

made. . . . From Parliament's perspective, this has expanded enormously the relationship between the Parliament and the Council Presidency. . . . Since the introduction of the co-decision procedure, encounters between members of Parliament and the ministers in the Council Presidency also take the form of hard bargaining.[91]

With the advent of the Amsterdam Treaty, the policy areas covered by the co-decision procedure more than doubled, making co-decision the most common legislative procedure in the EU. The demand for the Presidency as representative increased accordingly. But the new treaty revised the format of the procedure as well, enabling the parties to conclude an agreement already at first reading, following informal trialogue negotiations. This procedure allows the Presidency to accelerate proposals it would like to see enacted during its period at the helm. Member governments accept and support this system in the name of efficiency, fully aware of "the intrinsic disadvantage involved in so much activity taking place outside their direct vision at meetings to which they are not invited."[92]

Representation: assessing the institutional development

The area of external and internal representation offers the most decisive evidence in favor of a functionalist interpretation of the Presidency's institutional development. The initiation of interaction with third parties presented EU governments with the classic problem of representation: all states are of equal standing, yet not all states can participate in communication and negotiation with third parties, which requires that some form of representation arrangement be found. In both external affairs and internal policy-making, EU governments opted for the rotating Presidency as their choice of representative. The subsequent evolution of these representational powers closely reflects increasing EU involvement in world politics and intensified legislative bargaining with the European Parliament.

Instead of extending the Commission's authority as the external representative in trade and aid negotiations, national governments chose to appoint the Presidency as their spokesperson when establishing the EPC. Once agreement had been reached on how to respond to international events, it was the task of the Presidency to issue declarations and speak on behalf of EC governments in world affairs. Over time, this function took on growing proportions. The EU engaged in structured

---

[91] Corbett 1998, 4. See also Farrell and Héritier 2003b; Shackleton and Raunio 2003.
[92] Shackleton and Raunio 2003, 175.

dialogue with an increasing number of states and international organizations. Furthermore, member governments formulated more far-reaching
foreign policy ambitions. The delegation of negotiation authority to the
Presidency was a prominent knock-on effect.

The evolution of the Presidency's powers as internal representative
went hand in hand with the European Parliament's development into an
important interlocutor in budgetary and legislative affairs. The conferral
of budgetary authority on the Parliament in the 1970s created a functional pressure for representation to which governments responded by
engaging the Presidency as their spokesperson and negotiator. Similarly,
the delegation of meaningful legislative powers to the Parliament in the
second half of the 1980s led member governments to equip the Presidency with negotiation authority in this area as well. The strengthening
of the Parliament's legislative powers during the 1990s and early 2000s
intensified inter-institutional bargaining further, with implications for
the Presidency's function as representative. Legislative bargaining increasingly takes place through informal trialogues, where the Presidency
negotiates agreements on behalf of EU governments, but beyond their
immediate oversight.

The rotating Presidency: evaluation and contestation

In the preceding sections, I have demonstrated how the EU Presidency
has accumulated increasing powers of agenda management, brokerage,
and representation, in response to functional pressures in the decision-
making environment. Governments' conferral of additional functions
and responsibilities on the Presidency has been a process of constant,
incremental adjustments, in search of efficient modes of cooperation. In
this section, I turn to another aspect of the Presidency's institutional
design, namely, the principle of rotation. Whereas the rotation arrangement has remained in place since the creation of the Presidency in the
1950s, it has not been immune to criticism. Challenging arguments
about institutional path-dependency and inefficiency, this section demonstrates that the rotating Presidency has only been maintained after
careful considerations of alternative institutional models.

As shown earlier, rather than shifting to competing solutions,
European governments have decided to compensate for the weaknesses
of the rotation design through mechanisms of continuity. While originally limited in size, the secretariats of the EC and the EPC were subsequently strengthened and eventually merged, for purposes of providing
operational support and off-loading the administrative burden of
the Presidency. Similarly, the member states introduced measures

of cooperation between Presidencies – notably multi-annual legislative programs in the EC, the troika in EPC/CFSP representation, and rolling summit themes in the European Council. Whereas this survey provides an overview of the debate during the last three decades, it does not discuss in detail the reforms proposed by the 2004 Constitutional Treaty, which are addressed in Chapter 8.

When European cooperation was first initiated through the European Coal and Steel Community (ECSC) Treaty in 1951, the contracting states opted for a chairmanship office organized on the basis of three-month rotation. This chairmanship design set the ECSC apart from other post-world-war institutions, such as NATO (supranational chairman), the Organisation for European Economic Cooperation (OEEC) (elected state chairman), and the Council of Europe (six-month rotation). Rather than adopting chairmanship arrangements familiar from other organizations in which they participated, the negotiating states engaged in institutional innovation. The choice of rotation as the governing principle entailed a sharing out of the responsibility for chairing Council negotiations. The choice of three months as the allotted period secured the office against undue exploitation, and prevented effective leadership in the Council, which accorded well with the supranational orientation of the ECSC.[93]

When the six governments chose to deepen cooperation through the EEC Treaty and the Euratom Treaty in 1958, one of the few changes to the Council's organization pertained to the Presidency, which was extended from three to six months. Instead of transferring the pre-existing design of the Presidency institution to the two new communities, the member governments assessed the experience of the ECSC and revised the office accordingly. The extension of the Presidency term should be understood as an effort by the contracting states to strengthen the Council in relation to the Commission, which had constituted the center of power in the ECSC. "[The extension of the term to six months] permitted more time for business to be organised by the incumbent and opened the door for the Presidency to emerge as an important wielder of influence and as a vehicle through which a collective Council view could be achieved and expressed."[94]

The debate about the merits and demerits of the rotating Presidency has been ongoing since the early 1970s. Scholars and policy makers have

---

[93] Wallace 1985, 2; Nicoll 1998, 1.
[94] Wallace 1985, 3.

voiced three main concerns with the existing model.[95] First, by its very design, the system of rotation constitutes a source of discontinuity in internal EU politics and in Europe's relations to the rest of the world. Second, the expansion of EU policy making has made the task of chairing all formal and informal meetings a heavy administrative and economic burden, which all states may or may not be able to carry. Third, consecutive rounds of enlargement have prolonged the time between each state's periods at the helm, challenging the notion of diffuse reciprocity in the division of gains from this office, as well as the alleged socialization effect from holding the Presidency.

The reform debate has been especially intense at times of enlargement, when the system's ability to manage new members, and new members' ability to manage the system, has been questioned. Over the years, member governments and EU institutions have presented and debated three main alternatives to the existing design of the Presidency, mirroring the general chairmanship models available in international cooperation: modified rotating chairmanship, elected chairmanship, and supranational chairmanship.

The first set of proposals have sought a shift toward alternative rotation models, either through an extension of the Presidency period or through the introduction of some form of group Presidency. When presenting his 1976 report on institutional reform, Belgian prime minister Leo Tindemans proposed doubling the term to twelve months, for the dual purpose of strengthening the Presidency and achieving greater policy continuity.[96] At the time, the heads of state and government were unenthusiastic about the proposal. By now, the arguments against this idea are well rehearsed.[97] The twelve-month term would widen the gap between a state's periods at the helm, especially when combined with an increasing number of member states. This would expand the potential for private exploitation of the office, as well as undermine the notion of reciprocity, since other governments would be less inclined to accept disfavors in the present in exchange for uncertain benefits in the distant future. It would also reduce the socialization effects of holding the Presidency on a regular basis. Finally, it would extend the period of inefficient operation of the decision-making machinery, should

---

[95] See, e.g., Bulmer and Wessels 1987, 144–145; Taulègne 1993, 239–243; Reflection Group 1995; Hayes-Renshaw and Wallace 1997, 155–157; Sherrington 2000, 172–175; Council of the European Union 1999e, 2002a; Council Secretariat 1999, 2002.

[96] Tindemans 1976.

[97] Bulmer and Wessels 1987, 144; Hayes-Renshaw and Wallace 1997, 156; Sherrington 2000, 172.

the burden of holding the Presidency be too great for any particular member state.

The idea of an extended Presidency term re-emerged in a new format in the mid-1990s, when the prospect of Eastern enlargement led policy-makers to propose a "team Presidency."

French minister Alain Lamassoure proposed in 1995 that the Presidency be shared among several member states, which would serve to-gether for a longer period of time and divide the different sectors of Council work between themselves.[98] The idea of a team Presidency was also discussed in the Reflection Group charged with preparing the 1996–1997 IGC, but this gathered only limited support and was never put on the negotiation agenda of the conference.[99] The proposal gathered new support in the debate on institutional reform in the early 2000s, in view of the impending enlargement to twenty-five member states. In 2002, the Council Secretariat, in the so-called Solana report, mentioned rotation between five to six groups of states as an alternative chairmanship arrangement.[100] The idea of team Presidencies consti-tuted the favored reform alternative of certain member state representa-tives as well, among them Swedish prime minister Göran Persson.[101] According to its advocates, the team model would permit the EU to keep a rotating Presidency, while generating greater coherence, and decreas-ing the burden of holding the office. Yet, so far, member governments have considered this arrangement to be inferior to the existing design of the Presidency. The value of having one coherent actor coordinating Council business would be lost. Instead, the management of a team Presidency would require additional layers of coordination.

The second set of reform proposals have suggested a shift from rota-tion to a system of semi-permanent elected chairmen in the Council and the European Council. In fact, this model had already been tested by the EU in the Economic and Financial Committee. When it was established in 1958, this committee was equipped with an idiosyncratic institutional design, one element of which was a chairman elected for two years by the committee's members. In 1999, the Council Secretariat proposed in the so-called Trumpf-Piris report, that some committees and working groups in the Council should be granted the possibility to elect a chair-man for a period of two to three years, whereas the system of rotation

---

[98] For a discussion, see Westlake 1999, 49.
[99] Reflection Group 1995.
[100] Council Secretariat 2002. The report was nicknamed after the Council's secretary general, Javier Solana. See also Council of the European Union 2002a.
[101] Persson 2002.

should be kept for the ministerial level and the top-level preparatory organs.[102] The Council Secretariat presented this reform proposal anew in the spring of 2002, in the Solana report on preparing the Council for enlargement.[103]

Contrary to most other reforms, the move toward elected chairmen in committees and working groups would not require treaty changes, only a revision of the Council's rules of procedure. Yet member governments refrained from introducing such an arrangement when deciding on reforms to the Council's organization in 1999 and 2002.[104] While holding the promise of greater continuity and long-term leadership in individual bodies, a system of elected chairmen would threaten the notions of equality and reciprocity between the member states, as well as create problems of coordination between different Council bodies.[105] That said, the member states, in parallel to this reform process, introduced two new exceptions to the general rule, when creating the Military Committee and the Military Committee Working Group in 2001, both of which were equipped with elected chairmanships.[106] Moreover, outside the formal framework of the EU, the member states in the eurozone in 2004 decided to introduce an elected chairman for the informal Euro Group, who could give the euro countries a more prominent presence on the international financial stage.[107]

The idea of an elected chairman for the European Council has surfaced periodically in the debate. The first and most far-reaching suggestion was presented by Valéry Giscard d'Estaing, during and after his term as French president (1974–1981). Giscard d'Estaing proposed that the chairman of the European Council be elected by popular vote for a term of five years.[108] While presented by Giscard d'Estaing as holding the key to strong leadership and political legitimacy, the suggestion

---

[102] Council Secretariat 1999. The report was nicknamed after the Council's secretary general, Jürgen Trumpf, and the director general of the Council's Legal Service, Jean-Claude Piris, who functioned as chairman and vice chairman of the working group producing the report.

[103] Council Secretariat 2002.

[104] Council of the European Union 1999e, 2002a.

[105] Council Secretariat 2002; Council of the European Union 2002a.

[106] The chairman of the Military committee is appointed by the Council for a period of three years, on the recommendation of the committee meeting at the level of Chiefs of Defence Staff, and the chairman of the Military Committee Working Group is appointed by Coreper for a period of eighteen months, on the recommendation of the Military Committee.

[107] Luxembourg's prime minister, Jean-Claude Juncker was elected for a period of two years.

[108] See, e.g., Giscard d'Estaing 1984. For a discussion, see Taulègne 1993, 241–243; Werts 1992, 92, fn.

received very limited support among other member governments. Most notably, it was criticized for violating the principle of member state equality and for being politically unrealistic – Europe's citizens simply were not ready for a popularly elected president.[109] The suggestion re-emerged in a new format in the institutional debate in the early 2000s, when France, the UK, Spain, and Sweden advocated that the chairman of the European Council be elected by the heads of state and government for a period of five years. The proposal provoked immediate disapproval, mainly from the EU's small and medium-sized member states, who feared that the larger states would come to dominate the new position, and that a semi-permanent president would tilt the institutional balance of the EU in favor of the European Council, at the expense of the Commission. Yet, as I describe at greater length in Chapter 8, the advocates, with the help of Giscard d'Estaing in his position as chairman of the European Convention, managed to shepherd the proposal through the institutional reform debate in 2003–2004 and into the proposed Constitutional Treaty.

Finally, a third set of reform proposals have suggested that the rotating Presidency be replaced by a system of appointed supranational chairmen. Unsurprisingly, it is the Council Secretariat which has proposed that member governments grant the chairmanship of Council configurations, committees, and working groups to officials of the Secretariat. The 1999 Trumpf-Piris report suggested that the Council Secretariat be given the chairmanship of working groups and committees in the field of common foreign and security policy, as well as in groups concerned with technical and administrative questions.[110] This suggestion was repeated in general terms in the 2002 Solana report. Jealous of their prerogatives under the system of rotation, member governments have been reluctant to grant the Council Secretariat access to the chairmanship, even if there are some exceptions. As part of the reform package adopted in 2002, the member states delegated the chairmanship of five politically light working parties of administrative character to the Council Secretariat: the working parties on electronic communications, legal information, codification of legislation, information, and new buildings.[111] Furthermore, it was proposed in the 2004 Constitutional Treaty that a EU foreign minister, which would replace the existing high representative of the CFSP, should chair the planned Foreign Affairs Council.

---

[109] Bulmer and Wessels 1987, 145; Sherrington 2000, 173.
[110] Council Secretariat 1999.
[111] European Council 2002a, annex II.

This inventory of reform proposals demonstrates that maintaining the rotating Presidency has been anything but uncontested and self-evident. Rather, member governments have for at least three decades engaged in evaluation and contestation, debating the merits and demerits of rotation in comparison to alternative chairmanship arrangements. Still, the rotating Presidency remains fundamentally intact. With some exceptions, the notions of elected state chairmanships or appointed supranational chairmanships have been found to be inferior solutions. Instead, EU governments have sought to compensate for the drawbacks of the rotation design, by strengthening mechanisms of continuity in the Council. At the same time, it is evident that each enlargement round has spurred more intense discussions about the viability of the rotating Presidency. The proposals in the 2004 Constitutional Treaty to institute an elected chairmanship of the European Council and a supranational chairmanship of the Foreign Affairs Council constitute the latest and most profound challenges to this system. We will return to this reform process in Chapter 8. For now, suffice it to say that these proposals, regardless of whether they are put into practice or not, illustrate how European governments continuously seek to improve the efficiency of cooperation. They appear anything but trapped in the inevitable consequences of historical decisions.

Conclusion

This chapter has demonstrated that functional processes of institutional evolution best explain the development of the EU Presidency. This office has not gained its present powers and functions by historical accident, or because the empowerment of this institution has been seen as the normatively appropriate thing to do. Driven by a search for efficient institutional modes of negotiation and decision-making, EU governments have gradually adjusted and strengthened the mandate of Presidency as agenda manager, broker, and representative. This has not been for lack of alternatives. Rather, the Presidency office has been boosted in competition with other institutional solutions, such as the delegation of powers to the Commission. Where the rotation design of the Presidency has given rise to problems of discontinuity in the provision of these services, member states have established and strengthened mechanisms of continuity.

Only part of the Presidency's historical development is reflected in formal treaty texts; for the most part, it has consisted of an adaptation of political practices. "Treaty provision is minimal, and the office has grown organically. A mere reading of the Treaty would reveal only a little about the Presidency's formal functions: in practice, it is absolutely indispensable to the good working of the European Union."[112] The function of agenda management grew from limited procedural responsibilities into *de facto* policy initiation and prioritization. This development was driven by member states' inability to collectively ensure delimited and negotiable agendas in the absence of some coordinating force, especially as the EU's decision-making structures grew increasingly fragmented and complex. Partly, the Presidency's empowerment took place at the expense of the Commission, whose supranational ambitions national governments sought to keep in check. In a similar way, the Presidency evolved into the member states' preferred architect of compromise in response to increasing problems of negotiation failure and in competition with the Commission. To facilitate mediation and consensus building by the Presidency, member governments created specific brokerage practices that enabled the Presidency to obtain the privileged preference information it required for the engineering of viable compromise proposals. Yet nowhere are the functional pressures behind the evolution of the Presidency's tasks as evident as in the delegation of representational responsibilities. The power to speak, act, and negotiate on behalf of all member governments developed as a direct effect of an observable demand for an internal and external representative *vis-à-vis* third parties in the EU and world politics.

---

[112] Westlake 1999, 50.

4   The EU Presidency as agenda manager: shaping political priorities

The rotation of the Presidency gives every member state of the EU an opportunity to engage in agenda management, brokerage, and representation. Yet what are the political implications of this arrangement? Does the Presidency office constitute a power platform that permits the incumbent to pursue national interests through extraordinary means, or a burden that forces governments at the helm to sacrifice private concerns for the collective good? In this chapter and in Chapters 5 and 6, I turn to the question of how the powers of the Presidency office may be used to influence the direction of EU negotiations. I begin by analyzing the Presidency's function as agenda manager.

Existing literature is highly skeptical about the capacity of Presidencies to shape the EU agenda. Typically, three forms of arguments are advanced. According to the first argument, the office of the Presidency office has not been conferred any exclusive formal powers of initiative, and therefore cannot set the EU's policy agenda. In this vein, Richard Corbett stresses: "[T]aking on the Presidency does not mean acceding to an executive office but is merely the chairmanship of one of the EU institutions for a short period."[1] The second line of reasoning emphasizes the limitations on Presidencies' room for maneuver imposed by inherited agendas and unforeseeable events. In an early and widely cited assessment, Guy de Bassompierre asserts that "any Presidency, however worthy and able, can only influence, at best, 5–10 percent of the issues."[2] Substantiating this claim, David Neligan notes: "[T]he fact is that the great bulk of a Presidency's program will at all times consist of inherited and wholly foreseeable material. The 'spin' often put out, that a new departure is being marked when a different government takes over the helm, is never more than very partially true. The agendas and the accompanying files simply land on the new Presidency's table, many of

---

[1] Corbett 1998, 1.
[2] Bassompierre 1988, 103.

them with a dispiritingly dull thud."[3] Finally, a third argument stresses
the constraining effect of the norm of the neutral Presidency. Even if the
holder of the Presidency might enjoy the means to prioritize issues of
specific national importance, this argument goes, member states refrain
from such behavior, either because they have been socialized to behave
neutrally, or for fear of being ostracized.[4]

This chapter challenges the conventional wisdom by demonstrating
that the Presidency's agenda-management function carries distinct implications for the distributional consequences of EU decision-making.
While enabling Presidency governments to ensure that negotiations in
the Council do not suffer from overcrowded and uncoordinated
agendas, the powers and resources of the office may be exploited for
national political purposes as well. Discarding the narrow focus on
formal agenda setting that underlies the assessments of existing literature, I suggest that influence over the agenda may take a variety of
forms.[5] Presidencies engage in agenda setting when they introduce
initiatives or concerns on the agenda, either on their own or in collaboration with the Commission. Presidencies engage in agenda structuring
when they emphasize or de-emphasize issues already on the agenda,
thereby assigning priority to competing political concerns. Finally, Presidencies engage in agenda exclusion when barring issues from decision
agendas or collective deliberation. In the exercise of these forms of
influence, Presidencies draw on a broad repertoire of instruments.

This chapter is organized into three sections. The first section conducts an inventory of the power resources that Presidencies can draw on
as agenda managers, and identifies the most important institutional rules
with an enabling or constraining effect on the Presidencies' capacity to
shape the agenda. The second and third sections are devoted to two case
studies of agenda management: Finland's promotion of the Northern
Dimension initiative during its Presidency in the second half of 1999,
and Germany's removal of the directive of car recycling from the agenda
of the Council in the first half of 1999. The Finnish case offers an
example of how the Presidency office may be exploited to launch and
anchor a new policy initiative on the EU political agenda. Having carefully prepared the ground in the period prior to the Presidency, the
Finnish government used the time in office to consolidate the initiative.
The German case illustrates how agenda influence need not consist of
positive political action, but may just as easily take the shape of negative

---

[3] Neligan 1998, 7. See also, e.g., Hayes-Renshaw and Wallace 1997, 146.
[4] E.g., Metcalfe 1998; Whitman 1998; Elgström 2003a.
[5] For an in-depth discussion of alternative forms of agenda influence, see Tallberg 2003a.

political action, keeping issues away from the decision agenda. The German government made sure that the directive on car recycling was not adopted during its period at the helm, and managed to obtain changes in the proposal that made it more conformant with German interests.

Agenda management: resources and constraints

The Presidency endows the member state in office with a broad range of procedural instruments that may be used to shape the EU agenda. This section provides an inventory of the most central resources. In addition, it identifies formal agenda setting and decision rules, and explains how these institutional factors enable and constrain the Presidency in its agenda-shaping activities.

Power resources in agenda management

The Presidency's capacity to shape the orientation of the EU's political agenda rests with its asymmetrical control over decision procedure. By contrast, the kind of informational advantages that give Presidency governments a competitive edge in the execution of the functions of brokerage and representation are less prominent in agenda management.

First, the *political program* presented by each Presidency allows the government in office to assign priority to issues on the EU agenda. This document is generally the product of a long preparatory process at the national level, where government ministries and agencies canvass domestic interests, identify ongoing European policy processes, develop action plans, and issue priority papers.[6] When the program is presented shortly before the new Presidency assumes office, it takes the shape of an inventory of policy proposals and processes to be addressed during the next six months. Whereas the broad themes of the program tend to reflect the EU's general areas of activity, it is by no means neutral to the interests of the Presidency government or other member states. Some themes are given a more prominent position than others, and the more specific goals developed under each theme mark the prioritization of some policy concerns before others. New issues are included that would not have been part of another government's program, and some issues are excluded that another member state would have wished to promote. The relative weight this program assigns to alternative issues

---

[6] See, for instance, the country case studies in Elgström 2003b.

sets the political framework for the concrete actions of government officials during a particular Presidency period.[7]

A second procedural instrument is the possibility for the Presidency to plant or develop *concrete proposals for action*. As I will explain below, the Presidency's capacity to launch new initiatives is conditioned by the formal agenda-setting rules in EU decision-making, which determine whether the Presidency can act on its own, or must act through, and in agreement with, the Commission. Where the Commission enjoys a monopoly on policy initiation, the Presidency is dependent on the close cooperation of this institution. Whereas, formally, all member states enjoy the same right to lobby the Commission, the Presidency is recognized as "first among equals." As one Commission official and former French diplomat notes: "All member states try to influence the Commission, not just the Presidency. But there is a special relation with the Presidency."[8] As agenda manager, broker, and representative, the Presidency's support is essential for the Commission's ability to reach its own objectives. It is therefore easier for the Presidency to plant issues on the agenda through the Commission, than for other member states. Furthermore, this special relationship can be exploited to discourage the Commission from developing unwelcome policy proposals. As Rüdiger Wurzel notes: "The Commission is unlikely to spend scarce resources on a proposal if forthcoming Presidencies indicate that they will attribute only a low priority to particular dossiers."[9]

Where the member states enjoy formal agenda-setting prerogatives – either exclusively or together with the Commission – the Presidency may place its own policy proposals directly on the decision agenda. Formally, the Presidency does not enjoy any special advantages compared to other member states. In practice, however, the Presidency has developed into the dominant producer of proposals in these areas and its initiatives stand a better chance of success. As one observer notes with regard to the EU's foreign and security policy: "The Presidency is in most cases the driving force behind the pace and policy content of initiatives in the CFSP field. While other Member States and the Commission are also entitled to initiate proposals, the Presidency, because of its authority and because this role is generally expected of it, is in a stronger position to take such initiatives."[10]

---

[7] Interviews, Finnish government official, 15 May 2000; Swedish government official, 7 July 2001.
[8] Interview, 6 December 2000.
[9] Wurzel 1996, 227.
[10] Westlake 1999, 222.

A third kind of procedural instrument is the Presidency's authority to determine the shape of *actual meeting agendas*. It is the Presidency which prepares the agendas of the meetings at the various levels of the Council machinery, as well as the agenda of the European Council's summits. Ongoing negotiations set certain general parameters, but the Presidency still enjoys important leeway in the development of agendas. As in all decision-making organs, setting meeting agendas involves a set of strategic decisions: Which issues should be included on the agenda? Which items should be at the top of the agenda? Which issues require continued debate and which may be put up for decision? In the concrete preparation of Council meetings, the Presidency addresses these questions by distinguishing between A and B points. The first category consists of issues where decisions can be taken without further discussion, based on preliminary agreements between the EU ambassadors in Coreper (Committee of Permanent Representatives), whereas the second category is made up of issues that are deemed to require further deliberation before any decision can be taken.

The authority to determine meeting agendas may be exploited to exclude items from debate and decision-making in the Council or the European Council. Every Presidency offers examples of proposals that are quietly shelved for six months and decisions that are postponed until the next Presidency. To refuse to pick up a dossier during a six-month period is a sure way of stalling progress in an area. Though such overt manipulation is an invitation to criticism, Presidencies typically dismiss complaints by emphasizing the tall order of items that deserve prime attention, as well as time and resource constraints. In the preparation of European Council meetings, the Presidency often uses its control over the meeting agenda to leave out issues that some member state wishes to see included for domestic political reasons, or issues that call for attention because of unexpected events in the EU or abroad, but that would burden an already crowded agenda.

The Presidency's authority to set the *overall meeting schedule* for six months of political activity in the EU is an additional procedural source of agenda influence. To determine the number of opportunities for governments to consider an issue is a very concrete way of shaping priorities in EU decision-making. Historically, some of the more rare Council configurations have been convened only when states with specific interests in this area have held the chair. For instance, a Council configuration for cooperation on tourism was first established by the Greek Presidency in 1988, and was subsequently only convened when Mediterranean member states with key interests in this area held the

Presidency.[11] The number of meetings in more established Council configurations has also been known to vary depending on a Presidency's relative involvement. Even greater variation exists at the level of working groups, where meeting schedules are not as institutionalized as at the ministerial level. The political dimension of meeting-room distribution was emphasized by a Finnish government official, who explained that there were only seventeen meeting rooms available in the Council each day, forcing the Finnish Presidency to make a very concrete selection of what working groups to prioritize.[12]

One particular aspect of the meeting schedule is the Presidency's convocation of informal meetings in the home country. The Presidency government can invite the other member states to informal meetings at all levels of the Council machinery. Since these meetings take place at the initiative of the Presidency, and are funded by this state, the host government is at complete liberty to determine the theme. Up to 100 such meetings may be held during a Presidency.[13] These meetings are regularly used to raise the awareness among EU governments and institutions of concerns dear to the Presidency, or to push for progress on issues already on the EU agenda. The one informal meeting for which this discretion is becoming increasingly reduced is that of the European Council, whose agenda nowadays often is partly pre-defined by earlier summits.

Institutional constraints in agenda management

The institutional environment in which EU governments operate conditions the extent to which they can successfully exploit the Presidency's procedural resources for private gain.

Formal agenda-setting rules are regulated in the EU treaties. Slightly simplified, these treaties provide for two alternative arrangements, with direct implications for the Presidency's ability to develop and table new initiatives on the formal EU agenda. In the standard, supranational model of decision-making, the Commission enjoys a monopoly on agenda setting. No other actor – whether member state or EU institution – is permitted to initiate and table formal proposals for new legislation. This model is used in those areas of EU decision-making that traditionally have been referred to as the EC or the first pillar, comprising the internal

---

[11] Sherrington 2000, 38–39.
[12] Interview, 30 November 2000.
[13] See, e.g., the Swedish Presidency in the first half of 2001, which held some 80 informal meetings in Sweden. Tallberg 2001, appendix.

market, environmental policy, regional policy, agricultural policy, the Economic and Monetary Union (EMU), and a range of other policy domains.

In these areas, the Presidency is dependent on the close cooperation of the Commission for its agenda-setting activities. The Presidency cannot force the Commission to present a particular legislative initiative or to refrain from developing new proposals in an area. Instead, its capacity to influence the Commission's formal agenda setting is dependent on informal lobbying and pressuring – either through bilateral channels or through collective state efforts. Prior to the period in office, the incoming Presidency and the Commission compare working programs and policy priorities. Attempts by the incoming Presidency to convince the Commission of the need to present much-wanted policy proposals are a common ingredient of this process. An alternative way of encouraging the Commission to develop a specific policy initiative is to gain other member states' support for the need to send a strong collective signal to the Commission, by issuing a European Council request for new initiatives in a particular area.

Next to this supranational model of decision-making, the EU offers an alternative, intergovernmental model of decision-making in a number of policy domains. In this model, the member states enjoy the power of initiative – either exclusively or together with the Commission. This mode of agenda setting is used within the EU's common foreign and security policy, as well as in cooperation on justice and home affairs, often referred to as the second and third pillars of EU policy-making. Since these areas of cooperation were brought within the treaties in 1991, the agenda-setting arrangements have been subject to gradual evolution. Whereas, originally, the Commission was entirely excluded, this institution now shares the power of initiative in most parts of these areas.

The absence of a Commission monopoly on new initiatives greatly facilitates agenda setting by the Presidency. The government at the helm is now free to present new proposals and initiatives, and need not seek the support of the Commission, even if this institution can constitute a powerful ally. In addition, the agenda-setting competition from other governments tends to be limited. As noted above, the primary responsibility for new proposals has devolved upon the Presidency in these areas of cooperation. By the same token, it is relatively easier for the Presidency to keep issues away from collective deliberation in these areas of cooperation.

This brief inventory of agenda-setting arrangements generates predictions about variation across issue areas in the Presidency's capacity and methods to set the formal EU agenda. We would expect the Presidency to be more constrained in those areas where the Commission enjoys exclusive agenda-setting rights, than in those areas where the member states possess this power and the Presidency carries the main responsibility for new initiatives. At the same time, we should bear in mind that the tabling of new proposals only constitutes one of several ways for Presidencies to shape the EU agenda, and that Presidencies' use of alternative instruments is not equally constrained by formal agenda-setting rules. For instance, the nature of the formal agenda-setting arrangement is likely to carry less weight when a Presidency wishes to exclude an issue from the agenda. In such a case, it is of limited importance whether the dossier was originally put on the agenda by the Commission or another member state. The Presidency's decision to drop the issue from the agenda essentially constitutes a unilateral measure, relieved of formal regulation, even if it is likely to be seen by the other bargaining parties as a violation of the informal codes and working methods of the Council.

Formal decision rules shape the ease with which the Presidency can secure support for the policy initiatives it has put on the agenda, either on its own or through collaboration with the Commission. By contrast, these rules do not affect the Presidency's capacity to block or postpone decisions on a particular dossier. In effect, there are no non-decision-making rules. Slightly simplified, a consideration of decision rules generates the same predictions about cross-sectoral variation in Presidency influence as the inventory of agenda-setting arrangements.

In the broad range of areas that fall within the first pillar, decisions are generally taken through qualified majority voting in the Council. Under this decision rule, each state enjoys a particular number of votes, depending on the size of its population. Whereas the measure of a qualified majority has varied somewhat over time, as a result of enlargement rounds and treaty revisions, decisions have traditionally required around 70 percent of all votes. Qualified majority voting makes it comparatively easy for the Presidency to secure support for favored proposals (which, in these areas, generally originate from the Commission). The Presidency need not consider fringe states, but can concentrate its lobbying efforts on those states that are most positive and whose support is sufficient for adoption.

In the second and third pillars of EU cooperation, in the European Council, and at IGCs, it is the general rule that proposals must be adopted by all governments in the Council. The requirement of unanimity imposes a significant constraint on the Presidency's agenda-shaping efforts, since all states must now be convinced of the appropriateness of the Presidency's favored proposal (which, in these areas, is often its own).

Unanimity tends to cause a watering down of proposals, until all governments are prepared to sign on. Presidencies may therefore have to sacrifice elements of their proposals in order to secure agreement. Even if the Commission's support is not necessary for the preparation or adoption of a proposal, it is often central to the implementation of a policy. Presidencies therefore tend to go to considerable lengths to obtain the consent of the Commission, even if it is not formally required.

The Finnish Presidency and the Northern Dimension

The Finnish campaign to promote a northern dimension in the EU's external relations grew out of Finland's reorientation in the European security structure after the Cold War. The campaign was launched in 1997 with the aim of reaching fruition during the Finnish Presidency in the second half of 1999, when the initiative was to be consolidated and institutionalized. In this process, the Finnish government faced a set of challenges: raising the awareness of north European political concerns, securing unanimous support from EU governments and the liking of the Commission, and promoting a national interest without giving the impression of exploiting the Presidency for private purposes.

The Northern Dimension initiative

Finland's decision to launch the Northern Dimension initiative reflected a number of converging political and economic factors in the mid-1990s.[14] The end of the Cold War permitted a reorientation of Finnish foreign and security policy, which since the late 1940s had been formed in the context of the Friendship, Cooperation and Mutual Assistance (FCMA) Treaty with the Soviet Union. The decision to join the EU in 1995 constituted a central step in Finland's security orientation. Even if the EU could not offer Finland any hard security guarantees, acceding to the EU meant that Finland joined the Western security community. The Northern Dimension initiative was Finland's first active attempt to shape the direction of the EU's foreign and security policy to its liking. One researcher has described the initiative as an attempt to "customize" the EU to Finnish interests and concerns.[15]

The initiative's orientation toward soft security issues, rather than hard military concerns, reflected Finland's continued status as a

---

[14] Ojanen 1999, 13–15; Arter 2000, 680–682; Forsberg and Ojanen 2000, 119–124.
[15] Ojanen 1999.

non-aligned country. The Northern Dimension initiative later proved to be one of several steps taken in the late 1990s and early 2000s by Finland and its non-aligned neighbor Sweden, for purposes of promoting an EU development toward soft security, crisis management, and conflict prevention, rather than a joint European defense. The initiative's orientation toward northern Europe reflected Finland's interest in gaining EU acceptance for the particular regional concerns in this area. The development of a northern dimension in the EU's external policies would benefit Finland in both economic and security terms. It would enable Finland to secure EU funds for regional cooperation in northern Europe, and it would stimulate the development of a coherent EU policy toward Russia.

The Northern Dimension furthermore constituted a Finnish response to political initiatives taken by neighbors in northern Europe in the 1990s, in an effort to shape the post-Cold War structure in the region. Norway had been the leading initiator of the Barents Euro-Arctic Regional Council (BEAR), whereas Denmark and Germany had promoted the establishment of the Council of Baltic Sea States (CBSS). In these processes, Finland had found itself in a reactive position, responding to the initiatives, but not shaping them to its own security needs. The Northern Dimension was an attempt by Finland to define its regional security interests and to gain a leading role in the evolving Nordic security environment.

The Northern Dimension initiative was first presented by Prime Minister Paavo Lipponen in a speech in Rovaniemi on 15 September 1997, with the telling title "The European Union Needs a Policy for the Northern Dimension."[16] Yet this was not the first time that references had been made to a northern dimension. The concept had been mentioned by leading politicians as early as 1994, in the political processes prior to Finland's accession to the EU.[17] From the very beginning, the Northern Dimension functioned as an umbrella concept, whose limits were vague and whose contents would develop over time. A defining characteristic of the initiative, which contributed to its nebulous nature, was the ambition to build on and coordinate existing EU policy, rather than create new EU policy. The initiative was supposed to increase the EU's general awareness of specific northern concerns, and to make the EU's policies for this area more coherent and efficient.

---

[16] Lipponen 1997.
[17] Ojanen 1999, 15.

In his 1997 speech, Lipponen placed the emphasis on the geographical orientation of the initiative, on specific Nordic values, and on the particular climate conditions of the region. As the initiative evolved, the EU's relations with Russia emerged as the dominant component of the Northern Dimension.[18] Thematically, the Northern Dimension initiative sought to improve cooperation on a range of soft security concerns, including environmental problems, nuclear safety, and nuclear waste management, as well as create better opportunities for cross-border business in the region through cooperation in areas such as transport, investment, and telecommunications. The geographical focus on Russia and the thematic focus on soft security concerns and business opportunities in the region were very much in line with Finnish national interests. As Lipponen acknowledged in his speech: "Finnish national interests are very much involved. We need to enhance stability in this region. Finland will be developed as business center for the region, with global opportunities." The president's advisor similarly explained: "Our own policy on Russia is partly transforming into the Northern Dimension of the Union."[19]

Preparing for political breakthrough

When Finland initiated its campaign to promote the Northern Dimension initiative in 1997, its eyes were already set on the Presidency period in the second half of 1999. The aim of Finnish activities from 1997 and onwards was to prepare the ground for a political breakthrough during the Presidency. To this end, Finland adopted and pursued two strategies, where the first pertained to the timing of the initiative and the second to the contents of the initiative.

The Finnish campaign was based on an elaborate timing strategy. The launch in 1997 marked the first step in this strategy and was scheduled to allow Finnish policy-makers sufficient time to anchor the initiative on the EU agenda well in advance of the Presidency period. The second step consisted of Finnish attempts to gain the support of member states and EU institutions for the acceptance of the Northern Dimension as EU policy. The third step was the Presidency in 1999, when Finland wished to see further commitment to the initiative, as well as a concretization of its contents, preferably in the shape of a European Commission action plan. It is essential to understand that these three steps were

---

[18] Ojanen 1999, 15; Arter 2000, 684.
[19] Quoted in Forsberg and Ojanen 2000, 119.

part of a coherent strategy: "The strategy that Finland had planned for the advancement of the NDI project covered the whole decision-making process from the launch of the initiative through its acceptance as an official policy to the ministerial conference arranged during the Finnish Presidency."[20]

The timing strategy reflected Finland's wish to secure progress on the initiative, while avoiding being perceived as promoting national interests during the Presidency. Finland's reputation as a constructive European partner was a central concern of its government. "Finland saw the Presidency as an investment which would bring dividends in its EU work for years to come and had therefore mobilized the whole administrative machinery with one aim – running a successful Presidency."[21] Based on their own experience and on contacts with previous Presidencies, especially the Irish in the second half of 1996, Finnish policy-makers concluded that the best strategy for achieving a good reputation was to act as honest brokers and efficient managers, with only limited regard to national interests. The concrete effect of this strategy was that Finland had few national pet projects compared to other Presidencies – it mainly focused on the existing European agenda, and on some occasions even sacrificed national interests if this could facilitate agreement.[22]

The Northern Dimension was one of the few attempts by Finland to exploit the Presidency for the purposes of leaving its own imprint on EU structures. In order to escape this promotion of national interests with its reputation intact, Finland chose to launch the initiative before the actual Presidency. As one senior official stressed in an interview, "We learned that high profile initiatives during the term of office of the Presidency are not well received, especially not if they are very much in the zone of the Presidency's own interests."[23] Instead, the Presidency was now designed to give an important stimulus to an issue that could be presented as "European," since it was already part of the EU's broad policy agenda prior to the Presidency.[24]

In concrete terms, Finland's strategy to place the Northern Dimension on the EU agenda took the shape of bilateral contacts and lobbying *vis-à-vis* the European Commission and other member governments. The support of the Commission would be required at later stages, for

---

[20] Tiilikainen 2003, 110; see also Arter 2000, 692.
[21] Stubb 2000, 52.
[22] Stubb 2000; Tiilikainen 2003; interviews, Finnish government officials, 15 May and 30 November 2000.
[23] Quoted by Bunse 2000, 59.
[24] Bunse 2000, 59–60; Haglund 2002, 6; interview, Finnish government official, 30 November 2000.

the initiative to be implemented in practice. Since the Northern Dimension would fall within the ambit of the EU's intergovernmental foreign and security policy, it was also necessary to secure the unanimous support of the member states. The lobbying efforts were primarily aimed at other heads of state and government, since an endorsement by the European Council would provide a firm political ground for the continuation of the campaign.[25] Tours by Prime Minister Lipponen to other EU capitals in November 1997 paid off, and at the Luxembourg summit in December 1997, the European Council requested the Commission to submit an interim report.[26] This report was subsequently presented to the European Council in Vienna in December 1998, where the heads of state and government recognized the Northern Dimension as a dimension to be considered in EU policy.[27] Equally important, Finland managed to secure the support of the European Council for a ministerial conference on the Northern Dimension during its forthcoming Presidency. Finland's political basis for action was furthered bolstered when the European Council, at its meeting in Cologne in June 1999, opened up the possibility of requesting a Commission action plan in this area, should the ministerial conference be productive.[28] Everything was now set for the Finnish Presidency, whose task it would be to give substance to the Northern Dimension initiative.

Central to the Finnish success of gaining early approval was its strategy to market the policy content of the initiative in a way that would appeal to member governments and the Commission, or at least not give them sufficient reason to veto the initiative. Following the launch in 1997, Finland used several complementary marketing strategies.[29] The initiative was strategically couched in nebulous language in order to enable a broad appeal; the Northern Dimension should offer something for everybody. The Finnish government stressed that the project would benefit the EU as a whole, just like the Union's Mediterranean policy, and not solely be in the interest of its northern members. Finland emphasized that the Northern Dimension would bring "added value" to existing EU programs in the region, by better coordinating this activity, and refrained from using criticism of ongoing EU initiatives as a rationale for the Northern Dimension. The attendant advantage of this

---

[25] Bunse 2000, 61.
[26] European Council 1997.
[27] European Council 1998.
[28] European Council 1999a.
[29] Ojanen 1999, 16–17; Arter 2000, 685–686; interview, Finnish government official, 30 November 2000.

arrangement, Finland carefully underlined, was that the Northern Dimension would not cost anything, nor require the construction of new institutions: "[T]he Finns were extremely cautious in divising the initiative in such a 'harmless' way that it would not bring any new financial burdens to the European Union, knowing very well that any grandiose plans for new budget lines would be torpedoed by the other member states."[30]

This last point was of particular importance for securing acceptance, according to many observers.[31] Whereas the Commission at first was slightly skeptical, the EU executive later warmed to the idea and became a staunch supporter once it realized that the initiative would not require new resources or institutions, but instead held the promise of greater efficiency at no additional cost. The EU's southern members were concerned that the Northern Dimension would steer resources away from the Mediterranean, but yielded once they were given guarantees that this would not be the case. Remaining EU countries found no reason for opposing the initiative.[32]

The Finnish Presidency: from initiative to policy

The Finnish government's goal to establish the Northern Dimension as an important part of the EU's external relations involved a number of components.[33] Finland wished to successfully conclude the ministerial conference in November, whose aim it was to further substantiate the contents of the initiative. This was the singularly most important event planned for the promotion of the Northern Dimension. Finland also hoped that the ministerial conference would pave the way for a European Council decision requesting the Commission to develop an action plan for the Northern Dimension. To closely involve the Commission in the project was essential, since it was the Commission that would have to shoulder the executive responsibility for the initiative in practice. For similar reasons, the Finnish government wished to extract promises from forthcoming Presidencies that they were willing to include the Northern Dimension in their political programs, thus ensuring

---

[30] Haukkala 2001, 108.

[31] E.g., Ojanen 1999, 16–17; Arter 2000, 689–690, 693; Catellani 2001, 16–17.

[32] Note, however, that Denmark and Sweden, somewhat paradoxically, were only lukewarm at first. The main reason was not economic in nature, but rivalry between the Nordic EU members. Denmark and Sweden felt that Finland should have presented the Northern Dimension as a joint Nordic initiative. For discussions, see Ojanen 1999, 17–18; Arter 2000, 687–688; Joenniemi 2002, 8–9.

[33] Haglund 2002, 7; interviews, Finnish government officials, 30 November 2001.

a continuation of the political process. The office of the Presidency equipped the Finnish government with a range of procedural instruments for achieving these goals, including the control of the Presidency program, the right to determine the formal meeting schedule, and the authority to decide the theme of formal and informal meetings.

The Finnish government's political program for the Presidency period had been shaped over the course of two years. The Northern Dimension initiative had been included in the program at an early stage, but was not presented as one of the seven lead themes, since that would have risked provoking allegations of Presidency bias.[34] Instead, the Northern Dimension appeared as one priority under the general heading of "A Globally Active and Influential Union":

Promoting the new Union policy of a Northern Dimension will be an important objective for the Finnish Presidency. The aim is to get the Northern Dimension concept firmly incorporated into the external relations of an enlarging Union, especially with regard to Russia and the Baltic region. The Northern Dimension policy supplements and supports the Union's Common Strategy on Russia as regards northern Europe. In November, Finland and the European Commission will be organising a conference at foreign minister level which will offer an opportunity for political discussions on the content of the Northern Dimension between EU Member States and partners in the Northern Dimension – Iceland, Norway, Latvia, Lithuania, Poland, Russia and Estonia. During the Finnish Presidency, active support will be given to the Commission's work to make the Northern Dimension concept more concrete and to implement the Commission communication and Council recommendations. In accordance with the Presidency Conclusions of the Cologne European Council, the Helsinki European Council will study the possibility of drawing up an Action Plan.[35]

The ministerial conference in November achieved in substance what the Finnish government had hoped for, but did not become the political manifestation the Finns had expected.[36] The conference consolidated the initiative by clarifying the institutional framework, opening up a dialogue with the EU's partner countries in the region, and establishing joint policy priorities in a broad range of areas. Furthermore, it secured the future commitment of key political actors, notably the European Commission and the upcoming Swedish and Danish Presidencies in 2001 and 2002, respectively. As Commissioner Chris Patten concluded: "The Commission is determined to play an active part both in the preparation and implementation of the action plan that will be needed

---

[34] Bunse 2000, 74–75.
[35] Finnish Presidency 1999, 37.
[36] Bunse 2000, 76–79; Haglund 2002, 8–9.

to take forward this important initiative."[37] Finally, the Finnish Presidency managed to rally unanimous support around the conference conclusion that an action plan was needed to concretize the Northern Dimension and move the initiative to its implementation phase. The Presidency's major disappointment was the poor attendance by the EU states' foreign ministers, who instead sent their deputies in protest against Russia's war in Chechnya.

The European Council summit in Helsinki in December delivered the results the Finnish government had aimed for. Enough political pressure had been built up by the advocates of the Northern Dimension for the European Council to take the necessary decisions. The Commission had signaled that it was willing to develop an action plan, and whatever opposition had existed among member governments had been overcome. Sweden had decided to rally behind Finland, and managed to formally anchor its promise to hold a follow-up ministerial conference during its stint at the helm in the first half of 2001. The heads of state and government declared:

> The European Council welcomes the conclusions of the Foreign Ministers' Conference on the Northern Dimension held 11 and 12 November 1999 in Helsinki and the intention of the future Swedish Presidency to organise a high-level follow-up. The European Council invites the Commission to prepare, in cooperation with the Council and in consultation with the partner countries, an Action Plan for the Northern Dimension in the external and cross-border policies of the European Union with a view to presenting it for endorsement at the Feira European Council in June 2000.[38]

Whereas the ministerial conference in November and the European Council in December were the highpoints of the Finnish campaign for the Northern Dimension, the Presidency also devoted a range of other meetings to the promotion of this initiative.[39] Indeed, the Finnish government made it an explicit strategy to have the Northern Dimension addressed in as many European and international forums as possible. For instance, the Northern Dimension was placed on the agenda of a EU–Russia seminar on migration in July, a conference on the Barents region in July, the conference of foreign affairs committees in July, an expert seminar on the forest sector in October, the EU–Russia summit in October, an informal ministerial conference on energy and cooperation in the Baltic in October, the Health Council in November, and the Energy Council in December. The Finnish Presidency also held

---

[37] Patten 1999.
[38] European Council 1999b.
[39] Bunse 2000, 75–76; Haglund 2002, 10.

informal meetings with forthcoming Presidencies in order to guarantee their commitment, and formal meetings with the US and Canada in order to secure their continued engagement in the region.

With hindsight, it is evident that the Finnish Presidency in 1999 was vital for the shaping of the Northern Dimension initiative, as it later came to develop. The Finnish Presidency left a clear legacy both as regards process and contents. The action plan requested by the Helsinki European Council, developed by the Commission, and adopted at the summit in Feira in June 2000, became the central policy instrument of the Northern Dimension.[40] The action plan covered the period 2000–2003 and consisted of two parts, where the first identified the major challenges, priorities, and institutional instruments, and the second the concrete policy actions to be undertaken. The decision in Helsinki that Sweden would organize a follow-up conference translated into a concerted political effort by the Swedish Presidency, which generally is judged to have been successful in further elaborating the policy content of the Northern Dimension.[41] The third Nordic member state, Denmark, followed the Swedish example and arranged the third ministerial conference on the Northern Dimension during its Presidency in the second half of 2002. Following annual progress reports on the implementation of the first action plan, the Commission in 2004 presented a second action plan, covering the period 2004–2006.[42] Today, the Northern Dimension no longer qualifies as an initiative, but has gained the status of institutionalized EU policy.

The policy contents of the Northern Dimension corresponds well with the intentions of the original Finnish initiative.[43] The Northern Dimension is formulated as a policy for the entire Union, and its aims resemble those of the EU's policy toward the Mediterranean region. To a significant extent, the main areas of cooperation are those identified by Finland. Geographically, the Northern Dimension extends across the area envisaged by Finland, with a primary focus on the Baltic region and northwest Russia, even if Sweden reinforced the initiative's implications for the southern part of the Baltic. In sum, "Finland, being the promoter of the Northern Dimension, has had a pivotal role in shaping the initiative's content. The ND agenda has been, throughout the process, a largely Finnish oriented agenda."[44]

---

[40] Council of the European Union 2000a.
[41] Catellani 2001, 14; Haglund 2002.
[42] European Commission 2003.
[43] Catellani 2001, 2003; Heininen 2001.
[44] Catellani 2001, 12.

The power of the chair: assessing process and outcome

The Finnish Presidency in 1999 was vital for the transformation of the Northern Dimension from idea to policy. During its period at the helm, the Finnish government made effective use of the procedural powers of the Presidency. Simultaneously, Finland's strategies for launching and anchoring the initiative were shaped by formal agenda-setting and decision rules in the EU. The case further illustrates how informal norms about the conduct of the Presidency influenced the Finnish strategy.

In anticipation of its forthcoming Presidency in 1999, the Finnish government formulated an agenda-setting strategy consisting of a number of phases. As David Arter notes: "The NDI was an expansive project, carefully planned and industriously marketed which, it was hoped, would reach concrete fruition by the end of Finland's Presidency period in December 1999."[45] The initial steps of this strategy sought to raise the awareness of the Northern Dimension of the EU's external relations, create anticipation among other EU actors of the Finnish ambitions for the Presidency, and prepare the ground for advances during the Finnish period at the helm. The actual Presidency period was only to be used for the consolidation and institutionalization of the initiative. The Finnish agenda-setting tactics in the pre-Presidency period included bilateral lobbying *vis-à-vis* the Commission and member governments, strategic framing of the initiative, and efforts to insert formulations in European Council conclusions that could function as "hooks" for future steps.

A legitimate question in this context is whether lobbying in the period before a government assumes the Presidency actually qualifies for inclusion in the assessment of this government's influence as Presidency. In the case of agenda setting, the answer is yes. The process of shaping the EU's political priorities through the introduction of new political concerns is, by necessity, long term in nature. What the six months at the helm offer is an opportunity to formally anchor an initiative introduced in the pre-Presidency period, or to launch a new initiative that will only be brought to political fruition in the post-Presidency period. This is the reason why member states that wish to exploit the Presidency for agenda-setting purposes are advised to start preparing years in advance.

During the six months of the Presidency, the Finnish government made use of the broad range of procedural instruments that are generally at the disposal of the Presidency. It made sure that the Northern

---

[45] Arter 2000, 691.

Dimension was safely anchored in the political program for the Presidency. It placed the Northern Dimension on the agenda of informal and formal meetings, seminars, and conferences with EU and external partners. It scheduled a ministerial conference specifically devoted to the future of the Northern Dimension, and engineered support for a European Council decision on an action plan. It used the Presidency's position as liaison with other EU institutions to strengthen relations with the Commission and secure its continued commitment.

The Finnish government's agenda-setting activities prior to, and during, the Presidency were clearly influenced by the formal constraints that it faced. The initiative was shaped so as to maximize its use to Finland, while minimizing the risk of rejection. To secure the support of all EU governments, the initiative was couched in nebulous language, presented as being in the interest of the Union as a whole, and designed so as not to require additional financial means or institutions. This was a process that involved compromises on the part of Finland, brought on by the requirement of unanimous approval, and leading to a dilution of the most ambitious version of the initiative. By building on co-existing programs and promising greater efficiency, the Finnish government sought and managed to win the Commission over to its side. Forthcoming Presidencies constituted additional actors with veto power over the political future of the initiative, and were consequently courted by the Finnish government.

Simultaneously, the informal norm of the neutral Presidency shaped the Finnish campaign for the Northern Dimension. Yet there is little to suggest that the Finnish government's adaptation to the norm was based on an institutionalized perception of appropriate Presidency behavior. Instead, the evidence indicates that the Finnish government related strategically to this norm. It sought to avoid giving the impression of promoting national interests, in the expectation of future rewards for its good behavior. This approach to the Presidency was reflected in the Finnish government's timing of the campaign, which placed the major lobbying efforts in the period prior to the Presidency. The six months at the helm could then be devoted to low-profile nurturing of the initiative, without attracting criticism and risking Finland's good reputation.

Posing the counterfactual question of whether the outcome would have been different with another state at the helm, much speaks in favor of an affirmative answer. With the exception of Sweden and Denmark, which share Finland's interests in Baltic cooperation, it is unlikely that another member state would have spent scarce resources on the development of an initiative such as the Northern Dimension. Since the early 1990s, the development of the EU's relations to its neighboring regions has followed a distinct pattern, with EU governments prioritizing alternative regions, depending on geographical proximity, cultural affinity, and historical heritage. The exploitation of the Presidency has constituted a prominent vehicle for these campaigns. The Barcelona process of regional cooperation around the Mediterranean was launched by the Spanish Presidency in 1995 and subsequently carried further by other southern Presidencies. Similarly, Germany has been a strong advocate of a broad enlargement of the EU to include states in Central and Eastern Europe. Whereas other EU governments did eventually grant their support to the Finnish proposal, it is probable that they would have spent their political capital on developing cooperation in other neighboring areas than the Baltic and Barents region.

The German Presidency and car recycling

When assuming the EU Presidency in January 1999, the new red–green German coalition government was widely expected to promote environmental integration. Yet all steps taken by Germany for the furthering of environmental concerns were politically overshadowed by the Presidency's efforts to prevent the adoption of the so-called end-of-life vehicles directive, requiring car manufacturers to carry the costs of recycling used vehicles. Following intense pressure from the domestic car industry, the German government exploited the prerogatives of the chairmanship to postpone the decision and force a renegotiation of the directive. Germany's engagement in non-decision-making caused considerable frustration and consternation among its European partners, but successfully secured more favorable terms for the automobile industry when the directive eventually was adopted in September 2000.

The end-of-life vehicles directive

Historically, Germany has been conceived of as one of Europe's "environmental leaders," driving the process toward environmentally friendly regulation in the EU, and pulling along a group of "environmental laggards" toward higher levels of protection.[46] The election in 1998 of a new government, composed of the Social Democrats and the Greens, and the associated appointment of Jürgen Trittin as the first-ever Green environment minister, created further expectations of a strong German environmental profile in the EU. It was widely believed that Trittin's

---

[46] Héritier 1995; Sbragia 1996; Liefferink and Skou Andersen 1998.

chairmanship of the Environmental Council would be one of the most productive and least difficult parts of Germany's EU Presidency in the first half of 1999.

Hardly surprisingly, environmental issues ranked high on the German government's list of priorities for its six months at the helm. In the political program for the Presidency, the German government singled out environmental policy as one its five major objectives. The general ambition was "to develop a European environmental policy in the single market based on the principle of sustainability."[47] More specifically, the German environment minister sought to promote three main themes: (1) harmonization of environmental protection requirements, especially as regards energy taxation; (2) increased transparency and greater involvement of citizens and environmental groups in environmental policy-making; and (3) the integration of environmental considerations in other policy sectors.[48]

At the time, one of the initiatives for new and stringent environmental rules high on the EU's political agenda was the end-of-life vehicles directive – an ambitious package of car recycling measures scheduled for adoption during the German Presidency. The fifteen member states had come to an agreement in principle already in December 1998, at the final Environmental Council meeting held by the preceding Austrian Presidency. In the quantitative beauty contest that Presidencies regularly engage in, counting the number of acts adopted during their period in charge, the car recycling directive offered an easy gain for Germany.

The proposal for the directive had been presented by the European Commission in the fall of 1997.[49] In order to be adopted, the directive required the mutual agreement of the Council and the Parliament under the co-decision procedure. The adoption of the Council's common position required the support of a qualified majority of the member states. The aim of the proposal was to limit the negative environmental impact of vehicles "at the end of their life," by introducing measures to ensure the recycling of car components. The proposal was based on the polluter pays principle, which in this case would require car manufacturers to cover the cost of recycling. Furthermore, the proposal was formulated so as to induce manufacturers to produce increasingly more recyclable vehicles. The basic formula of the proposal was an obligation for car owners to deliver vehicles to particular recycling facilities, for car producers to reimburse owners of the costs of this delivery, and for

[47] German Presidency 1999, 3.
[48] Wurzel 2000, 29.
[49] European Commission 1997a.

producers to design cars in such a way that an increasing share of the vehicle actually could be recycled.

Slightly simplified, there were four contentious elements in the proposal on which proponents and opponents differed. First, should the costs of recycling be borne only by the car producers or by a combination of actors? Second, how much of the vehicle should have to be recycled? Third, should the rules have retroactive effect or only apply to new cars produced after a certain date? And fourth, when should the rules enter into force?

The proposal met with strong dislike from European and international car producers. The European Automobile Manufacturers Association (ACEA) was hostile to all versions of the proposed directive, and claimed that it would have serious cost implications for the European automobile industry.[50] The Japanese Automobile Manufacturers Association similarly complained that "[t]he Commission proposal is not really market-oriented. The danger is that it will add to costs and get us into the business of dismantling, which is an area where we do not want to get involved."[51] By contrast, environmental lobbies, such as the European Group of Automotive Recycling Associations (EGARA), warmly welcomed the Commission's proposal.[52]

The German Presidency: non-decision-making at work

The Environmental Council was scheduled to meet three times during the German Presidency: a formal meeting in March, an informal meeting in May, and a concluding formal meeting in June. Since the closing of the dossier on car recycling only required the formal adoption of the Council's informal December agreement, the end-of-life vehicles directive was included on the agenda of the first meeting in March. In the week prior to the meeting, the *European Voice* newspaper reported: "Union environment ministers are expected to agree a compromise deal on the European Commission's proposals for an 'end-of-life vehicles' directive at their meeting next Thursday (11 March)."[53]

Yet the German Presidency had other plans in mind. The German government let it be known shortly before the Council meeting that it would withdraw its support for the proposal, and then exploited its privileged control over the agenda during the meeting to force a

---

[50] *European Voice*, 4–10 March 1999, 4.
[51] Ibid., 8.
[52] Ibid., 4.
[53] Ibid.

postponement of the adoption. Formally, there was nothing to prevent the other member states from proceeding without German support, since only a qualified majority was required for the adoption of the common position. But for another member state to call a vote against the explicit wishes of the chairman would have constituted a challenge against the authority of the Presidency, and a violation of the working method in the Council.

The German turnaround reflected a combination of massive lobbying against the directive from the automobile industry, and political interference by the German chancellor on behalf of these interests.[54] As the home of car producers such as Volkswagen, Mercedes-Benz, and BMW, Germany was expected to be hardest hit by the new directive. Volkswagen, Europe's largest manufacturer, had most to lose and lobbied strenuously for its cause. According to newspaper sources, the German government was exposed to "an unprecedented lobbying campaign by Ferdinand Piëch, chief executive of giant German car manufacturer Volkswagen."[55] Serving concurrently as the president of the ACEA, Piëch spoke not only on behalf of Volkswagen, but for the entire European car industry. Next to the general interest that governments normally take in the fortunes of important national industries, German chancellor Gerhard Schröder's prior involvement in Volkswagen helps explain the receptiveness of the German government to the demands of the car manufacturers. When serving as prime minister of Lower Saxony, Schröder had been a member of Volkswagen's supervisory board, and he retained an interest in the company.[56] Whereas Trittin allegedly would have favored continued German support for the draft directive, "Schröder made use of his prerogative as Chancellor to determine the policy guidelines for his government. He instructed Trittin to postpone the decision on the ELV directive until the June Environmental Council in order to allow time for finding a compromise solution acceptable to the automobile industry."[57]

The German government's crude exploitation of the chairmanship for national political purposes shocked its European partners and was condemned by member state representatives, the Commission, the environmental lobby, and the media.[58] In the press release from the tumultuous meeting, the Council Secretariat skillfully summarized the event in the

[54] See Wurzel 2000, 30–31, for a detailed analysis.
[55] *European Voice*, 17–23 June 1999, 6.
[56] Wurzel 2000, 30–31; *European Voice*, 1–7 July 1999, 4.
[57] Wurzel 2000, 31.
[58] Ibid.

diplomatic garb appropriate for official documents: "The German delegation, while re-stating its support for the Directive, requested to postpone the decision on the common position by three months; this would give time for clarification through talks with the economic operators concerned by the Directive and allow a decision to be taken in June on the present text."[59]

During the spring of 1999, Germany used the time it had gained to lobby other member governments for the purpose of achieving a minority of states capable of blocking the adoption of the common position. The intention, according to German officials, was not to veto the directive in principle, but rather to create the political preconditions for a compromise that could better accommodate the interests of the automobile industry.[60] In order to form a blocking minority, Germany had to secure the support of another sixteen votes, according to the weighted voting system of the Council. In concrete terms, this meant that the support of another two large member states would be sufficient to prevent adoption. This explains why the German government specifically targeted France, the UK, and Spain.[61] Yet to convince other member states to backtrack on their previous commitments to the December agreement proved difficult. When the Environmental Council met for an informal meeting in the town of Weimar in early May, the German government was still in the process of lobbying other states, and used its prerogative as Presidency to exclude the controversial car recycling proposal from the agenda of the deliberations.

In the run-up to the formal Council meeting in June, Germany's chances of securing the required support looked slim. As *European Voice* reported: "Germany looks set to cave in to pressure from other EU governments and drop its opposition to controversial proposals which would set binding targets for recycling and reusing car parts. – National officials say Bonn recognises that it cannot go on blocking the measure on its own, but is hoping that other member states will voice misgivings about the proposals, justifying a further delay."[62] However, at the eleventh hour, Germany's political pressure eventually yielded results, as the UK and Spain shifted sides. The British volteface was the result of a trade-off between Bonn and London, where Germany agreed to support the UK in a dossier negotiated in the

---

[59] Council of the European Union 1999a. See also *European Voice*, 18–24 March 1999, 22.
[60] Wurzel 2000, 35.
[61] *European Voice*, 17–23 June 1999, 6.
[62] Ibid., 6.

Internal Market Council in return for British support in blocking the car recycling directive.[63] Whether Germany offered anything in exchange for the Spanish support is less well known. One observer explains the shift in Spain's position with its relative disinterest in environmental issues and the fact that Spain is the host of one of Volkswagen's subsidiaries, SEAT.[64]

The events of the June meeting of the Environmental Council are unusually well documented. Following new rules intended to open up Council decision-making, the meeting was conducted in public. When the end-of-life vehicles directive came up on the agenda, chairman Trittin ordered the Council to move to "restricted session," which meant that all national aides and media representatives had to leave the room. By accident, however, one camera was still recording and transmitting sound to the pressroom. The reactions to Germany's successful welding of a blocking minority quickly made it into the media: " 'What are you doing trying to talk *us* into a compromise when *you* are the problem?' asked Austrian Environment Minister Martin Bartenstein. Denmark's Sven Auken was almost screaming with anger and France's Dominique Voynet boomed: 'We cannot leave this room to tell the press and the public that we have dropped our trousers for the car industry.' "[65]

The Council Secretariat's press release from the meeting reproduces the concluding remarks of chairman Trittin:

(1) I note that there is a blocking minority against the current draft. A common position is therefore impossible today. (2) I note that the Council sees the possibility of a compromise and that the Commission does not fundamentally reject this possibility. (3) A solution could consist of bringing forward the date of entry into force of the obligation to take back new vehicles and postponing the date in respect of vehicles already on the market. (4) I note that the incoming Presidency intends, in agreement with the Commission, to schedule a further discussion of and a decision on the draft Directive within the Council.[66]

Having successfully used the agenda-management powers of the chair to postpone a decision, and subsequently gained the support of the UK and Spain, the German government concluded its Presidency by opening the door to a future compromise more in line with the interests of its domestic automobile industry.

---

[63] *European Voice*, 1–7 July 1999.
[64] Wurzel 2000, 42, fn. 54.
[65] *European Voice*, 1–7 July 1999, 24.
[66] Council of the European Union 1999b.

Accommodation and conclusion

The German government's exploitation of the Presidency office during the first half of 1999 continued to shape the negotiations on the car recycling directive even after the Finnish government had taken over the chair of the Council. The conditions for an agreement had been permanently altered during the German period at the helm. This was recognized by the Finnish government, which sought to balance competing demands and broker a compromise as soon as it had taken office: "The incoming Finnish presidency has vowed to push for swift agreement on EU-wide car recycling measures despite German intransigence over the issue. Helsinki is under intense pressure from the outgoing European Commission to undo the damage caused by Bonn when it scuppered hopes of a deal at last week's meeting of environmental ministers."[67]

The Finnish Presidency directed its brokerage efforts at the potential solution outlined by Jürgen Trittin in his concluding statement at the turbulent June meeting, namely, to postpone the dates from which car producers would have to cover the costs for the free delivery of used vehicles to recycling facilities. The deadlock was broken by a Finnish compromise proposal tabled at a meeting of Coreper on 22 July, and the proposal was subsequently rushed to the General Affairs Council for adoption by written procedure on 29 July, before the EU's summer recess.[68] The compromise moved forward the dates of the free take-back, effectively delaying the introduction of the proposed legislation from 2001 to 2006. The agreement saved the automobile industry important time and money, while simultaneously rescuing the proposed directive from the scrap heap. Germany had succeeded in extracting important concessions, but nevertheless voted against the common position, possibly for domestic political reasons.[69] In the explanatory note that accompanied the adopted legal text, the Council openly recognized its internal disagreements and indirectly requested the Parliament not to touch this sensitive part of the deal in its response to the Council's common position: "The Council agreed on this solution after a very difficult discussion, taking into account the specific problems voiced during the final negotiations."[70]

---

[67] *European Voice*, 1–7 July 1999, 4.
[68] Council of the European Union 1999c. See also the press release from the meeting: Council of the European Union 1999d.
[69] Council of the European Union 1999d. The Council's common position was adopted by a qualified majority, Germany voting against and the Netherlands abstaining.
[70] Council of the European Union 1999c, 31.

Traditionally, the European Parliament has been the more environmentally progressive institution of the two co-legislators, pushing the Council toward greener EU legislation. In the case of the car recycling directive, the roles were less clearly defined, mainly because of a strong and vocal group of business-oriented MEPs. German Christian Democrat Karl-Heinz Florenz was appointed *rapporteur* of the dossier, and the proposed amendments presented by Florenz to the Parliament's Environmental Committee in early 2000 were intended to further dilute the impact of the directive.[71] More specifically, Florenz suggested that the costs of recycling vehicles be shared between car producers and buyers, which meant surrendering the polluter pays principle. Socialist Bernd Lange allied with Florenz, and together the two German MEPs managed to gain the support of the conservative European People's Party, smaller right-wing parties, as well as a number of socialists.[72] Yet the majority of the Parliament still opposed weakening the approach agreed by EU governments. The legislative resolution adopted by the full Parliament in early February went a fair way toward respecting the delicate compromise in the Council, leaving mainly minor disagreements to be settled in conciliation negotiations between the two institutions.[73]

In late May 2000, the delegations of the Council and the Parliament could agree on a joint text in the conciliation committee, subsequently confirmed by a qualified majority in the Council and an absolute majority in the Parliament. The conciliation negotiations resulted in noteworthy changes of the terms previously agreed in the Council.[74] The dates from which car producers would have to cover the costs for the free take-back of vehicles were postponed another 18 months, to 1 July 2002 for vehicles put on the market as from this date and 1 January 2007 for vehicles put on the market before 1 July 2002. However, to make this additional concession to the automobile industry politically more digestible, the directive also referred explicitly to the possibility that member states may apply the provisions of the directive in advance of these dates. The directive on end-of-life vehicles was formally signed and adopted by the Parliament and the Council on 18 September 2000.[75]

---

[71] *European Voice*, 6–12 January 2000, 2.
[72] *European Voice*, 27 January–2 February 2000, 6.
[73] European Parliament 2000.
[74] Council of the European Union 2000c.
[75] European Parliament and Council of the European Union 2000.

The power of the chair: assessing process and outcome

The maneuvering of the German Presidency in the spring of 1999 fundamentally shaped the most controversial provisions of the EU's new rules on car recycling. The case provides an illustration of the Presidency's capacity to engage in agenda exclusion. By exploiting the Presidency's powers of procedural control, the German government managed to prevent the EU's member states from adopting a common position during its period at the helm, and permanently altered the conditions for such an agreement in the post-Presidency period. Whereas formal institutional rules shaped the actions and effects of the German government, informal norms about appropriate Presidency behavior carried little weight.

In its attempts to steer the negotiations toward an outcome which was more compatible with the interests of its influential automobile industry, the German Presidency made effective use of the procedural power resources of the chairmanship. Whereas non-decision-making is known to be less observable than decision-making, a comparison with the Finnish campaign for the Northern Dimension reveals how the exercise of agenda exclusion truly constitutes a mirror of agenda setting. Instead of exploiting the control over meeting agendas to include new issues for debate, Germany dropped a dossier scheduled for decision from the list of items, thus producing a postponement. Where Finland used its responsibility for the meeting schedule to arrange formal and informal sessions devoted to its national priority, Germany refrained from scheduling negotiation sessions where the crisis it had given rise to could be solved, and abstained from raising the car recycling dispute at the informal meeting in Weimar. Rather than drawing on its procedural toolbox for purposes of brokering a compromise at the concluding meeting of the Environmental Council, the German Presidency just let it be known that a blocking minority existed and a common position thus could not be adopted.

Formal institutional rules shaped the German government's capacity to exploit the Presidency office for national purposes. While there is no indication that the rules for formal agenda setting constrained the German government in its exercise of non-decision-making, the nature of the decision rule clearly affected the Presidency's capacity to permanently change the political landscape for the adoption of the proposed directive. Had the Council's common position required unanimous agreement among the member states, rather than the support of a qualified majority, the German Presidency could have permanently killed the proposed directive when backtracking on its previous commitment to the deal brokered by the preceding Austrian Presidency. Instead, Germany was forced to seek the support of allies it originally did not have, but which it gained through diplomatic pressure, side payments, and political trade-offs.

There is no empirical evidence to indicate that the German government took notice of the norm of the neutral and impartial Presidency, let alone allowed this norm dictate its behavior. As Wurzel concludes in a study of the German Presidency's performance in the area of environmental regulation: "The disregard for the role of the EU presidency and blatant support of national economic interests by the German government with regard to the ELV directive tarnished its overall record in the Environmental Council and arguably overshadowed its entire presidency."[76] The German government crudely exploited the office of the Presidency to pull apart an existing agreement and shift the outcome toward a distribution of gains that better served its national political objectives, fully aware that it violated established norms of appropriate behavior. Even if the German government had been uncertain as to what the reaction of the member states would be when it first chose to postpone the decision, there could have been no doubt the second time around. The perseverance of the German Presidency in the face of vocal protests suggests that the perceived benefits of a renegotiated deal in this case surpassed the perceived costs of a tarnished reputation. This interpretation is strengthened by evidence that the German Presidency tailored its behavior depending on the dossier under negotiation, displaying a more constructive approach on environmental dossiers that were domestically less unpopular.[77]

Is it likely that the negotiations would have arrived at the same outcome with another member state in the chair? The empirical evidence clearly speaks in favor of a negative answer. The Council had already reached a preliminary agreement during the Austrian Presidency. In the absence of German maneuvering at the March meeting, this agreement would have become the Council's common position. No other member state had revealed any intention of surrendering the December agreement before Germany began to exert considerable political pressure on the UK and Spain, which only came on board after much hesitation and the exchange of political favors.

[76] Wurzel 2000, 38.
[77] Wurzel 2000, 2001.

Conclusion

EU governments have delegated agenda-management powers to the Presidency as a means of avoiding overcrowded and badly organized agendas. This chapter has demonstrated how these procedural instruments, while raising the general efficiency of decision-making, simultaneously may be used to shape the political priorities of the EU. Presidencies influence outcomes by introducing new concerns on the EU agenda, emphasizing or de-emphasizing issues already on the agenda, and even excluding items from negotiation. Rather than as an office hamstrung by its weak formal agenda-setting position, its required attention to an inherited agenda, its exposure to disruptive external events, and its obligation to remain neutral, the Presidency appears in this chapter as a power platform that offers governments in office the possibility to affect policy outcomes through alternative forms of agenda shaping. As the gardener of the European agenda, the Presidency creates favorable conditions for those plants it wishes to see in full bloom, while neglecting or removing those that would compete for light and nourishment.

Following an inventory of the most central power resources and institutional constraints in agenda management, this chapter offered two case studies, each exemplifying one of the prominent ways in which Presidencies shape the EU's policy priorities. The Finnish promotion of the Northern Dimension illustrated how an incoming Presidency, for tactical reasons, may choose to launch political initiatives well in advance of its period in office, use the time until the Presidency to prepare the ground, and then exploit the powers of the office to give its favored initiative the decisive push required for institutionalization and long-term survival. The German case demonstrated that agenda influence just as well can consist of the exclusion of unwanted issues from the political agenda. Dissatisfied with the existing proposal for a directive on car recycling, which would have been exceedingly costly to its domestic industry, the German government exploited its agenda-management resources to keep this dossier away from the Council's decision agenda and force a renegotiation of its terms.

5 The EU Presidency as broker: constructing intergovernmental bargains

In the previous chapter, I showed how the function of agenda management offers opportunities for Presidencies to shape the EU's policy agenda. In this chapter, I turn to the second of the Presidency's principal functions in EU cooperation: brokerage. My central argument is that the Presidency's brokerage resources permit the government at the helm to construct and shape agreements that otherwise may not have come about. The Presidency's influence over these negotiated outcomes is two-dimensional. By collecting private information on state preferences and structuring negotiations in ways that encourage convergence, Presidencies can unveil the underlying zone of agreement and engineer viable compromises. Presidency brokerage helps to explain why negotiation failure is a reasonably rare phenomenon in the EU, despite a tendency among governments to be secretive about their preferences and to adopt tactical negotiating positions that reduce the zone of agreement. At the same time, Presidencies are tempted to use their informational and procedural power resources for private gain. Typically, they exploit the position as broker to favor the outcomes they desire. If the zone of agreement permits a number of efficient outcomes with varying distributional consequences, Presidencies promote the agreement closest to their own preferences.

The argument in this chapter challenges the dominant understanding of Presidency brokerage in existing research. Typically, this literature asserts that the responsibility as broker carries adverse consequences for the Presidency government's capacity to secure national interests. The logic of this argument revolves around the norm of the honest broker, which is said to constrain Presidencies by prescribing impartial mediation and proscribing efforts to favor national interests.[1] As the Council Secretariat's handbook for Presidencies states: "The Presidency must, by definition, be neutral and impartial. It is the moderator for

---

[1] For good discussions, see Metcalfe 1998; Schout 1998; Elgström 2003a.

discussions and cannot therefore favour either its own preferences or those of a particular member state."[2] Whereas it is expected and legitimate that other Member States pursue national interests in EU negotiations, the Presidency should refrain from such behavior during its six-month period. According to this norm, the interests of the Presidency government should even be sacrificed if they make agreement more difficult. By consequence, holding the Presidency does not offer new opportunities, but instead carries a price.

The chapter is divided into three sections. The first part conducts an inventory of Presidencies' power resources in the function as broker, and delineates the institutional constraints under which they operate. The second and third sections present two case studies: the negotiations of the Agenda 2000 reform package during the German Presidency in the first half of 1999, and the negotiations on the Nice Treaty during the French Presidency in the second half of 2000. In both cases, I offer a reinterpretation of these negotiation processes, paying specific attention to the role of the Presidency in achieving and shaping the outcome. The German Presidency is often seen as having sacrificed key national interests for purposes of delivering an agreement. However, a closer examination of the multiple dossiers under negotiation yields a more balanced verdict, pinpointing several areas of German negotiation success. The French Presidency's handling of the IGC in 2000 has attracted significant criticism from policy-makers and academics, who blame the French for having produced an incoherent treaty through a biased process. Yet popularity mattered little for the French government, which was intent on delivering an agreement in Nice and ensuring that terms conformed to central French interests. The criticism only reflects the extent to which the French government was successful in this endeavor.

Brokerage: resources and constraints

The rules and practices of the Council grant the Presidency asymmetrical control over information and procedure, which may be used to broker and shape agreements among member governments. This section identifies the sources of the Presidency's privileged information about state preferences, its instruments for controlling the negotiation process, and the formal rules that condition the Presidency's brokerage activities.

---

[2] Council Secretariat 1997, 5.

Power resources in brokerage

The Presidency enjoys access to a set of actors and practices that enable it to gain privileged information about EU governments' preferences, beyond what is available to other Member States. This information enables the Presidency to identify the zone of agreement within which deals can be constructed.

The *General Secretariat of the Council* plays a central role in the Presidency's gathering of information, and works side-by-side with the Presidency throughout negotiations.[3] The Council Secretariat primarily provides three kinds of information to the Presidency, thus granting the chair a competitive edge. First, and most importantly, the Council Secretariat tracks the preferences and negotiating positions of all member governments. Through the long-term involvement in a dossier and informal communication with government representatives, the Secretariat gains an in-depth and horizontal picture of state preferences. Second, no actor is as familiar with the complex decision-making procedures of the EU and the formal instruments available to the Presidency as the Council Secretariat. Tactical advice on negotiation procedure is part and parcel of the Secretariat's support function, as is legal advice on possible courses of action. Third, the Council Secretariat constitutes a source of expertise on the content of dossiers under negotiation. Much like the Commission's officials gain intimate knowledge of a subject when preparing a proposal, the civil servants of the Secretariat develop an issue-specific expertise when tracing a dossier through the Council machinery.

The Council Secretariat communicates its information on preferences, procedure, and contents to the chair through so-called *notes au Président*. These confidential documents are drawn up exclusively for the Presidency and generally contain information on the background of the proposal, its legal basis, the voting procedure, the state of play in the negotiations, governments' negotiating positions and room for concessions, tactical brokerage advice, and alternative compromises that the Presidency may want to investigate. The great value of these briefs is well illustrated by the mixed feelings with which outgoing Presidencies give up this privilege. As one Belgian diplomat testifies: "Relief over shedding the work load is often combined with a tinge of regret at no

---

[3] Hamlet 2002; Stubb 2002; Beach 2004; interviews, Commission official, 6 December 2000; Council official, 7 December 2000; Council official, 8 February 2001.

longer . . . enjoying the exclusive privilege of the excellent presidential briefing papers."[4]

The second important source of privileged information is bilateral talks initiated by the Presidency. The so-called *confessional* is a bilateral encounter between the Presidency and a member state, designed to break deadlocks in negotiations. Confessionals may be convened either during the course of negotiations, by simply adjourning plenary talks for bilateral discussions with individual delegations, or in preparation for negotiation sessions. As suggested by the term confessional, these encounters are strictly confidential: "The President is under oath not to reveal a Member State's 'confessed' position to any other Member State, but his secret and privileged knowledge of the positions and the degree of flexibility of all Member States can enable him to make winning compromise proposals."[5] The sharing of private information is the most important function of the confessional, but it also provides an opportunity to put additional pressure on recalcitrant delegations, and to offer unofficial side payments.

The Presidency practice of *tours des capitales* serves the same purpose of collecting information and putting pressure to bear. These shuttle diplomacy tours take place at a number of levels in the political machinery. In addition to the prime minister's visits to all EU capitals prior to summits, which generally receive massive attention, less high-profile tours are undertaken by the ministers for foreign and European affairs, as well as senior civil servants. The format of the bilateral encounter enables prime ministers to share information about their bottom lines with the Presidency, without granting the same favor to other bargaining parties, thus improving the chances of agreement at the summit without exposing themselves to exploitation.

The Presidency's second major resource as broker is its asymmetrical control over negotiation procedure and sessions. As one close observer of Council negotiations testifies: "[A]ll Council sessions are essentially stage-managed by the Presidency."[6] The Presidency's command of the negotiation process rests on a broad repertoire of procedural instruments.

First, the Presidency is central in determining *the pace of Council negotiations*. The Presidency fixes the meeting schedule, and even if tradition imposes certain limits, the chair can shape the number and frequency of formal and informal negotiation sessions. The effect is a

---

[4] Bassompierre 1988, 107.
[5] Westlake 1999, 115.
[6] Sherrington 2000, 45.

well-documented variation across Presidencies in the number of meetings in different working groups, committees, and ministerial configurations.[7] Control over the meeting schedule grants the Presidency a capacity to improve the chances of agreement, by speeding up negotiations. "If a chairman senses that a deal is near, he may call further meetings at short notice to keep up the momentum and to put potentially recalcitrant delegations under pressure."[8] Similarly, the Presidency may use its control over the meeting agendas to allow greater room for negotiations on some dossiers rather than others. The Presidency's position in the negotiations may also be used to impose time pressure on the parties, as a means of encouraging agreement. For instance, it can create a sense of urgency by reminding all parties of the detrimental effects of not coming to an agreement, and it can warn like-minded governments of the probable consequences of leaving this issue for the next Presidency to conclude.

The Presidency's formal prerogative to decide *the format of negotiation sessions* constitutes a second procedural instrument. The standard format of a negotiation session at the ministerial level is a formal meeting in the Council's Brussels headquarters, each minister being accompanied by an impressive tail of officials, often making the total number of people in the room over one hundred. To facilitate agreement on sensitive issues, the Presidency frequently chooses to shift meetings into restricted session, when only three representatives from each state are allowed, or even super-restricted session, when only the minister and the EU ambassador remain at the table. The main advantage of the restricted negotiation format is the greater room for maneuver that it grants to the ministers, in the absence of watchful officials. Another variation on the negotiation format is the informal meetings that the Presidency may convene in the home country. The purpose of these meetings is to provide a more relaxed and congenial atmosphere which can improve the chances of reaching an agreement. Finally, the Presidency may choose to activate the "Friends of the Presidency" – an informal, *ad hoc* group of like-minded officials, whose composition varies depending on the subject area, and which is convened by the Presidency to address complicated issues or solve specific conflicts.

A third procedural resource is the so-called *Presidency compromise*.[9] The existence of a specific term for compromises proposed by the chair reflects the Commission's original role as mediator and the Presidency's

---

[7] Sherrington 2000.
[8] Westlake 1999, 308.
[9] For discussions, see Hayes-Renshaw and Wallace 1997, 146–147; Nicoll 1998, 5–6.

subsequent development into the preferred broker. Part of the explanation rests with the Presidency's unusual capacity to conclude package deals, owing to its position as a link between the different bargaining arenas in the Council. Such deals may consist of a conventional trade of concessions within the same issue area, but the true value-added of the Presidency as a broker is the ability to stitch together unorthodox deals that stretch across a number of issue areas. As I describe below, the relative ease with which the Presidency can establish its own compromise proposal as single negotiating text and gain sufficient support for this text to be adopted, depends on the agenda setting and decision rules in the particular policy area.

The establishment of the Presidency's text as the basis of negotiation grants the government at the helm significant room for maneuver. Since it is also the Presidency's responsibility to determine when an issue is ripe for decision, negotiations generally continue until the Presidency assesses that a sufficient number of member states are on board. Typically, the Presidency does not make use of its authority to call a vote, but instead proceeds by noting the existence of sufficient support, and if nobody objects, the proposal is considered to be adopted. As one EU official explains: "He who proposes is in the driver's seat. Member states only say no if they totally cannot buy it, which grants the Presidency quite some room to shape deals to its own liking."[10] This discretion is also reflected in the kind of tactical advice given by the Council Secretariat:

If no solution has been found, which is most likely, the Chairman may conclude by noting that the Presidency's proposal seems to be the one most likely to achieve general acceptance. If the countries have agreed on a solution, then this can be presented to the others for general acceptance. If this is not acceptable to the others, the Chairman can again go back to the Presidency's text and note that it seems to be the one most likely to achieve general acceptance.[11]

Institutional constraints in brokerage

The formal institutional environment in which the Presidency operates exerts an enabling and constraining effect on its brokerage activities, determining the source of compromise proposals, the zone of agreement, and the Presidency's room for maneuver.

---

[10] Interview, European Parliament official, 2 July 2001.
[11] Quoted in Hamlet 2002, 46.

Formal agenda-setting rules affect the Presidency's capacity to present its own compromise as the single negotiating text of the negotiations. In the areas of cooperation that follow the supranational model of decision-making, where the Commission enjoys a monopoly on political initiative, the Presidency's compromise text competes with the original legislative proposal of this institution. The Commission's proposal for new legislation is the first candidate for a single negotiating text around which bargaining can converge. Yet, sometimes, the Commission's original proposal is not sufficiently attuned to the wishes of EU governments. Even if this does not preclude that negotiations proceed using the original text as the basis for discussion, it may be more efficient to move to an alternative compromise text, drafted by the Presidency. To the extent that the Presidency's compromise document attracts more support, it *de facto* supplants the Commission's original proposal as the single negotiating text. In this case, the Commission is put under pressure to revise the formal proposal along the lines suggested by the Presidency.

In the areas of cooperation that follow the intergovernmental model of decision-making, where the member states possess formal agenda-setting powers, the Presidency's compromise document faces less competition for the position as single negotiating text. Even if other EU governments can present initiatives as well, the principal agenda-setting role in these areas has devolved to the Presidency. In most cases, therefore, the Presidency functions both as formal agenda setter and as informal architect of compromise. Should other governments present proposals, the Presidency is still in a favorable position to assume the role of broker.

This survey of agenda-setting arrangements suggests that it is relatively easy for the Presidency to place its own text at the center of negotiations where these follow the intergovernmental, rather than the supranational model of decision-making. Once the Presidency's compromise text has been established as the basis of negotiation, the chair's ability to engineer agreement around its preferred outcome expands considerably. Yet, to be adopted, the Presidency text must pass the more or less stringent decision rules specified by the treaties.

Formal decision rules condition the chair's ability to construct an agreement and to promote its own ideal solution. As explained in Chapter 4, unanimity is used in those areas that operate according to the intergovernmental model of decision-making, i.e. the second and third pillars of EU cooperation, as well as decision-making in the European Council and at IGCs. Majority voting is the norm in those areas that operate according to the supranational mode of decision-making, in practice, most areas of EU cooperation.

When unanimous consent is required, the Presidency must take into consideration the interests of all member states. Since even outliers must be brought on board, the Presidency is forced to seek solutions that accommodate the position of the most conservative state, wishing the least change to the status quo. Unless the Presidency's own position is close to that of the most conservative state, the capacity of the chair to promote its own preferred solution simultaneously is reduced. The Presidency's best chance of delivering agreements that go beyond lowest-common-denominator solutions rests with its ability to construct package agreements. If the Presidency can compensate outliers through side-payments, it can conclude agreements that upgrade the common interest.

When only a qualified majority of the member states is necessary for agreement, the Presidency's room for maneuver expands. It becomes easier to construct viable compromises, and to guide negotiations in the Presidency's favor. The effects of extreme positions are mitigated, since outliers can be overruled. Even if actual voting rarely occurs, negotiations take place "in the shadow of the vote." The absence of voting is best explained by the Presidency practice of declaring an act to be adopted once it has gathered sufficient support. As one Council official explains: "You note that there is a qualified majority in favor of the Presidency proposal, you invite the remaining states to join and you propose minor modifications in order to increase acceptance, and then you make it clear that it is time to take a decision. Usually, the minority then accepts the proposal without a vote."[12]

This inventory of decision rules modifies the expectations about Presidency influence generated by the consideration of agenda-setting rules. Whereas the intergovernmental model makes it easier for the Presidency to gain the position as principal architect of compromise on a particular dossier, the stringent decision rule in this mode of cooperation makes it more difficult for the Presidency to secure its most favored outcome. Conversely, it is easier for the Presidency to construct and shape final agreements where supranational decision-making is used, given that the Presidency has managed to establish its compromise document as the single negotiating text.

---

[12] Interview, Council official, 8 February 2001. This was confirmed in interviews with Commission official, 6 December 2000; Commission official, 8 February 2001; Danish government official, 9 February 2001. For recent data on the occurrence of voting in Council decision-making, see Hayes-Renshaw, van Aken, and Wallace 2005.

The German Presidency and Agenda 2000

The major brokerage challenge for the German Presidency in the spring of 1999 was the conclusion of the Agenda 2000 reform package. Not only were the parties' negotiating positions wildly at odds with each other, but Germany also held firm and extreme preferences in many of the issues. Add the requirement of unanimous agreement, and the odds for a successful conclusion during Germany's period at the helm looked very poor. Yet, making full use of the brokerage instruments at its disposal, the German government succeeded in forging a package agreement that was acceptable to all parties. Simultaneously, and contrary to what some observers suggest, the Presidency managed to safeguard German interests in several of the key areas under negotiation.

The Agenda 2000 reform package

In the mid-1990s, the EU embarked on the process of preparing its policies and institutions for the forthcoming enlargement of the Union to include countries mainly from Central and Eastern Europe. The Agenda 2000 reform package was an integral part of these efforts. The package targeted the EU's major spending policies: the Common Agricultural Policy (CAP) and regional policy, the former consuming approximately 50 percent of the EU budget and the latter about 35 percent. The third key component was the proposal for a new financial framework for the EU, covering the period 2000–2006. The driving concern behind this reform package was the financial implications of admitting ten to twelve new states, all less wealthy than the existing members, many of whom had large and inefficient agricultural sectors. The challenge for EU governments was to decide on the degree and orientation of reform, and to determine the division of contributions to, and gains from, the EU budget over the next financial period.

The policy areas covered by the reform package belong to those parts of EU cooperation where the supranational model of decision-making is used. In its function as formal agenda setter, the Commission formulated and presented the proposals for reform in 1997 and 1998.[13] Even if the adoption of some proposals only required the support of a qualified majority, other parts of the package – notably, the financial agreement setting the parameters for the policy reforms – required unanimous

---

[13] European Commission 1997b.

support. In practice, the reform package was therefore treated as one single undertaking, to which all governments had to agree. The Commission proposed: (1) reducing price support for agricultural products and modifying the system of direct income payments to farmers; (2) concentrating the resources of the EU's regional funds to the areas of greatest need; and (3) capping the annual budget at 1.27 percent of total EU GNP.

The proposals were extremely contentious and exposed a number of deep rifts among the member states.[14] The suggestions on agricultural reform were criticized by the UK, Denmark, and Sweden for being insufficiently far-reaching. While a step in the right direction, the reforms were far from the complete liberalization of the market for agricultural products that these countries would have preferred. Germany and France, by contrast, were completely opposed to any kind of agricultural reform, questioning the alleged problems and the proposed solutions. Both states were major beneficiaries of CAP support, and both governments faced vocal and well-organized agricultural interests domestically. The proposed changes in the area of regional policy pitted the majority of member states against Greece, Ireland, Portugal, and Spain, which insisted on keeping the special favors they enjoyed in this area. The most contentious issue of all was the financial perspective and the question of budgetary imbalances between the member states. Four major net contributors to the budget – Germany, the Netherlands, Sweden, and Austria – demanded a rebalancing of the system and a considerable reduction of their burden, whereas the major net beneficiaries from the budget opposed such a reorientation.

Progress in the negotiations was slow during 1998, with member governments mainly reiterating their initial positions without any significant movement. The most important event during the first half of 1998 was the decision to impose a deadline of March 1999 for the conclusion of the negotiations. Even so, few advances were made during the fall of 1998. A major explanation for this was the German general election in September 1998, which had a paralyzing effect on the reform discussions. The ruling Conservative government was reluctant to make concessions before the election, and there was little point in striking difficult bargains if these could be unravelled by a new government. Only after the Social Democratic victory in the elections in late 1998 did the negotiations pick up speed.

---

[14] For good discussions, see Galloway 1999a; Ackrill 2000; Schwaag Serger 2001.

The German Presidency: developing the negotiating box

When Germany took over the Presidency in January 1999, the government declared Agenda 2000 to be its top priority. With less than three months left before the deadline, it was essential to achieve movement in the negotiations and the gradual approximation of governments' competing positions. The Presidency program, outlining Germany's objectives for its period at the helm, underlined the government's commitment to an early agreement, and stressed the need for a package-deal approach:

> The German Presidency will make every effort to have the reforms in Agenda 2000 areas adopted before the end of its term of office. If this is to be achieved, political agreement must be reached on the entire package no later than March 1999. . . . In the German Presidency's view, it will be possible to achieve a solution within the framework of a comprehensive balancing of interests and overall compromise involving all Member States and all sectors only if we ensure that Agenda 2000 continues to be treated as a package.[15]

In early January, the Presidency introduced its major strategy for achieving unanimous agreement on this complex package over the coming three months: a draft document dubbed the "negotiating box," essentially conforming to a single negotiating text or the first stage of a comprehensive Presidency compromise.[16] The document was organized around the issues of the negotiations, rather than member state positions, and constituted "a skeletal pre-draft of what would eventually become the Berlin European Council Conclusions."[17] The language of this shell accord was developed in those areas where governments agreed, but otherwise bracketed. The purpose of the procedure was to ensure a package-deal approach in the negotiations, and to steer work forward through successive revisions of the box. The result of this strategy was a shift in focus from the demands of outliers to areas of potential compromise: "As a result [of the negotiating box], nobody is even genuflecting before isolated Spanish positions. . . . Instead, discussion papers prepared by the presidency for Member States' ambassadors to the Union before weekly negotiating sessions have focused on finding accommodations between the differing shades of opinion held by the majority of governments."[18]

---

[15] German Presidency 1999, 4.
[16] Galloway 1999a, 15–17; *European Voice*, 7–13 January 1999, 6. The negotiating box mirrored the method used in the run-up to the Edinburgh European Council 1992, which had decided on the previous financial package.
[17] Galloway 1999a, 15.
[18] *European Voice*, 4–10 February 1999, 11. See also Galloway 1999a, 15; Laffan 2000, 740.

Over the next two and a half months, the Presidency fleshed out the contents and filled in the gaps of the box. The essential elements of the Presidency's brokerage approach were compromise proposals based on consultations with the Council Secretariat, bilateral meetings with member governments to sound out concerns and reactions, weekly negotiations by the EU ambassadors in Coreper, and ministerial discussions in the Council of particularly divisive political issues. In addition, the Presidency supplemented the formal institutional structure of the Council with a number of extraordinary high-level groups that were to prove instrumental in the process of reaching agreement, especially in the area of agriculture.[19]

For Germany, the task of brokering a deal was complicated by the fact that it held strong – and not easily compatible – preferences on agricultural reform, finances, and enlargement. Bundling these issues into the same set of negotiations put Germany in an awkward position. "Germany faced the dilemma of pursuing a restrictive policy for the EU budget on the one hand, while opposing any reforms of the CAP aimed at eventually reducing agriculture expenditure of the EU, on the other."[20] Germany's strategy for reconciling its interests was to stress that agricultural reform, while possibly cost-cutting in the long term, in fact involved a short-term increase in agricultural spending, which was undesirable given the general support – and Germany's preference – for budget discipline. In addition, Germany held a strong interest in the enlargement of the EU, which would be best served by an early Agenda 2000 agreement.

As soon as Germany had taken over the chair, the negotiations on agriculture became centered on the financial aspects of reform.[21] German ministers sought to gather support for a capping of the agricultural budget at the current level in real terms. German ministers first sought support for a capping of the agricultural budget, and once the preliminary agreement had been obtained, the negotiations were directed toward methods of budget restriction.[22] The Presidency sought to engineer support for the alternative of limiting or postponing reform measures as a way of reducing the expected costs of reform. Late February and early March witnessed a number of Presidency compromise proposals, coupled with bilateral talks. In order to signal that

[19] Laffan 1999.
[20] Schwaag Serger 2001, 52. See also Maurer 2000, 46–47.
[21] Galloway 1999a, 24–26; Laffan 2000, 737–741; Schwaag Serger 2001, 106–125.
[22] *European Voice* 14–20 January 1999, 1; 28 January–3 February 1999, 16; 4–10 February 1999, 11.

Germany was not prepared to disregard its national interests, just because it held the Presidency, the German government took the unusual measure of presenting a national position paper on 5 March. Based on governments' reactions to all these initiatives, the Presidency eventually formulated a compromise proposal, which gathered the support of agriculture ministers on 11 March. The compromise restricted or postponed reform in important areas, but exceeded the agreed budget ceiling by seven billion euros.

In the negotiations on regional policy reform, the early months of 1999 witnessed gradual convergence on a final compromise.[23] The four privileged countries first criticized the Commission's original proposal, arguing that its formula for the distribution of regional funds in a future EU of twenty-five or more member states would undermine the level of aid to the current member states. But when this group of countries realized the comparative generosity of this offer, they adopted the Commission's proposed levels of support as their bargaining position. By contrast, the advocates of a rigorous budget approach, among them Germany, considered the Commission's offer too generous, and questioned whether Spain, Portugal, and Ireland were actually eligible for more aid under the so-called cohesion fund. In a classic concession-and-convergence negotiation, the parties abandoned the initial positions of about 240 and 190 billion euro over the next financial period, to seek agreement in the mid-range of the spectrum. In the week prior to the Berlin summit, the two sides were judged to be close to a deal.[24]

In the negotiations on the financial perspective, it proved easy to gain support for the objective of budgetary discipline. By contrast, rebalancing was difficult.[25] In the early months of its Presidency period, the German government continued to push hard for some kind of budgetary adjustment mechanism, supported by the other net contributors.[26] This could be achieved through a number of different measures, and the end negotiations consisted of Germany testing alternative approaches on other governments. The alternative most favored by the net contributors – a general correction mechanism – met with strong objections from the other member states. The net contributors then directed their efforts at the special budget rebate enjoyed by the UK since 1984. If the UK agreed to give up part of, or the entire, budget rebate of three billion

[23] Galloway 1999a, 26–27; *European Voice*, 18–24 March 1999, 2.
[24] *European Voice*, 18–24 March 1999, 2.
[25] *European Voice*, 4–10 February 1999, 11; 25 February–3 March 1999, 1, 10; Galloway 1999a, 28–32.
[26] *European Voice*, 7–13 January 1999, 6; 28 January–3 February 1999, 16.

euros annually, these funds could be used to finance a reduction for the net contributors. Though the UK declared the issue non-negotiable, the British rebate was the focus of discussion from late February up and until the summit in Berlin.

The Berlin agreement

In its efforts to prepare the ground for a final agreement in Berlin, the German Presidency attempted to raise the intensity and perceived urgency of the negotiations.[27] Formal Council meetings were almost exclusively devoted to Agenda 2000 negotiations, and other issues were put on the back burner. In addition, the Presidency used the possibility of calling informal meetings in Germany, often with restricted participation. Simultaneously, Germany tried to instill a sense of urgency in the negotiations, by warning of the risk of negative repercussions for the newly-born euro currency and Europe's international standing, in the absence of a deal. As Schröder declared: "If the EU were to create no reasonable financial planning for the years 2000–2006, then that could, and I deliberately choose my words with care, have repercussions on the international financial markets on the quality of the euro."[28] When the Commission unexpectedly resigned on 16 March, following allegations of corruption, the German Presidency was granted an additional reason for its crisis warnings and calls for unity.

The concluding European Council summit in Berlin on 24 and 25 March constituted a forty-eight-hour bargaining session, shifting between multilateral negotiations and bilateral talks between the Presidency and member governments. In the end, the German Presidency managed to weld a package compromise, which was sufficiently appealing to all parties, though markedly shaped by the positions of the most recalcitrant states.

The already existing agreement of the Agriculture Council was re-negotiated by the heads of state and government, for the purpose of keeping agricultural spending below the agreed budgetary ceiling. Eventually, the proposals for CAP reform became so watered down that budget stability was achieved. The two winners from this negotiation were France and Germany, which managed to secure outcomes close to their initial positions on almost all key issues.[29] France had taken a no-reform position throughout the negotiations, which forced the other

---

[27] *European Voice*, 25 February–3 March 1999, 1; Ackrill 2000; Schwaag Serger 2001.
[28] Quoted in *European Voice*, 24–30 June 1999. See also *European Voice*, 25 February–3 March 1999, 1, 9, 10; Ackrill 2000, 347; Schwaag Serger 2001, 127–129.
[29] Ackrill 2000, 346–348; Schwaag Serger 2001, 126–146.

parties toward less and less ambitious reform alternatives. The German Presidency had secured support for the principle of budget stability, which had then been used successfully as an argument against reform. In fact, the final agreement corresponded closely to the German national position paper tabled in early March.

On regional policy reform, the German Presidency could secure unanimous agreement for the level of 213 billion euro, almost exactly the mid-point between the initial bargaining positions of the cohesion group and the advocates of budgetary restraint. The greatest obstacle to reform in this negotiation, and arguably its greatest winner, was Spain. Staunchly opposed to reform, the Spaniards pursued what one diplomat described as a "no, no, no, no, no approach."[30] When all other parties at the summit had given their consent to the final agreement, the Spanish held out, and were generously awarded for their recalcitrance.[31] Instead of losing the support of the cohesion fund, Spain secured terms granting it 62 percent of this fund over the next financial period.

When governments finally came to an agreement on the financial perspective for 2000–2006, this deal was designed to meet the concerns of the net contributors, without fundamentally shifting the burden of financial responsibility.[32] The package contained three central elements: an approach of discipline and stabilization with regard to the overall EU budget; a set of specific measures on the resources and expenditure sides targeted at individual net contributors; and a revision of the financial key for the UK rebate, reducing the contribution of Germany, the Netherlands, Austria, and Sweden to the financing of this rebate to 25 percent of their normal share. The net contributors certainly had not achieved as much as they desired, but neither had the net beneficiaries been able to uphold the status quo in terms of budgetary growth and redistribution. The state that emerged as the winner from the negotiations was the UK, which managed to keep its budget rebate intact. This outcome is partly explained by the late interest of the net contributors in keeping this arrangement, once the rebate had become the means for reducing these countries' net contribution to the EU budget.

The power of the chair: assessing process and outcome

The German Presidency made use of the full range of brokerage instruments available to it in its position as chair, and thereby steered the

---

[30] *European Voice*, 4–10 February 1999, 11.
[31] *European Voice*, 24–30 June 1999, 9; Stein 2000, 38.
[32] Galloway 1999a, 28–32.

negotiations toward a concluding compromise deal. As one observer commented: "*Agenda 2000* would still be under negotiation if a firm hand had not been used in managing the negotiation process."[33] Exploiting its powers of procedure, the Presidency shaped the negotiation process by intensifying the formal meeting schedule, moving Agenda 2000 to the top of meeting agendas, and calling informal negotiation sessions. The Presidency adopted a specific brokerage formula – the negotiating box – that functioned as a single negotiating text, encouraging a focus on issues and trade-offs rather than positions and ultimatums. The Presidency unlocked outstanding issues of contention, particularly at the end stage, through a combination of bilateral confessionals that unveiled the bottom lines of the parties, and follow-up papers that outlined new compromise alternatives. The Presidency exploited the power of the pulpit and political turmoil in the EU to create a sense of urgency and crisis that facilitated agreement in Berlin. In the end, the Agenda 2000 deal was considered the main achievement of the German Presidency.[34] It is another example of the Presidency as architect of compromise in major EU package agreements.

The procedural and informational advantages of the Presidency were instrumental, not only for stitching together a compromise deal, but also for safeguarding German interests in the terms of that agreement. Whereas some observers, especially in the German media, argued that the Presidency emerged as a loser from the Agenda 2000 negotiations, these statements are based on a one-sided focus on the rebalancing of the budget, and unrealistic expectations as to what Germany could possibly achieve.[35] A comprehensive and more realistic assessment yields a more balanced verdict, pointing to German negotiation success in several areas. The deal that eventually emerged from the negotiations corresponded closely to the German positions on agricultural reform, reflected the German demands for budget discipline over the next financial period, contained provisions for targeted cuts in Germany's net contribution, albeit not as extensive as desired, and balanced the competing demands on regional spending. In addition, Germany reached the goal of concluding a political agreement in March, which kept the enlargement process on track.

---

[33] Galloway 1999a, 34. Emphasis in original.
[34] Lankowski 1999; Laffan 2000, 740; Maurer 2000, 46.
[35] For instance, *Die Welt* commented: "At Berlin Schröder's European partners showed him how national interests should be protected. France got their billions for agriculture and Spain got their structural funds. The UK didn't have to give up their rebate. From a national point of view the Berlin summit was anything but a success." Quoted in Stein 2000, 39. See also, e.g., Laffan 1999.

The German government's brokerage activities were shaped by formal institutional constraints. This is the primary explanation for the problems experienced by the Presidency in brokering an agreement and defending its own interests in select areas. Whereas the formal agenda-setting rules imposed few constraints – the Presidency's negotiating box quickly replaced the Commission's original set of proposals as the single negotiating text – formal decision rules shaped the negotiations in clear and identifiable ways. The requirement of unanimity for the Agenda 2000 package worked in favor of those states least interested in reforms of existing arrangements: France and Germany in agricultural policy, Spain in regional policy, and the net beneficiaries and the UK on the financing of the budget. These states had no incentive to agree to proposals that yielded less than the existing arrangements, and the German Presidency consequently experienced problems in stitching together solutions which went beyond the lowest common denominator. This necessity to acquiesce to the demands of the most conservative states similarly reduced the Presidency's capacity to steer the negotiations toward its most preferred outcome in those areas where Germany itself was in favor of reform, such as the rebalancing of the budget and regional spending.

There is little empirical evidence to suggest that Germany was constrained by the norm of the honest broker. Throughout the negotiations of Agenda 2000, Germany was explicit about its national objectives, both in the bargaining sessions and in the media. Though several observers note that the German government's behavior in the end game was influenced by the responsibilities of the Presidency office, it was not the requirement of neutrality that affected German behavior, but the expectation on results. Partly, Germany had only itself to blame. The strong commitment to a deal in Berlin and the active attempts at instilling crisis awareness meant that Germany, in the end, had to shoulder the responsibility of chairman and deliver an agreement, even if this meant compromising its own objectives on the rebalancing of the budget.

Is it likely that the Agenda 2000 negotiations would have ended in this particular way had another member state had access to the power platform of the Presidency? It is not unreasonable to think that the negotiations on regional policy reform, which followed a concession-and-convergence pattern, would have yielded a similar outcome under another Presidency. By contrast, the German government's active interference in other areas, to make sure that certain options were on the table and that others were never considered, suggests that the end result would have been different had a government with an opposing position directed the negotiations instead. This is most evident in the talks on agriculture, where Germany skillfully steered the negotiations away from the reforms advocated by several member states and toward an outcome closely in line with German financial and agricultural interests. Whereas Germany, because of its veto, probably would have been able to limit the degree of agricultural reform even in the absence of the Presidency platform, it is less likely that unanimous agreement would have been engineered around a solution whose terms effectively corresponded to a German position paper. Furthermore, the process for arriving at this solution was distinctly marked by the German government's ambition to reconcile its preferences for budget restriction and against agricultural reform – a preference combination not held by any other party in the negotiations.

The French Presidency and IGC 2000

The most important dossier during the French Presidency in the fall of 2000 was the conclusion of the intergovernmental conference initiated earlier that year. Member state positions diverged sharply on the key elements of the proposed treaty, and for France – just as for Germany in the Agenda 2000 negotiations – the brokerage task was complicated by its own extreme preferences and the requirement of unanimity. Yet, through an often criticized exploitation of the Presidency's privileged arsenal of weapons, France engineered agreement on a new treaty – the Nice Treaty – that both gained the support of all parties and was surprisingly conformant to the French government's preferences.

The intergovernmental conference 2000

The IGC convened and concluded in 2000 constituted an additional step in the EU's preparations for enlargement. If the purpose of the Agenda 2000 negotiations had been to adapt the EU's major spending policies, the rationale of IGC 2000 was to prepare the EU's institutions for an enlarged Union. This constitutional conference was motivated by the realization that the institutions, in their existing format, would be unable to function properly with an additional ten to twelve member states. The conference addressed four key issues: the size and composition of the Commission, the weighing of votes in the Council, the possible extension of qualified majority voting in the Council, and the methods of enhanced cooperation or flexible integration.[36] The

---

[36] For background discussions, see Best, Gray, and Stubb 2000; Galloway 2001.

issues were extremely controversial, and it was no coincidence that the governments had failed to find acceptable solutions when these issues were first considered during the IGC in 1996–1997.

In the existing system, the Commission was composed of twenty members, where each of the small and medium-sized member states nominated one commissioner, whereas the five large states – Germany, France, Italy, Spain, and the United Kingdom – nominated two. A simple extrapolation of this system would result in an unwieldy Commission after enlargement, and member governments therefore had to agree on ways of reducing the number of commissioners. The size and composition of the Commission was explicitly linked to the weighing of votes in the Council through a protocol attached to the Amsterdam Treaty. If the large member states were to lose one of their two commissioners, they would have to be compensated with greater voting weight. Since the late 1980s, successive IGCs had expanded the number of areas where decisions could be taken through majority voting. Yet governments still retained the capacity to veto agreements in a substantial number of areas. The need to consider a further extension of qualified majority voting was fueled by the fear of decision paralysis in these areas in an enlarged EU of ten to twelve additional veto players.

Prior to the French Presidency in the second half of 2000, the deliberations centered almost exclusively on the agenda of the conference. Member states agreed on the need to tackle the first three issues, but disagreed as to whether any further institutional issues should be brought on board. Advocates of a narrow agenda feared that additional issues would lead to a lengthy IGC and eventually a postponement of enlargement, whereas proponents of a broad agenda emphasized the advantages of rendering further unnecessary IGCs in the near future. The combined effect of the Finnish Presidency in the fall of 1999, charged with preparing the IGC, and the Portuguese Presidency in the spring of 2000, which opened the formal IGC negotiations in February, was to include enhanced cooperation or flexibility as a fourth negotiation item.[37]

When the Portuguese government handed over the EU Presidency to French president Jacques Chirac and French prime minister Lionel Jospin in July 2000, the IGC agenda had been fixed, but little movement had taken place in the substantive negotiations on the four dossiers. The concluding report of the Portuguese Presidency illustrated "the complexity of the institutional issues on the agenda, the deep divergence of

---

[37] See, e.g., Dinan and Vanhoonacker 2000a, 2000b; Gray and Stubb 2001, 8–10.

opinion among Member States, and the extent to which the IGC has yet to get off the ground."[38]

The French Presidency: provoking conflict and producing progress

For France, the conclusion of the IGC during the fall and the achievement of a treaty in Nice was the foremost priority.[39] In the official working program, institutional reform was presented as one of three key objectives for the French Presidency:

> The French Presidency will do all it can to ensure that the Conference reaches a satisfactory agreement at the Nice European Council in December. . . . The French Presidency will endeavour to obtain broad agreement between all the Member States on all these subjects, which are decisive for European construction, and its primary objective will be the effective and legitimate functioning of the Union with the prospect of its forthcoming enlargement.[40]

France held key interests in the issues under negotiation. In addition, it was clear that institutional reform constituted the basis on which the French Presidency would be assessed. When the IGC talks were relaunched in July under French chairmanship, the Presidency chose to proceed by way of a new negotiation approach. This approach was composed of a partially new structure of the overall negotiation process, as well as a specific brokerage strategy.

The French government announced a fuller schedule of IGC meetings and a new format for the negotiations.[41] Next to the existing negotiation levels of state representatives in the Preparatory Group, foreign ministers in the General Affairs Council, and heads of state and government in the European Council, the Presidency added a fourth tier of extraordinary ministerial conclaves. Four such conclaves were held during the fall of 2000. In addition, the French Presidency made the IGC negotiations the focus of informal ministerial meetings, for instance, the foreign ministers' informal meeting at Evian, the finance ministers' informal meeting at Versailles, and the European Council's informal summit at Biarritz.

The French brokerage strategy consisted of a number of consecutive steps.[42] Rather than moving directly to the stage of article drafting, the

---

[38] Dinan and Vanhoonacker, 2000b, 1.
[39] *European Voice*, 5 June–29 July 2000, 15–19; interview, French government official, 9 February 2001; Costa, Couvidat, and Daloz 2003.
[40] French Presidency 2000, 23.
[41] Dinan and Vanhoonacker 2000c; Galloway 2001, 31–34.
[42] Galloway 2001, 33–36; Gray and Stubb 2001, 11; Schout and Vanhoonacker 2001, 12–13.

French began by issuing oriented questionnaires, to sound out state concerns. Over time, these questionnaires turned into papers that gradually acquired the form of draft treaty language. In early November, these papers were merged into a summary document that constituted a first outline of a draft treaty, which then was shaped over the coming month into the draft submitted for final negotiation in Nice. In terms of substance, the French Presidency devoted most of the early work to the less sensitive issues of QMV extension and flexibility. By contrast, the size of the Commission and the reweighing of votes were largely left for the European Council summits in Biarritz and Nice. The fact that some agenda items were interlinked opened up for trade-offs and package deals. Yet, in contrast to previous IGCs, the exclusive focus on institutional issues in this round of negotiations meant that no financial side-payments existed that could be used to persuade recalcitrant states.

The issues under negotiation had been French key concerns for a long time, and there was no denying that France preferred certain outcomes over others. It was equally clear that these key interests would guide French behavior in the chair, even if this was in conflict with the expectation of a neutral Presidency. Before the beginning of the Presidency, the French government formulated a central strategy for its period at the helm, communicated to all key negotiators.[43] The first priority was to safeguard the country's core institutional interests, the second concern was its responsibility as honest broker, and the third was French policy interests of secondary importance. As the chief advisor to the European affairs minister stated: "It would be hypocritical to pretend that we can put our national priority concerns in brackets, but we can drop secondary preoccupations."[44]

Already at the previous IGC France had insisted on a Commission with a limited number of members. France wished to secure a reweighing of votes that would compensate large Member States for their likely loss of one commissioner, as well as maintain French voting parity with Germany. France was in favor of an extension of majority voting, yet was concerned to keep the national veto for provisions pertaining to visas, asylum, and immigration, as well as the common commercial policy. France was one of the strongest proponents for new rules that would make it easier for groups of member states to engage in enhanced cooperation or flexible integration.

---

[43] Costa, Couvidat, and Daloz 2003, 123.
[44] Quoted in Costa, Couvidat, and Daloz 2003, 123–124.

The size of the Commission quickly became the most controversial and conflict-ridden issue in the negotiations. The French Presidency presented a discussion paper at the first ministerial conclave in July that was criticized for favoring the option of a limited Commission, where each member state would not be allowed to keep a commissioner, as desired by the smaller states.[45] Tensions increased further when French European affairs minister Pierre Moscovici persisted in centering the negotiations around this alternative, accused small member states of trying to weaken the Commission, and threatened to blame an eventual failure on small-state recalcitrance.[46] While criticized by many as unproductive, this move exposed the underlying fault line and prepared the ground for the summit in Biarritz. The negotiations in Biarritz produced surprising progress, when the French Presidency managed to gain the support of the other four large states for equal rotation, that is, alternation between all member states of the posts in a restricted Commission. By declaring their own willingness to lose their final commissioner, and promising equal treatment of all member states, the large states firmly placed the ball in the court of the small states. This proved to be a major breakthrough in the negotiations, which then shifted to the format of such a capping in the number of commissioners.[47]

The negotiations on the reweighing of votes lay dormant for much of the fall. This was the most important issue for the large member states, but was the dossier on which the least amount of time was spent before the Nice summit. When France took over the chairmanship, two camps had formed. A first group of primarily smaller states supported a system of dual majority, where a decision would require both a majority of states and a majority of the EU population. A second group of mainly large states supported a simple reweighing within the existing system, to the advantage of the larger members. These alternatives and a range of in-between solutions were aired during the fall. But real bargaining was postponed by the Presidency to the concluding session in Nice, since any solution to this highly sensitive issue would require concessions that only heads of state and government could make.[48]

When France took over the Presidency, the negotiations on QMV had produced a list of about forty articles that could be considered for a shift to majority voting. From early September, the Presidency devoted considerable time to the issue and the parties engaged in a detailed

---

[45] *European Voice*, 20–26 July 2000, 6.
[46] *European Voice*, 21–27 September 2000, 1, 11.
[47] *European Voice*, 19–25 October 2000, 8; Gray and Stubb 2001, 15.
[48] Gray and Stubb 2001, 15; Schout and Vanhoonacker 2001, 20.

consideration of each provision.[49] In order to facilitate trade-offs at later stages, the Presidency took the tactical decision of keeping as many articles as possible on the list until the end phase, even if it was unlikely to secure support for many of them. In reality, the negotiations were centered on a fairly limited number of articles, since the introduction of majority voting for many articles on the list was either uncontroversial or out of the question. Where articles were subject to proper bargaining, the negotiations often concerned the possibility of moving part of the subject matter to majority voting, while retaining unanimity for the remaining part. The Presidency engaged in the time-consuming work of developing consecutive draft proposals, in an effort to find texts that would respect national sensitivities, yet achieve maximum extension of majority voting.[50] This work was particularly delicate in those areas where France itself held the strongest reservations; for instance, the article on common commercial policy saw the greatest number of options, redrafts, and proposals during the entire IGC. France's fight to keep the veto in nationally sensitive areas did not go unnoticed, and the Presidency was accused of hypocrisy.[51]

Enhanced cooperation was put high on the agenda when France took over the chairmanship. The first ministerial conclave was partly dedicated to the issue, as were five of the first eight meetings of the Preparatory Group. The attention to the issue yielded quick results. The French Presidency's handling of the dossier is generally considered to be a strong contributing factor.[52] Once agreement had been reached that flexibility would not be applicable in the core areas of the internal market and economic and social cohesion, relaxing the conditions for enhanced cooperation proved less controversial. In fact, the European Council summit at Biarritz reached political agreement on all parts of this dossier, save enhanced cooperation in foreign and security policy.

The Nice Treaty

As the end stage of the negotiations approached, the French Presidency sought to prepare the ground for a comprehensive agreement in Nice. Formal negotiations were increasingly supplemented by informal bargaining and brokerage.[53] The Preparatory Group held two informal

---

[49] *European Voice*, 1–13 September 2000, 3; Galloway 2001, 101–111.
[50] Interview, French government representative, 9 February 2001.
[51] *European Voice*, 5–11 October 2000.
[52] Gray and Stubb 2001, 11; Schout and Vanhoonacker 2001, 14–15; Stubb 2002, 115–122.
[53] Gray and Stubb 2001, 12.

meetings in Paris and Val Duchesse in an attempt to settle outstanding key issues. For purposes of probing member governments' bottom lines and exploring potential compromises, the Presidency engaged in bilateral talks at three levels. In Brussels, the Presidency held confessionals with the EU ambassadors in the Preparatory Group. European affairs minister Moscovici met his counterparts in other governments on a *tour des capitales*. Shortly before the summit, President Chirac undertook a similar tour to the capitals of Europe, meeting fourteen heads of government in ten days. The likelihood of a deal in Nice improved considerably when Chirac and German chancellor Schröder, after a bilateral *tête-à-tête*, could announce that they had agreed to agree. Until then, French insistence on voting parity despite Germany's greater population had been seen as a potential impediment to a final agreement.

The concluding negotiations in Nice on 8–11 December proved extremely tough and have generally been described as a tug of war over national interests, devoid of the honoured Community spirit. The talks began on the Friday night with bilateral confessionals between the French Presidency and the delegations, on the basis of which a new draft treaty was distributed for negotiation on Saturday morning. This draft was discarded by the small member states, which considered it biased in favor of large state positions, both as regards the size of the Commission and the reweighing of votes.[54] A second draft was presented on Saturday afternoon and a third draft on Sunday morning, the main outstanding question being the reweighing of votes. During Sunday afternoon and evening, the multilateral deliberations were interrupted eight times for bilateral consultations with delegations and, one by one, member governments came on board.[55] To facilitate the last necessary compromises, the Presidency moved the negotiations to restricted session, excluding all but the heads of state and government. The negotiations were concluded early on Monday morning, once Belgium had given its consent following side payments from the Presidency.

Member governments reached the compromise that each state would maintain one commissioner until the EU reaches twenty-seven members, when the number of commissioners will be capped at a lower level than the number of Member States and an equal rotation system will be introduced. While temporarily satisfying the small Member States' insistence on one commissioner each, the compromise is best considered a victory for the French line of reasoning. After the conclusion of the

---

[54] *Svenska Dagbladet*, 9 December 2000; *Dagens Nyheter*, 10 December 2000, A7.
[55] Gray and Stubb 2001, 13.

previous IGC in 1997, it was generally expected that the large states would lose their second commissioner, but all states would keep one. The French campaign for capping the number of commissioners, and the rallying of other large states around the principle of equal rotation, explains the turn of events. "The role of the French Presidency in reaching the agreement has been crucial. France was not so much a broker distilling a compromise from the various discussions – something which was almost impossible seen the opposing views between small and big Member States – but it used its position in the chair to direct the debate in a particular direction and toward a specific result."[56]

The final outcome of the hard negotiations on the reweighing of votes was a complicated triple-majority compromise. According to the new rules, the adoption of an act by QMV requires the support of a qualified majority of votes, a majority of member states, and at least 62 percent of the EU's population. This complex outcome reflected a set of interlinked bargains, rather than a coherent approach, though "[i]nterestingly, the final result does not differ dramatically from the first proposal tabled by the French Presidency in Nice."[57] The large states obtained the expected rebalancing of voting weight in their favor, and France managed to gain the hotly desired German acceptance of continued parity in votes. The price for formal parity was the new demographic criterion, whereby Germany in effect, but not as visibly, was compensated in power for its larger population. As a French diplomat acknowledged, "it was the only way to pay Germany."[58] Yet, in order to gain small-state support for the demographic criterion, the Presidency had to introduce the new majority-of-states requirement. To ensure unanimous support, the Presidency also engaged in *ad hoc* deal making at the end. Notably, Spain gained additional votes, as did the Netherlands in comparison to Belgium, which in turn was bought off with the decision that European Council meetings would take place in Brussels in the future.[59]

Member governments eventually agreed to transfer about thirty articles from unanimity to majority voting. This was generally regarded a success in numerical terms, but less impressive in substantive terms, since some were institutional articles of limited importance, whereas key legislative articles remained under unanimity. For instance, QMV in taxation issues and social security coordination was blocked by the UK, and QMV in decisions on regional aid were prevented by Spain. In

---

[56] Schout and Vanhoonacker 2001, 19.
[57] Gray and Stubb 2001, 15.
[58] Interview, French government representative, 9 February 2001.
[59] Interview, French government representative, 9 February 2001.

addition, the French government refused to surrender its national veto on key parts of the articles pertaining to visas, asylum, and immigration, as well as the common commercial policy.

The question of enhanced cooperation had largely been solved before the summit. The only outstanding issue to consider after the political agreement at Biarritz was whether flexible cooperation should be possible in foreign and security policy. Governments eventually limited the scope in this area, only permitting enhanced cooperation for the implementation of certain foreign policy instruments, while excluding matters with military or defense implications.

The power of the chair: assessing process and outcome

In the process of steering the negotiations toward a conclusion in Nice, the French Presidency made active use of the procedural and informational advantages of the chair. When taking over the Presidency, the French government exploited its control over the negotiation process by intensifying the formal meeting schedule, introducing a fourth tier in the negotiations, and moving the IGC to the top of the agenda of both formal and informal Council meetings. Toward the end of the process, the Presidency invited the negotiating parties to specific, informal negotiation sessions, in order to prepare the ground for a final agreement. Throughout the process, the Presidency's documents functioned as single negotiating texts. The negotiation process was structured so as to solve the easiest questions first – extension of majority voting and enhanced cooperation – and save the exceedingly thorny matters – size of the Commission and reweighing of votes – to the heads of state and government.

The chair's control over negotiation sessions was used to collect information about state preferences, put pressure on recalcitrant parties, and present revised compromise proposals. The Presidency obtained open information about member state preferences through questionnaires, and sought private information about the parties' resistance points through confessionals and *tours des capitales*. New compromise texts were formulated in response to reactions and new information, and the chair's prerogative of summing up negotiation sessions was used to steer the deliberations in the direction desired by the Presidency. In order to cajole recalcitrant parties into agreement at the end stage, institutional side payments were invented and distributed, in the absence of the traditional money purse.

France exploited its position as chair to advance its own national interests as well – a source of significant criticism. While resolute in its ambition to deliver a treaty, the French government was equally adamant on the content of such a deal. It is striking how the French government scrupulously used the position of the chair to advance proposals that essentially constituted national position papers framed as Presidency compromises. "France took its own proposal as a basis for discussion and assumed that any point on which objections were not raised had been accepted. Contrary to other Presidencies that would consider the different delegations' stands on a particular point, France contented itself with stating its views and asking opponents to stand up."[60]

The open use of the Presidency's assets to this end, and the alleged arrogance in response to other parties' criticism, resulted in much negative publicity, which some observers interpret as a sign of failure for the French government.[61] Yet, if we assess the substantive outcome of the negotiations, the French were remarkably successful in protecting their own interests. "France succeeded in what really mattered to her: holding the bottom line on issues of vital national interest."[62] The French government managed to produce a treaty in Nice, achieved a future capping in the number of commissioners, secured a rebalancing of voting weight in favor of large states and formal vote parity with Germany, prevented QMV in nationally sensitive areas, and reached the goal of facilitating enhanced cooperation.

The Presidency's capacity to deliver an agreement and to secure a specific distribution of gains was conditioned by formal institutional rules. Whereas the IGC format granted all member states equal agenda-setting powers, the task of producing proposals and single negotiating texts devolved upon the Presidency, as so many times before. The exception to this general pattern was the negotiations on the extension of majority voting, where the French Presidency voluntarily abstained from formulating compromise proposals for those nationally sensitive articles where it wished to see no changes, and where the Commission and Finland stepped in to fill the breach. The requirement of unanimous agreement for all provisions of the treaty left predictable imprints on the outcome. On the size of the Commission and the reweighing of votes, the brokerage efforts of the Presidency were facilitated by the absence of a status quo alternative. No agreement would mean no arrangement for the institutions after enlargement, and all states were therefore anxious to come to some sort of deal. By contrast, concrete status quo

---

[60] Costa, Couvidat, and Daloz 2003, 124.
[61] See, e.g., Ludlow 2001; Ross 2001.
[62] Meunier and Nicolaïdis 2001, 7; see also interview, Commission official, 8 February 2001.

alternatives, in the shape of a continuation of the existing modes of decision-making, existed as regards QMV and enhanced cooperation. This meant that the requirement of unanimity favored the most conservative states: the UK on taxation and social security, Spain on regional policy, and France on visas, asylum, and immigration, as well as the common commercial policy. Except where France itself benefited, this logic reduced the Presidency's capacity to steer the negotiations toward its most preferred outcome.

Cognizant of the expectations on neutrality, the French government paid certain lip service to the principle of the honest broker, but let its behavior be guided by other considerations. As dictated from the central level before the beginning of the Presidency, French negotiators prioritized core national interests over conformance to norms about appropriate behavior: "In fact, whenever France's core interests were at stake, its role of arbiter was unquestionably relegated to a position of secondary importance – all its energy being devoted to the defence of its own interests."[63] When accused by other member states and the Commission of partiality, arrogance, and misuse of the Presidency, the French government referred to the necessity for achieving results.

To address the counterfactual question of whether this particular outcome would have been likely with another government at the helm, we can conclude that this probability is low. The empirical analysis reveals how the French government used the power resources of the Presidency at key points in the negotiations to favor certain outcomes rather than others. For instance, it is unlikely that one of the EU's small or medium-sized states, had they enjoyed access to the Presidency position, would have tabled proposals and steered the negotiations toward a deal that eventually would leave them without a commissioner at all times – a key concern for these countries. Similarly, it is highly improbable that any other member state would have structured the end game of the negotiations so as to achieve the French objective of formal vote parity with Germany, which required the creation of a complicated triple-majority system for qualified majority voting and the invention of institutional side payments. Indeed, it may even be the case that another Presidency government would have preferred to postpone the closure of the negotiations, rather than conclude an agreement in Nice on the terms promoted by France.

---

[63] Costa, Couvidat, and Daloz 2003, 124.

Conclusion

When EU governments' bargaining positions are incompatible and no zone for agreement can be discerned, the Presidency's brokerage efforts can help governments avoid negotiation failure. The sources of the Presidency's influence are its privileged access to information about state preferences and its instruments of procedural control. The resourceful Council Secretariat, confidential confessionals, and the practice of *tours des capitales* make it possible for the Presidency to obtain private information about bottom lines and possible concessions. To facilitate convergence and agreement, the Presidency can draw on its broad repertoire of procedural instruments, which includes the authority to call formal or informal meetings, restrict participation in negotiation sessions, and draft single negotiating texts.

Yet, as demonstrated in this chapter, these power resources may just as well be used to promote the Presidency government's national interests. Typically, Presidencies steer negotiations away from their worst alternative and toward their preferred outcome. The privileged information about state preferences is exploited to extract concessions from the Presidency's adversaries. The command over the negotiation process is used to formulate compromise proposals that keep certain options on, and others away from, the negotiation table. As one former EU ambassador testifies, it is "almost impossible" for the Council to arrive at decisions that go against the desires of the Presidency.[64]

The Agenda 2000 and IGC 2000 negotiations well illustrate the capacity of EU Presidencies to affect both the efficiency and distributional implications of comprehensive EU agreements. Despite negotiating conditions that worked against the capacity of the Presidency to engineer agreement and shape distributional outcomes, the German and French governments managed to strike accords that simultaneously secured key national interests. In neither case does the empirical evidence point to the widely cited norm of the honest broker as a determinant of German and French behavior, forcing these governments to abstain from actions that would serve national priorities. Rather, where Germany and France were unsuccessful in their attempts to steer the negotiations toward their preferred outcomes, this is explained by the formal requirement of unanimous consent, which forced the Presidency to accommodate those member states least interested in financial or institutional reform.

[64] Quoted in Troy Johnston 1994, 25.

6   The EU Presidency as representative: negotiating on behalf of others

The previous two chapters have explored the EU Presidency's capacity to shape political outcomes as agenda manager and broker. This chapter turns to the third and final of the Presidency's key functions – representing the member states in negotiations with third parties. The EU Presidency negotiates on behalf of member governments in two principal contexts. It functions as the Council's representative in interinstitutional negotiations with other EU bodies. In particular, it engages in legislative negotiations with representatives of the European Parliament as part of the co-decision procedure, the dominant legislative procedure in the EU. Furthermore, the Presidency acts as the member states' representative in certain international negotiations. The area where the function as external negotiator is most institutionalized is accession negotiations with countries that wish to become members of the EU.

The central argument in this chapter is that EU governments' engagement of the Presidency as their representative leads to a classic principal–agent problem, with divergent preferences, incomplete control, and agent discretion. This claim shares important affinities with arguments about delegation and agency in other contexts where collective principals have delegated powers of representation to an executive agent, for instance, international trade negotiations.[1] In the EU, the member governments have delegated the authority to negotiate agreements to an actor with its own interests and stakes in the outcome. Simultaneously, they have refrained from establishing mechanisms of complete control, since the Presidency must be able to negotiate with some flexibility in order to arrive at external agreements. The discretion accorded to the Presidency serves the general interests of EU governments when permitting the government at the helm to conduct and

---

[1] See, e.g., Mnookin and Susskind 1999; Nicolaïdis 1999; Meunier 2000; Pollack 2003, ch. 5.

conclude efficient negotiations with third parties. Yet this discretion may also be used by Presidencies to shape the terms of the agreements negotiated with external counterparts, by permitting Presidencies to strategically channel preference information, play off recalcitrant parties against each other, and negotiate *fait accompli* agreements.

This chapter challenges the conventional wisdom about the Presidency's room for maneuver as internal and external negotiator. Typically, existing literature describes the Presidency as constrained by norms of neutral behavior and interstate disagreements. When acting on behalf of EU governments, the Presidency is expected to represent and defend the collective position of this group, not present its own political preference as the EU's negotiation position. In this vein, Richard Whitman emphasizes: "States which appear to engage in the 'aberrant' behaviour of nakedly pursuing national foreign policy objectives ahead of those of the EU face heavy criticism and a difficult Presidency. Thus, paradoxically, the Presidency may not provide a good opportunity for advancing national foreign policy objectives."[2] Furthermore, the existence of disagreements among national governments is generally taken as a source of weakness for the Presidency, not least in external affairs, by reducing the authority of the Presidency to speak of behalf of the EU as a collective.

The chapter consists of three sections. The first identifies the informational and procedural resources of the Presidency as representative, and explains how formal institutional rules enable or constrain the Presidency in the pursuit of private and collective interests. The second and third sections of the chapter present two case studies: the legislative negotiations on new rules for public access to EU documents during the Swedish Presidency in the first half of 2001, and the conclusion of the enlargement negotiations with ten candidate countries mainly from Central and Eastern Europe during the Danish Presidency in the second half of 2002. The two cases offer important evidence of the Presidency's capacity to influence outcomes in the two primary bargaining contexts where it negotiates on behalf of EU governments. Despite a strong secrecy-oriented majority in the Council, the openness-friendly Swedish Presidency managed to conclude an agreement on new transparency rules that greatly expanded the public's access to EU documents. With little regard to norms of neutrality, the Swedish government used the extreme transparency position of the Parliament as a lever against the Council's secrecy hawks, and exploited the room for maneuver in informal bargaining to negotiate a deal that was subsequently presented as

---

[2] Whitman 1998, 15.

a *fait accompli* to the other governments. The Danish government made effective use of its position as EU representative to realize its number one foreign policy priority – a big bang enlargement of the EU in 2004. Drawing on the resources of the Presidency office, the Danish government played off recalcitrant member states against stubborn candidate countries, and negotiated bilateral deals beyond its mandate.

Representation: resources and constraints

Positioned at the interface between internal and external negotiations, Presidencies enjoy access to privileged information and procedural instruments that give them a certain autonomy and flexibility in the shaping of outcomes. Simultaneously, formal decision rules and the preferences of external counterparts condition the extent to which the government at the helm can steer outcomes in its own favor. Even if there are notable differences between the two contexts in which the Presidency acts as the member governments' collective representative, the resources and constraints are similar in kind.

Power resources in representation

In its function as representative, the Presidency can draw on two forms of information asymmetry. These informational advantages constitute an important asset for the Presidency in the difficult process of stitching together a deal that is acceptable both to the governments in the Council and its external counterpart. At the same time, the Presidency can exploit these informational advantages to maneuver negotiations in a particular direction.

First, the Presidency enjoys access to the same *privileged information about state preferences* that is central to the execution of its brokerage function and which I described in Chapter 5. Representation rarely consists of simply forwarding the joint position of the member states to an external third party. More often, it involves a process of brokering an internal agreement before external negotiations are initiated, renegotiating this position in light of the other party's counter-demands, and eventually seeking member states' support for a final deal involving new compromises.

In this process, the Presidency can draw on the Council Secretariat and established mediation practices for purposes of obtaining the privileged information about state preferences that is necessary to identify the underlying zone of agreement. Confidential, bilateral talks between the Presidency and individual member governments are the most central source of such privileged information. The Presidency can call member states to confessionals in order to probe their bottom lines and test the acceptance of alternative negotiation mandates. The *tours des capitales* conducted by Presidency representatives may also be used to elicit information and support on high-profile issues.

Second, the Presidency enjoys *superior information about its own contribution* to the negotiated outcome. This kind of information asymmetry is a standard feature where one actor is engaged to negotiate on behalf of others.[3] So that the Presidency has the flexibility required to find creative bargaining solutions with third parties, member governments have abstained from seeking full control over their negotiator. As a consequence, the Presidency's actions are seldom fully observable to the principals in the Council, which find it difficult to ascertain whether any other deal could have been made. Was this the best possible agreement the Presidency could reach in order to satisfy the majority of member states in the Council, or did the Presidency exploit its room for maneuver to steer the negotiations toward its own preferred outcome?

Both as internal and external representative, the Presidency engages in informal, bilateral negotiations with its counterpart. These informal talks should be distinguished from the formal procedures prescribed for negotiations with third parties, which tend to be more cumbersome and involve a greater degree of control over the Presidency. Formally, enlargement negotiations take place in intergovernmental conferences between all existing member states and the candidate country in question. Similarly, legislative disagreements should formally be settled in the conciliation committee, where the Presidency is accompanied by representatives from all other member states. In practice, neither of these arrangements gives the Presidency and its counterpart the leeway required to hammer out agreements on sensitive issues. Just like agreements among EU governments often require the use of confessionals, the chances of concluding an external deal improve significantly if the Presidency is permitted to enter into bilateral talks with the other side.

Legislative negotiations with the Parliament offer the most illustrative example of the room for maneuver the Presidency gains when negotiations are shifted from formal to informal venues. Instead of meeting in the crowded conciliation committee, the representatives of the Council, the Parliament, and the Commission seek to settle legislative conflicts in two informal negotiation forums with highly restricted membership. Both are denoted trialogues. The first kind of trialogue is convened at

---

[3] Mnookin and Susskind 1999.

the first reading of the legislative procedure as a way of seeking fast-track agreement on new legislation, to try and avoid time-consuming conciliation altogether. The second kind of trialogue is convened at the third and final reading of the legislative procedure to informally negotiate an agreement that can be formally adopted in the conciliation committee.

Composed only of key officials from the Presidency and select representatives of the Parliament and the Commission, these trialogues put other member states at an informational disadvantage and grant the Presidency significant room for maneuver. As one regular participant of the Parliament's delegation expresses it: "The Presidency clearly has scope for determining how much to tell the member states about negotiations with the Parliament, for instance, whether to present the Parliament position as a bottom line or something up for negotiation, depending on what serves the Presidency best."[4] The closed nature of the trialogue is illustrated by the European Parliament's frequent criticism that negotiations in this forum carry negative democratic implications, since they undermine openness and accountability in EU decision-making.[5]

Closely related to these informational advantages are a set of procedural resources that can be used by the Presidency to improve the conditions for an agreement that is acceptable to all, but particularly satisfying to the Presidency government itself. These procedural resources enable the Presidency to decide when and how to exploit its informational advantages for strategic purposes.

First, the Presidency can shape *the format of negotiations with third parties*, and can thus decide when to shift to informal negotiations that expand its own room for maneuver. In enlargement negotiations with candidate countries, it is the Presidency's call whether bilateral talks must be initiated to solve particularly divisive issues. In legislative negotiations with the European Parliament, the creation of the fast-track trialogue in the late 1990s greatly expanded the Presidency portfolio of procedural tricks.[6] The Presidency is now at liberty to initiate informal negotiations at several stages of the legislative procedure, whereas before, the trialogue could only be convened at the conciliation stage. In fact, the Presidency may even enter into negotiations with the European Parliament before the Council has come to a common position, which opens up additional opportunities for the Presidency to

---

[4] Interview, European Parliament official, 2 July 2001. See also Farrell and Héritier 2003a, 9; Bjurulf and Elgström 2004, 260–262.

[5] Farrell and Héritier 2003a, 22–23; Shackleton and Raunio 2003, 177–179.

[6] Shackleton 2000; Farrell and Héritier 2003a; Shackleton and Raunio 2003.

shape outcomes. Moreover, the fast-track nature of this method of legislative bargaining makes it possible for the Presidency to push through proposals it wishes to see enacted during its limited period in office. As one interviewee expressed it: "The Presidency has in this legislative world a choice to say what they consider a priority."[7] Henry Farrell and Adrienne Héritier draw the same conclusion: "On the Council's side, the Presidency's power and influence is clearly enhanced. Coreper may be sidelined by the successful attempts of the Presidency to dominate the policy making process in the thrashing out of early agreements. The latter offers it a unique possibility to realize its policy agenda within six months."[8]

Second, the Presidency's position at the nexus of two negotiation arenas grants this actor a possibility to *play off internal and external negotiating parties against each other*. The Presidency can exploit the two-level game character of the negotiations, extracting concessions from external parties by referring to internal Council positions, and conversely, achieving internal movement by referring to the tough stance of its external counterpart. That positions will have to be shifted is clear to all parties, but whose positions and how far are partly open questions, whose answers can be molded by the Presidency.[9] As Farrell and Héritier note:

Where the Member States have not yet reached a Common Position, the country holding the Presidency may be in a position of unique influence within the Council, reporting the Member States' negotiating positions to the Parliament, and the Parliament's position to the other Member States. It may potentially use this leverage to affect other actors' perceptions of what is possible and what is not, and thus bring through outcomes which reflect its own preferences rather than the preferences of the Council as a whole.[10]

Third, the Presidency can negotiate external deals that are presented as *fait accompli agreements* for EU governments to adopt on a take-it-or-leave-it basis. Even if the Presidency acts on the basis of a negotiating mandate from the Council, it possesses the autonomy and authority as representative to strike agreements that entail further concessions. EU governments cannot be summoned to consider all possible twists and turns in the negotiations. Instead, the Presidency enjoys an informal fast-track authority that permits it to negotiate deals that subsequently are presented to the member states for adoption or rejection. One director

---

[7] Interview, European Parliament official, 2 July 2001.
[8] Farrell and Héritier 2003a, 24–25.
[9] Interview, Swedish government official, 2 July 2001.
[10] Farrell and Héritier 2003a, 9.

general in the Commission compared the Presidency position to that of the supranational executive in external trade negotiations, where the Commission enjoys fast-track authority: "On each and every occasion, you [the Presidency] have to bully member states. You negotiate first and then you present them with the facts."[11] Reluctance to reopen negotiations, time pressure, and political pressure from other member states put EU governments in a situation where it is extremely difficult to reject deals that a majority can support. As two observers note: "when [trialogue negotiation] works successfully, the Parliament and Council do little more than sign off on a deal that has already been negotiated among a small group of actors."[12]

Institutional constraints in representation

The formal institutional environment in which the Presidency operates conditions its influence as representative. Whereas agenda-setting rules carry limited implications for the Presidency's autonomy in this two-level negotiation game, decision rules are of manifest importance, as is the distribution of preferences among the bargaining parties on the two arenas.

Formal decision rules influence the strategic context of Presidency representation in important ways. The internal decision rules in the Council determine the level of support required for the adoption of the eventual agreement presented by the Presidency, which in turn shapes the room for maneuver of the government at the helm. Where unanimous support is required, the Presidency must conduct the negotiations with the recognition that all states eventually must give their consent. This decision rule therefore tends to produce lowest-common-denominator solutions and give particular weight to the position of the most conservative state, wishing the least change to the status quo. Unless the Presidency itself constitutes the most conservative government or holds similar preferences, the unanimity rule will reduce its chances of delivering an agreement that satisfies its own interests. At the same time, it is a well-known bargaining paradox that internal constraints can give the negotiator unusual bargaining strength in external negotiations.[13]

Where only a qualified majority of the member states is required for the adoption of an externally negotiated agreement, the Presidency's room for maneuver expands considerably. Majority voting reduces the

---

[11] Interview 9 July 2001.
[12] Farrell and Héritier 2003a, 24.
[13] Schelling 1960; Putnam 1988.

constraining effect of the internal bargaining arena on the Presidency's external negotiation behavior, by making it possible for the Presidency to engineer an external agreement which does not require the support of all principals in the Council. While expanding the Presidency's room for maneuver internally, it makes it more difficult to extract concessions from the external counterpart through references to inflexibility in the Council.

In this respect, legislative negotiations with the European Parliament and enlargement negotiations with candidate countries present the Presidency with varying strategic contexts and possibilities for securing its own interests. As a rule, the co-decision procedure goes hand in hand with qualified majority voting as the decision principle in the Council. The Presidency's negotiation mandate – the Council's common position – need only be supported by a qualified majority of the member states, as does the eventual compromise reached with the Parliament. By contrast, unanimity is required in enlargement negotiations. The Presidency negotiates formally and informally with candidate countries fully aware of the need to gain all member states' support for the final deal.

The distribution of preferences among internal and external bargaining parties conditions the effect of decision rules on the Presidency's room for maneuver. What merits attention are the Presidency's preferences and the external counterpart's preferences relative to each other and to the spectrum of preferences in the Council. Compared to strictly intergovernmental negotiations in the Council, bargaining with a third party can both improve and worsen the Presidency's chances of obtaining its preferred outcome. The effect is best illustrated if we picture a situation where the Presidency is positioned at one end of the spectrum of preferences in the Council. If the external party holds preferences at the same end of the spectrum as the Presidency, its involvement expands the Presidency's room for maneuver. By referring to the need for external agreement, the Presidency can extract internal concessions and move outcomes toward its own ideal point. If, by contrast, the external party holds preferences at the other end of the spectrum, this circumscribes the Presidency's room for maneuver significantly. The external arena cannot offer the Presidency any additional ammunition in its attempts to swing the internal opinion. Instead, the Presidency will have to fight a rearguard battle against opposing forces, both internally and externally.

The Swedish Presidency and EU transparency

The negotiations on new rules on openness and public access to EU documents posed both a challenge and an opportunity for the Swedish

Presidency in the first half of 2001.[14] Whereas Sweden advocated far-reaching transparency reforms, the majority of member states opposed such a development, which presented obvious problems for Sweden in its function as Council representative in the negotiations with the European Parliament. Yet, exploiting the procedural and informational resources of the Presidency office, as well as the Parliament's radical transparency position, the Swedish government managed to achieve an agreement close to its own preferred outcome.

Toward new EU transparency rules

Since the early 1990s, the EU has been under increasing political pressure to make its decision-making more open and to improve public access to EU documents. Driving actors in this process toward greater openness have been the European Parliament, a set of transparency-oriented member states – especially the Netherlands and the Nordics – the European Ombudsman, the European Court of Justice, and a range of pressure groups. In contrast, the Commission and the majority of member states in the Council have been reluctant to open up EU decision-making. During the 1990s, the proponents of transparency gained ground, slowly but steadily, and enhanced openness was increasingly seen as a means of reducing the EU's "democratic deficit."

The Commission's presentation in February 2000 of a legislative proposal for new EU rules on public access to documents of the Parliament, the Council, and the Commission constituted a response to these developments. When negotiating the Amsterdam Treaty in 1996–1997, EU governments had agreed on the need to formulate new EU transparency rules, but had delegated the actual formulation of these rules to the EU institutions. According to the Amsterdam Treaty, the Council and the Parliament were obliged to decide on new public access rules by 1 May 2001, at the latest. The legislative negotiations were to be conducted according to the co-decision procedure, which meant that the Commission's proposal had to be jointly adopted by the Parliament and the Council. The challenge for the Presidency was to engineer internal agreement in the Council, requiring the support of a qualified majority, while simultaneously negotiating an external agreement with the Parliament.

Even if governments agreed on the need for new transparency rules, they disagreed forcefully on the extent to which the public should be

---

[14] The presentation of this case draws on the research conducted by my project collaborator Bo Bjurulf, published in Bjurulf 2001; Bjurulf and Elgström 2004.

granted access to EU documents and the specific legal and political means for achieving this. This complex dossier contained up to six different conflict dimensions: (1) the degree of public access to sensitive documents in security and defense matters, (2) the degree of public access to documents in the preparatory stage of the legislative process, (3) the degree of harmonization in transparency rules across the EU, (4) the degree of control to be exercised by the original source of a document, (5) the degree of service offered to citizens wishing to obtain documents, and (6) the extent to which the European Parliament should enjoy the right to monitor the implementation of the rules.[15]

Simplifying slightly, institutions and member states fell into four main camps.[16] The Commission particularly wished to avoid public access to its preparatory documents and costly service commitments. The Council majority sought only limited moves toward increased transparency and generally wished to keep proceedings and documents confidential. The desire to avoid public access was particularly intense in relation to sensitive security and defense documents. The Council minority, comprising Denmark, Finland, the Netherlands, and Sweden (and in some cases Ireland and the UK), wished to establish public access to EU documents as the general principle, subject only to few exceptions. The transparency advocates further emphasized the need to offer extensive service to citizens in search of EU documents. The European Parliament was the most openness-oriented actor of all, essentially adopting the maximalist position on all conflict dimensions.[17] The Parliament's enthusiasm was based partly on a wish to uphold citizens' right to information, partly on the fact that enhanced transparency would allow the Parliament better insight into Commission and Council decision-making.[18]

The Commission's proposal was designed to appeal to both secrecy and transparency advocates.[19] However, the compromise document instead met with fierce disapproval in both camps. For the advocates of transparency, concessions were insufficient, but they were equally unacceptable to the secrecy-oriented Council majority. The transparency

---

[15] Bjurulf 2001; Bjurulf and Elgström 2004.

[16] Bjurulf and Elgström 2004.

[17] When I speak of the Parliament's preferences, I refer to the preferences held and expressed by those actors acting on behalf of the Parliament. It should be noted that the Parliament, just like the Council, was internally divided and represented in the negotiations by those members (the *rapporteurs*) most enthusiastic about new and far-reaching transparency rules.

[18] Jacobs 2001, 4.

[19] European Commission 2000. For an analysis, see Bjurulf and Elgström 2004, 255–256.

advocates were further provoked by the Commission's unashamed protection of its own self-interest as regards public access to preparatory documents. The negative reception to the proposal shifted the political initiative from the Commission to the Presidency, which had the main responsibility for brokering a deal in the Council and in relation to the Parliament.[20] Yet actual progress was slow under the secrecy oriented Portuguese and French Presidencies in the first and second half of 2000. Officials with insight into the process point to this case as a textbook example of how skeptical Presidencies can stifle progress in negotiations by assigning low political priority to a dossier.[21] The concluding December document of the French Presidency reflected the state of play in the Council, with several issues outstanding in the internal negotiations.[22] The Council had not yet entered into deliberations with the Parliament, which first had been able to reach a common basis for negotiation in late November.

The Swedish Presidency: informal negotiations and fast-track agreement

When Sweden assumed the Presidency in January 2001, the Council gained a chair with radically different interests in the transparency dossier than the two preceding occupants of the office. Next to "the three Es" – enlargement, employment, environment – transparency was the highest priority for the Swedish Presidency.[23] The Swedish freedom of information act – *Tryckfrihetsförordningen* – dated back to 1766 and enjoyed constitutional status. Among politicians, the media, and in the population at large, this act was widely conceived of as a fundamental feature of Swedish democracy. Compared to transparency regimes in other EU countries and the EU institutions, the Swedish freedom of information act was the most far-reaching and encompassing. Domestically, there was a widespread fear that Sweden's EU membership would force the country to surrender its traditional transparency policy. Sweden's strong support for new, ambitious transparency rules in the EU thus served a double purpose: spreading transparency norms favored by Sweden, and averting the threat to the domestic transparency regime.

---

[20] Bjurulf and Elgström 2004, 256.
[21] Interviews, Council Secretariat official, 8 February 2001; Portuguese government official, 7 February 2001. The progress that indeed was achieved during this period, notably the so-called Solana *coup*, tended to favor the secrecy-oriented faction in the Council. See Bjurulf and Elgström 2004, 256–258.
[22] Council of the European Union 2000b.
[23] Tallberg 2001.

In its Presidency program, the Swedish government described its ambitions for the transparency dossier:

It is of fundamental importance to the Swedish Presidency that the vision of a more open Union is realised. More transparent working methods must be introduced and information must be more readily available so that citizens can obtain real insight into European cooperation. . . . Sweden attaches great importance to ensuring that the relevant legal instrument that is to be adopted not later than May 2001 leads to improved access to documents kept at EU institutions.[24]

However, promoting transparency was easier said than done. The dossier presented the Swedish Presidency with a number of dilemmas. The Council majority was hostile to the ambitious Swedish transparency goals, and viewed the incoming Presidency with great suspicion. As one high-level Commission official noted: "Sweden may have some problems with transparency. There is an enormous suspicion against Sweden in this field because other member states know the Swedish positions."[25] The Swedish government felt the pressure of the majority relationships in the Council and was aware of the norm that Presidencies should behave neutrally in the pursuit of collective agreement. Brokering internal agreement without sacrificing national interests posed an obvious problem. In addition, Sweden faced the challenge of representing a Council whose dominant positions it did not support, in negotiations with a Parliament whose perspective it generally shared.

The Swedish Presidency's strategy for reconciling its private interests with the collective objective of agreement was to exploit its position as representative at the interface between internal and external negotiations.[26] Instead of following the standard practice of seeking an internal Council position before engaging in deliberations with the Parliament, the Swedish Presidency invited Parliament representatives to informal trialogue talks, so that negotiations were held in both arenas at the same time. In these negotiations, the Presidency used the transparency-oriented position of the Parliament as a weapon against the secrecy-oriented majority in the Council, while simultaneously threatening the Parliament with the unlikelihood of equally favorable deals during the coming Belgian and Spanish Presidencies.

The recent entry into force of the Amsterdam Treaty had created the possibility of a co-decision agreement already at first reading, and thus

---

[24] Swedish Presidency 2001, 27.
[25] Interview, 8 February 2001; see also interviews, Portuguese government official, 7 February 2001; Council official, 8 February 2001.
[26] Bjurulf and Elgström 2004.

offered Sweden a chance to conclude the negotiations during its own period at the helm. Next to speeding up the process toward an agreement, the trialogue talks expanded the Presidency's discretion. The absence of a common position in the Council meant that the Presidency was less constrained by the actual majority relationships among the member states, and enjoyed more room for maneuver in the negotiations with the Parliament. In addition, the Presidency could benefit from its exclusive position and informational advantages. While skeptical of the trialogue's closed format, the Parliament accepted the invitation: Sweden as counterpart offered the possibility of achieving results it would be difficult to obtain in negotiations with other, more secrecy-oriented, Presidencies.[27]

The spring of 2001 witnessed intense contacts between the representatives of the Council and the Parliament, including a series of four trialogue meetings.[28] Simultaneously, the member states in the Council negotiated the transparency dossier in the working party on information and in Coreper. In the early rounds of the trialogue negotiations, only limited progress was made. The Parliament's negotiators demonstrated little willingness to budge from their radical amendment proposals. Even if the Swedish Presidency shared many of the Parliament's positions and was willing to put pressure on the Council, it was obvious that an agreement between the two institutions would have to include concessions on both sides.

The Parliament's readiness to consider compromises increased with the appointment of Graham Watson, the chair of the Parliament's Committee on Citizens' Rights and Freedoms, as chief negotiator.[29] Watson was more flexible than other Parliament representatives and recognized the potential for the Parliament of a certain degree of collusion with the Swedish Presidency. One official involved in the negotiations even speaks of an alliance between the Parliament and the Swedish Presidency, represented by EU ambassador Gunnar Lund.[30] Watson and Lund entered into intense, private negotiations, interrupted by occasional consultations with their principals in the Parliament and the Council. In his reports to the Council, Lund explained the Parliament's demands, pointed to its concessions, and emphasized the need for the Council to compromise as well, if the EU were to adopt new transparency rules by the May deadline prescribed in the Amsterdam

---

[27] Interview, member of the European Parliament, 18 June 2001.
[28] Shackleton and Raunio 2003, 179.
[29] Bjurulf and Elgström 2004, 262.
[30] Interview, European Parliament official, 2 July 2001.

Treaty.[31] In his talks with Watson, Lund underlined that the deal Sweden could offer would be better than anything the Parliament would ever be able to get if the negotiations were to continue into forthcoming Presidencies. The secrecy-oriented Council majority continued to regard the Swedish Presidency's handling of the negotiations with great suspicion, especially as they were unable to directly monitor the closed and informal sessions between the Presidency and Parliament representatives.

The new transparency regulation

The Swedish Presidency's strategy for reaching an agreement was to propose a package deal in which the Council would have to accept a high service level and parliamentary oversight, and the Parliament accept secrecy in the handling of sensitive security documents.[32] The Presidency hoped that the secrecy-oriented majority in the Council could be convinced to accept the general movement toward increased transparency if it was given assurances that sensitive documents would be protected. The Swedish government recognized that not even the transparency advocates in the Council supported full transparency in the areas of security and defense. Defending the position of the Council majority and extracting concessions from the Parliament in this area was the Swedish Presidency's best chance of gaining the Council's support for the other provisions in the regulation. As a disappointed Parliament *rapporteur* later recognized: "They had to give the secrecy advocates something in order to save the general principles."[33]

The Swedish Presidency managed to gain the support of the Parliament's representative for the package deal. Yet, when the proposed agreement was presented to the other member states in the Council, the negotiations became extremely tough. The package deal met with objections from a range of secrecy-oriented states, notably France and Germany. Exploiting his position as chairman, Ambassador Lund went to some lengths to keep important elements of the package agreement on the table, while making sure that other alternatives were never considered.[34] Furthermore, Lund stressed the impending deadline for complying with the treaty provision of enacting transparency legislation by

---

[31] Swedish EU Committee 2001.
[32] Bjurulf and Elgström 2004, 262.
[33] Interview, member of the European Parliament, 19 June 2001.
[34] Interviews, Commission official, 18 June 2001; Council official, 18 June 2001; Swedish government official, 4 July 2001.

May 2001 at the latest. When accused by the German ambassador in Coreper for violating the norm of Presidency neutrality, Lund responded by turning off the ambassador's microphone, giving himself the word, and explaining at length the benefit of increased transparency for the EU at large. Complained another German official: "Sweden sided with the European Parliament when expected to speak for the Council!"[35]

After frantic last-minute contacts between Lund and Watson, a deal was eventually reached that could be accepted by both sides.[36] Despite the level of tension in the negotiations, the ambassadors in Coreper granted their support to the final version of the package agreement, as did the Parliament's Citizens' Rights and Freedoms Committee. The agreement was later formally adopted by the full Parliament without recourse to vote in the Council, and was subsequently issued as a regulation on 30 May 2001.[37] The negotiated outcome constituted a carefully balanced compromise between the Council and the Parliament, where both the secrecy-oriented majority in the Council and the radical transparency advocates in the Parliament had had to make substantial concessions. The true winner in these negotiations was the openness-orientated Council minority, led by the Swedish Presidency.[38]

The secrecy-oriented Council majority had gained its much-wanted provisions in the area of sensitive security and defense documents. While skeptical of the transparency reforms in other parts of the regulation, the secrecy-oriented states had been offered what they wanted in the area of greatest concern to them. The package agreement did not give them sufficient grounds to seek the construction of a blocking minority in the Council; the perspective of the Parliament was unlikely to change and the Swedish Presidency had indeed constructed a package that met the Council's and the Parliament's key concerns in time for adoption by the deadline prescribed by the Amsterdam Treaty.[39]

The Parliament had achieved the general movement toward greater transparency that it had advocated for some time. Public access was instituted as the general principle, the institutions would be obliged to offer extensive service to citizens in search of EU documents, and the Parliament would have a seat in the inter-institutional committee that had been created to monitor the application of the rules. Yet, the price for these reforms had been significant exceptions to the rules, notably,

---

[35] Interview, 3 July 2001.
[36] *European Voice*, 19–25 April 2001.
[37] European Parliament and Council of the European Union 2001.
[38] For discussions of the outcome, see Bjurulf 2001; Jacobs 2001.
[39] Interviews, Council official, 18 June 2001; Commission official, 18 June 2001.

the exclusion of sensitive documents and a compromise on access to preparatory documents. Even if the most radical transparency advocates in the Parliament were skeptical of these exceptions, an overwhelming parliamentary majority found the deal sufficiently attractive.[40]

The deal met most wishes of the transparency-oriented member states. As Bo Bjurulf and Ole Elgström conclude in their detailed analysis of the transparency negotiations:

> The Council minority, including the Swedish Presidency, had reason to be very satisfied with the result. Its major concerns were all met, although not always to the extent to which it had aspired. The Presidency had been able to use its mediator position and the possibilities created by the co-decision procedure and the trialogue to construct a package which it could accept with satisfaction.[41]

Compared to the Parliament, the transparency-oriented Council majority had few or no problems with the exception of sensitive security documents and preparatory documents. For the Swedish government, the most problematic compromise was the solution in the area of harmonization, where Sweden had desired clear assurances that national transparency rules would not be affected by the European regime, but where the regulation's provisions were contradictory and ambiguous. Yet this did not overshadow the fact that the Swedish government had achieved a highly satisfying outcome in a domestically sensitive issue. Most observers had predicted Swedish defeat before the Presidency, in view of the prevailing perspective of the majority of Member States in the Council.

The power of the chair: assessing process and outcome

As representative of the Council in negotiations with the Parliament, the Swedish Presidency was situated at the interface between two nested bargaining arenas. This offered the Swedish Presidency a set of procedural and informational advantages, which it used for private and collective gain. In contrast to its French predecessor, the Swedish Presidency sought to speed up the negotiations by initiating inter-institutional negotiations with the Parliament even before the Council had formed a common position. Exploiting its discretion as Council representative, the Swedish government pushed for agreement at the first reading of the co-decision procedure and initiated trialogue meetings with Parliament

---

[40] Shackleton and Raunio 2003, 179; interviews, members of the European Parliament, 19 June 2001.
[41] Bjurulf and Elgström 2004, 263.

representatives to this end. The format of the trialogue offered the Presidency informational advantages in relation to other member states. The concluding negotiations took place in an even more restricted format, involving only chief negotiators Lund and Watson.

The Presidency played off the secrecy-oriented majority in the Council against the transparency extremists in the Parliament. Extracting concessions in both internal Council negotiations and in external negotiations with the Parliament would be necessary for an eventual agreement, but they also served the Swedish aim of finding a solution which met the interests of the transparency-oriented minority in the Council. "The Swedish strategy was thus to use the wide gap between Council and Parliament to its own benefit by acting as a mediator between the two legislative actors. As the Swedish standpoint was in between the two positions, although far closer to the Parliament's side, it could manoeuvre to seek a compromise that suited its own (and the Council minority's) preferences."[42] The outcome of the negotiations, in the shape of a transparency regulation, reflected the success of this strategy. In the internal Council negotiations in Coreper, the Swedish representative exploited the procedural toolbox of the Presidency to focus negotiations on certain issues and alternatives, while steering clear of others.

The efforts of the Swedish Presidency to reach a collective agreement which satisfied its private interests were greatly facilitated by the formal rules and procedures that structured the negotiations. Majority voting as the decision rule in the Council made it relatively easy for the Presidency to gain support for its proposed package agreement. Unanimity would have invited lowest-common-denominator bargaining, thus producing an internal agreement structured in favor of the most conservative – secrecy-oriented – states and rendering external agreement more difficult to achieve. Instead, the threat of a vote helped the Swedish Presidency to convince even its staunchest opponents to endorse the package, once a majority prepared to accept the final take-it-or-leave-it proposal had formed.[43]

The requirement of agreement between the two co-legislators made it possible for the Presidency to use the position of the Parliament to extract concessions from the secrecy-oriented majority in the Council. This strategy would have been less effective under any other potential legislative procedure, all of which give the Parliament a weaker formal

---

[42] Bjurulf and Elgström 2004, 260.
[43] Bjurulf and Elgström 2004, 264.

position. The conclusion of an agreement during the Swedish Presidency was further dependent on the recently opened possibility to conclude legislative negotiations at the first reading. Had the earlier rules applied, the Swedish Presidency could only have made a preliminary contribution to a negotiation likely to continue to a third reading and conciliation negotiations under a less transparency-oriented Presidency.

By contrast, the widely claimed neutrality norm exerted little or no influence on the Swedish Presidency's handling of the transparency dossier. When faced with the choice between neutral representation and sacrifice of central national concerns, on the one hand, and protection of the same constitutional interests and negative reputational consequences, on the other, the Swedish Presidency chose the latter. EU and state officials with insight into the negotiations in Coreper testify to significant, but fruitless, criticism against Swedish partiality. Yet, to deflect this criticism and minimize its negative consequences for Sweden's reputation as a cooperative partner, Swedish negotiators paid certain lip service to the norm of the neutral Presidency. Notably, Sweden emphasized the value of a more transparent EU to all Member States, well aware that many governments did not share that interpretation.

Posing the question of whether the outcome would have been different under another Presidency government, much suggests that it would have. Even if the extreme position of the Parliament relative to the Council majority would have required some form of movement toward greater transparency under any Presidency, it is unlikely that it would have been as far reaching as that obtained by the Swedes. If a member of the secrecy-oriented majority had chaired the Council, it is quite improbable that the Presidency would have colluded with the Parliament to seek agreement at first reading, thus concluding the negotiations in time for the May deadline. Instead, we could have expected reluctant foot-dragging of the kind displayed by the preceding Portuguese and French Presidencies, a mobilization of the secrecy-oriented majority, and successful attempts to resist more than symbolic concessions to the Parliament.

The Danish Presidency and EU enlargement

Ever since the fall of the Berlin Wall in 1989, the enlargement of the EU to include Central and Eastern Europe had been Denmark's number one priority in the EU. Its Presidency in the second half of 2002 presented the Danish government with an opportunity to actively work to realize this goal, in its capacity as the EU's external representative in the negotiations with the candidate countries. Exploiting the Presidency's room for maneuver at the junction between internal and external arenas, Denmark succeeded in driving the negotiations toward a conclusion in Copenhagen in December 2002. To secure the agreement of all fifteen member states and ten candidate countries, Denmark had to make effective use of a broad range of procedural and informational instruments in its Presidency toolbox.

Eastern enlargement

The fall of communist regimes in Eastern Europe in 1989 and the end of the Cold War opened up the possibility of a politically united European continent. One of the first initiatives of the newborn Central and Eastern European democracies was to declare their interest in joining the EU. In 1993, at the European Council summit in Copenhagen, the EU opened the door to membership and laid down three conditions for accession, the so-called "Copenhagen criteria." First, the acceding state must have stable political institutions, guaranteeing democracy, rule of law, and respect for human rights and minorities. Second, it must have a functioning market economy, capable of coping with the market forces and competitive pressures within the EU. Third, it must have the ability to take on, and comply with, existing obligations in the EU, the so-called *acquis communautaire*.

In December 1997, the EU decided to initiate membership negotiations with the first group of candidate countries: Poland, Hungary, the Czech Republic, Slovenia, Estonia, and Cyprus.[44] The war in Kosovo in 1999, demonstrating the frailty of political stability in the former Eastern bloc, and progress in those states that had not been included in the first round, led the EU to expand the negotiations to a second group of states in December 1999: Latvia, Lithuania, Slovakia, Romania, Bulgaria, and Malta.[45] On the same occasion, Turkey gained the status as a candidate country, even if the EU declared itself unwilling to proceed to negotiations before Turkey had undertaken additional reforms to secure respect for human rights.

In practice, the negotiations between the EU and the candidate countries pertained primarily to the third membership criterion – the means, standards, and exceptions in the candidate countries' incorporation of EU law into national law. After the expansion to twelve candidate countries in 1999, the negotiations were based on the principle of

---

[44] European Council 1997.
[45] European Council 1999b.

differentiation, which meant that each state was judged on its own merits and could thus improve its chances of joining the EU by making progress in the talks. The negotiations covered a total of thirty issue areas or "chapters" and were conducted in bilateral, intergovernmental conferences between the EU and the individual candidate countries. As representative of the existing fifteen member states, the Presidency held a central position on two interlinked bargaining arenas. In the internal negotiation game, the Presidency had to broker compromises and engineer agreement around the EU's common position in relation to the candidate countries. Even if the bulk of the adjustment burden was on the candidate countries, enlargement also required reforms of existing policies and practices, which reopened historical compromises and conflicts among the EU states. In the external negotiation game, the Presidency was charged with presenting and defending the EU position *vis-à-vis* the candidate countries. In these talks, the Commission assisted the Presidency and played an important role through its technical expertise in the dossiers under negotiation and its information on the situation in the candidate countries.

For Denmark, Eastern enlargement had been a top priority since the velvet revolutions in 1989. As Prime Minister Anders Fogh Rasmussen stated shortly after the conclusion of the negotiations, the incorporation into the EU of the Central and East European countries had constituted "the main objective of nearly 15 years of Danish foreign policy."[46] Eastern enlargement in general, and the accession of the three Baltic countries in particular, carried significant economic and political advantages for Denmark. It held the promise of increased trade and the building of a secure community in the Baltic Sea area. It was a EU initiative for which Danish politicians could count on massive domestic support from an otherwise EU-skeptic nation. It was likely to move the EU in a direction more in line with Danish intergovernmental conceptions of European cooperation.

The Danish Presidency: *"enlargement, enlargement, enlargement"*

When Denmark assumed the Presidency on 1 July 2002, substantial progress had been achieved in the enlargement negotiations. For ten of the twelve candidate countries – all but Bulgaria and Romania – only a limited number of chapters still remained open. At its meeting in Göteborg in June 2001, the European Council had set two important

---

[46] Rasmussen 2003.

targets: the conclusion of negotiations with the most advanced candidate countries by the end of 2002, and subsequent accession to the EU in 2004 for these states.[47] Yet completing the negotiations during the fall of 2002 with up to ten candidate countries would be anything but simple. The remaining chapters contained the most controversial parts – both for the EU internally and for the candidate countries – and had been deliberately saved until the end of the negotiating process.

The main challenge for the Danish Presidency was to achieve an internal EU agreement on the financial terms the candidate countries would be offered in the EU's regional and agricultural policies, and then to arrive at an external agreement with the candidate countries on these terms. An eventual conclusion would require the unanimous support of all states involved in the negotiations. In addition, Denmark wished to achieve the maximum possible progress in the negotiations with those candidate countries with which no conclusion would be reached, and continue the work of bringing Turkey closer to the EU.[48]

The Danish government was unambiguous in its commitment to enlargement as the number one Danish priority for the six months at the helm:

Enlargement is the absolutely vital task facing the Danish Presidency. It is the Presidency's goal to conclude accession negotiations with up to 10 countries before the end of 2002. Maximum progress must also be made in the negotiations with those countries which will not be concluding their negotiations during the Danish Presidency. The conditions for EU accession – the so-called Copenhagen criteria – were laid down at the European Council meeting in Copenhagen in 1993. Now, barely ten years later, we have an opportunity to close the circle: From Copenhagen to Copenhagen.[49]

Paraphrasing the Swedish Presidency's motto of "the three Es," Danish minister of foreign affairs, Bertel Haarder summed up his government's priorities as "enlargement, enlargement and enlargement."[50] The symbolic importance of concluding the enlargement process that first had been set in motion in Copenhagen in 1993 at the Copenhagen European Council summit in December 2002 escaped no one, least of all the Danish government.

The Danish government made effective use of the procedural arsenal of the Presidency office for purposes of focusing its own and the EU's

---

[47] European Council 2001.
[48] Danish Presidency 2002a.
[49] Danish Presidency 2002a, 8.
[50] Quoted in Friis 2003, 2.

efforts on the enlargement dossier.[51] "All other major issues, such as, reform of the Common Agricultural Policy (CAP) and the ongoing 'Convention on the Future of Europe' were basically put 'on the back-burner' so that they did not detract the Presidency's top priority of enlargement."[52] For the negotiations as such, the Danish Presidency outlined a strategy consisting of three consecutive phases.[53] First of all, the Presidency would attempt to close the remaining technical chapters. Then it would aim for an internal EU agreement on the financial package in association with the mid-term, informal European Council meeting.in Brussels on 24–25 October. Finally, it would enter into negotiations with the candidate countries on this package, with the aim of producing a concluding agreement at the European Council summit in Copenhagen on 12–13 December 2002. The Danish prime minister suspected that the crucial, final deals would be struck at the level of heads of state and government, and Rasmussen therefore issued a strict order to his cabinet colleagues that none of them was allowed to refer issues to the European Council if they ran into problems in their own Council negotiations.[54] The attention of the heads of state and government should be devoted exclusively to enlargement, and not be wasted on less important dossiers.

As planned, the Danish government spent the early months of its Presidency clearing away technical negotiation issues.[55] Pre-negotiations on the financial issues only got under way after the German elections in late September. The negotiations leading up to the Brussels summit were heavily dominated by a row between Germany and France. Together with a group of net contributors to the EU budget – Sweden, Netherlands, and Great Britain – Germany sought to use enlargement as an argument for changing the financial conditions in the EU's agricultural policy, as agreed in Berlin in March 1999 (see Chapter 5). France, as the main beneficiary of the EU's agricultural policy, staunchly opposed any tinkering with the Berlin agreement and announced that CAP reform, as planned, should take place only after 2006. The Danish Presidency issued repeated warnings that any failure to come to an agreement would lead to delays in the enlargement process.[56] The Danes saw significant dangers in the link sought by Germany and others

---

[51] Bengtsson, Elgström, and Tallberg 2004.
[52] Friis 2003, 3.
[53] Danish Presidency 2002b.
[54] Friis 2003, 3.
[55] Danish Presidency 2002b, 7; Ludlow 2004, ch. 7.
[56] *EU Observer*, 22 October 2002.

between enlargement and CAP reform, since this risked making the process contingent on the renegotiation of a notoriously controversial dossier. The Presidency further signaled its determination to find an agreement in Brussels by emphasizing that it would be willing to continue the summit until a solution had been found, regardless of the scheduled conclusion date of 25 October.[57]

Just hours before the opening of the Brussels summit, France and Germany struck a bilateral deal that effectively paved the way for an agreement at the informal European Council meeting. Two days of summit negotiations yielded a clear mandate for the Danish Presidency, consisting of three parts.[58] The first was a common position on the terms to offer the candidate countries in the area of agricultural policy, and on the overall evolution of EU expenditure in this area in the period 2007–2013. This agreement was very close to the bilateral Franco-German deal, but also satisfied the wish of the Danish Presidency to de-link enlargement and agricultural reform. The second component was the EU offer in the area of regional policy. The third part was an agreement on a budgetary compensation mechanism for the years 2004–2006 – effectively, a lump-sum offer to the candidate countries so that no acceding state would be worse off in the EU than under the financial pre-accession arrangements.

The Copenhagen agreement

The Danish government's presentation of the EU's negotiation offer on the Monday after the Brussels summit marked the beginning of seven weeks of intense negotiations with the candidate countries, before the parties eventually came to an agreement at the Copenhagen meeting of the European Council in mid-December. The goal of the Danish Presidency in this process was to "find solutions that were acceptable to the candidate countries and to the EU Member States, while at the same time respecting the decisions taken at the Brussels European Council."[59] The candidate countries welcomed the fact that the EU had been able to form internal negotiation positions on the financial issues, but correctly interpreted this position as a first, rather than final, offer from the EU side.

Negotiations took place at a number of levels and through parallel channels over this period. In late October, the Danish Presidency

---

[57] *EU Observer*, 24 October 2002.
[58] European Council 2002b.
[59] Danish Presidency 2002b, 8.

organized a special mini-summit in Copenhagen to debate the EU offer with all the candidate countries. Early to mid-November witnessed additional high-level negotiation meetings with the candidate countries in Brussels, including a meeting of twenty-five foreign affairs ministers on 18 November, within the framework of the General Affairs Council. Simultaneously, the Danish Presidency conducted formal meetings and informal consultations with individual candidate countries.

For purposes of achieving approximation in the negotiations, and thereby improve the potential for a concluding deal in Copenhagen, the Danish Presidency took the unusual step of presenting a revised version of the EU's offer on 25 November, without consulting the other fourteen EU governments. The compromise package contained important concessions compared to the offer formulated by the EU at the Brussels summit. Hardly surprisingly, the other fourteen EU governments expressed strong discontent with the fact that the Presidency had presented them with a *fait accompli*.[60] The strongest resistance came from Germany, France, and the United Kingdom. German chancellor Gerhard Schröder, for instance, stated that the financial package "does not live up to our expectations."[61] However, the Danish Presidency maintained that both sides would have to offer concessions if the negotiations were to be concluded in Copenhagen: "It is difficult for the EU-15 to swallow, but I hope that they will at the end. Denmark believes that sacrifices are necessary if the negotiations are to be brought to an end."[62]

The candidate countries, for their part, welcomed the compromise package as a step in the right direction, but raised central objections to the new offer as well, thus signaling their willingness to negotiate until the very end.[63] Poland, Slovakia, Hungary, and Malta were particularly critical of the Danish offer. In the case of Poland – the most recalcitrant candidate country – the Peasant Party threatened to withdraw from the ruling government coalition and campaign in favor of a no to EU membership if Polish farmers did not get a better deal. Prime Minister Rasmussen responded to these demands with appeals, warnings, and threats: "I urge the candidates to do their utmost to conclude negotiations. I warn against raising demands too high, as there is the risk that negotiations will not be concluded at Copenhagen, which would postpone enlargement for many years. We are prepared to conclude

---

[60] Ludlow 2004, 235–245.

[61] Quoted in Institut für Europäische Politik 2003, 24; see also *EU Observer*, 4 December 2002.

[62] Danish official, quoted by *EU Observer*, 28 November 2002.

[63] *EU Observer*, 27 and 28 November, 2, 3, and 4 December 2002.

negotiations with the candidate countries that are ready. No candidate country should wait for the others."[64]

To strengthen the Presidency's hand in the negotiations before and during the upcoming summit, Rasmussen used the traditional pre-summit *tour des capitales* to rally support around the Presidency's latest offer and sound out concerns and resistance points among the existing EU members. Rasmussen testified to clear support for the proposed package, but limited room for maneuver in the final negotiations.[65] As a result of these consultations, Schröder publicly endorsed the package as the basis for negotiations, while emphasizing that this was the very limit. Yet, in his bilateral talk to Rasmussen, Schröder went even further and shared important private information with the Presidency. Germany would be willing to make further concessions to Poland, but only at the Copenhagen summit and if it was absolutely necessary for the conclusion of a deal.[66]

The final chance to conclude negotiations before the summit itself was the meeting of the General Affairs Council on 9–10 December, to which the ten candidate countries had been invited. At the meeting, eight of the ten candidate countries decided to accept the financial terms proposed by the Danish Presidency, even if some had minor technical issues left to settle. By contrast, Poland and Malta continued to raise major problems and objections. Poland's presentation of a list of requirements to be dealt with in Copenhagen led Danish foreign minister Per Stig Møller to declare: "If Poland does not want to be a EU member, I can accept that."[67]

At the Copenhagen summit of the European Council on the 12–13 December, the Danish Presidency engaged in intensive bilateral and multilateral negotiations with both candidate countries and existing member states.[68] Eventually, these negotiations produced a new compromise package that was acceptable to all twenty-five states.[69] Negotiating simultaneously on two interlinked arenas, the Danish Presidency was instrumental in the achievement of an enlargement agreement. In an insightful analysis of these negotiations, Lykke Friis points to three elements of the Presidency's strategy that proved particularly important

---

[64] Quoted by *EU Observer*, 8 December 2002.
[65] *EU Observer*, 8 December 2002.
[66] Danish Television 2003.
[67] *EU Observer*, 10 December 2002.
[68] For a detailed account, see Ludlow 2004, chs. 21–22.
[69] European Council 2002c.

in securing the outcome.[70] All three elements drew on the procedural and informational resources of the Presidency office.

First of all, the Danish Presidency framed the Copenhagen summit as a now-or-never occasion for enlargement. This tactic was aimed at both candidate and member countries. In relation to the candidate countries, Presidency representatives kept emphasizing that any state making un-realistic demands (read: Poland) would face the risk of being left behind. Yet equally, it was essential to convince existing EU member states that any failure to reach an agreement would lead to a postponement of the enlargement, and that further concessions would therefore have to be considered. To underline this point, Rasmussen informed his colleagues prior to the summit that the Danish Presidency had made practical arrangements for a continuation of the negotiations past the weekend, should this be necessary.[71] "Where other Presidencies may have tried to play down the need to agree on accession – in order to protect them-selves from defeat – Denmark did the exact opposite. It placed all its eggs in one basket and put the screws on its fellow Member States. This 'time pressure' forced other EU countries to reveal their actual preferences."[72] Notably, it became difficult for pro-enlargement Germany to credibly threaten to block a deal with reference to additional financial conces-sions to the candidate countries. "Ultimately, none of them were so worried about enlargement that they were willing to take the blame for postponing it."[73]

The Presidency's second instrumental move was to construct a final compromise offer to the candidate countries that contained additional "sweeteners." Whereas Poland, at the opening of the summit, had demanded an additional 2 billion euro in budgetary compensation over the 2004–2006 period, the Presidency put together a package that would give Poland 1 billion euro and the other nine candidate countries 300 million euro altogether. While 1.3 billion above the member states' Brussels agreement, this offer was still below the financial ceiling for enlargement decided in Berlin in 1999, which made it easier for the net contributors to the EU budget, especially Germany, to accept.[74] The decision to offer additional concessions to the candidate countries was based on information, gained in bilateral consultations, that these gov-ernments were under tough domestic pressure and had to be able to

---

[70] Friis 2003. See also Institut für Europäische Politik 2003, 18.
[71] Danish Presidency 2002c.
[72] Friis 2003, 6.
[73] Friis 2003, 7.
[74] *EU Observer,* 14 December 2002.

point to some kind of improvement in the EU's proposal. Just like the November compromise package, the Danish Presidency made this new offer without seeking prior consent from the other fourteen governments. In addition, it made sure to confirm the candidate countries' approval before it presented the concluded deal to the other existing member states. Though understandably upset by its methods, the other fourteen governments did not oppose the Presidency's deal, at least not enough to force a risky renegotiation of the deal.

The third Presidency tactic consisted of a deliberate sequencing of the negotiations during the Copenhagen summit, to put maximum pressure on Poland. By structuring the bilateral talks at the summit so that final agreements first could be closed with all other candidate countries, the Danish Presidency sent a strong signal to Poland that it risked being left behind. Yet this strategy was complicated by the fact that some candidate countries – the Czech Republic, Slovakia, and Hungary – saw the opportunity at the summit to gain additional favors by adopting the Polish extortion tactic. This explains why all candidate countries, not just Poland, obtained additional budgetary compensation in the final agreement, even if the financial negotiations with the other candidates were supposed to have been concluded prior to the summit.

The power of the chair: assessing process and outcome

The Danish government skillfully used its position as the EU's representative to move the negotiations toward a concluding deal that satisfied the collective interests of member states and candidate countries, as well as Denmark's private interests. As Friis concludes: "Throughout its Presidency, Denmark consistently used all procedural and informational instruments in its toolkit and hence affected the 'contract zone' of the candidate countries and the member states."[75] The procedural powers were exploited to provide the best possible circumstances for a conclusion of the enlargement negotiations during the fall of 2002. The Presidency chose to put other urgent EU concerns on the back burner, thereby focusing its own efforts and the EU's negotiation resources on enlargement. The summits of the European Council were reserved exclusively for enlargement negotiations, since the Presidency judged that only heads of state and government could make the controversial concessions necessary for closure. On a number of occasions, the Presidency transformed the regular meetings of the EU's General Affairs

[75] Friis 2003, 8–9.

Council into collective negotiation sessions with twenty-five states at the table.

The Danish Presidency's central position in the two interlinked bargaining processes offered additional instruments. It engaged in informal, bilateral consultations with both member governments and candidate countries, to testing resistance points and gain the information necessary to construct an acceptable agreement. It used its simultaneous access to both bargaining areas to play off the most recalcitrant parties against each other, and threatened delays and postponement if the parties did not consider concessions. It sequenced the negotiations with the candidate countries to turn up the pressure on Poland. It exploited the discretion within the representational function to offer compromise proposals to the candidate countries that had not been condoned by the principals in the Council, but which the Presidency judged would be accepted by the member states when presented to them on a *fait accompli* basis.

In the aftermath of the Copenhagen summit, the Danish Presidency was unanimously praised for having produced a balanced compromise agreement which was acceptable to all parties, despite the significant obstacles identified in the beginning of the fall.[76] Yet more important for Denmark than praise was the fact that it had achieved its long-sought national objective of a quick and broad enlargement round, including all three Baltic countries. In addition, the final compromise agreement satisfied Danish short-term interests as a net contributor to the EU budget, by keeping expenses for 2004–2006 below the previously agreed Berlin ceiling.

Formal rules shaped the process and outcome of the enlargement negotiations. The formulation of EU negotiation positions and the final acceptance of an enlargement agreement required the unanimous consent of the EU's fifteen member states. This shaped the Danish Presidency's strategy in a number of ways. It forced the Presidency to pay special attention to the interests of member states with particular interests at stake – France on agricultural reform, Spain on regional policy, and Germany on the EU budget. Yet the multidimensional character of these states' interests in the enlargement process helped to reduce the constraining effect of their veto power. Most importantly, Germany's budget interests were overshadowed by its overall support for enlargement, based on long-term economic and geostrategic calculations. The

---

[76] *EU Observer*, 14 December 2002; *Financial Times*, 16 December 2002; Institut für Europäische Politik 2003.

requirement of unanimity further shaped the negotiations by strengthening the Danish Presidency's hand in the negotiations with the candidate
countries. By limiting the EU's domestic win-set – the range of agreements acceptable to all fifteen governments – the unanimity requirement
made it possible for the Presidency to extract concessions through
reasonably credible threats of EU rejection, likely to result in a
postponement of enlargement.

In the external negotiations, the Danish Presidency sought to exploit
the fact that enlargement could proceed with fewer than ten states, and
that each country's accession was dependent on an agreement with the
EU. In plain language: Poland did not enjoy veto power over the fate of
the other candidate countries. While correct in formal terms, this was
unrealistic in political terms, which effectively meant that an overall
enlargement deal would require the unanimous consent of all candidate
countries. This informal unanimity requirement influenced the final
negotiations by forcing the Danish Presidency to meet Poland halfway
and to offer additional sweeteners to the other candidate countries, once
the Czech Republic, Slovakia, and Hungary had jumped on the Polish
bandwagon.

The Danish Presidency's handling of the enlargement negotiations
does not provide evidence of a strong constraining norm of neutrality.
Well aware of the negative reaction this would elicit, Denmark went
beyond the negotiation mandate dictated by EU governments in Brussels. Neither did the criticism publicly expressed by Germany and other
member states after the first incident prevent the Danish Presidency
from repeating this maneuver in Copenhagen. As Peter Ludlow notes:
"As Rasmussen toured the capitals, he received several reminders of the
disquiet that the Presidency's tactics had caused . . . These complaints,
which were echoed once again in the final meetings of Coreper and the
GAERC in the week before the European Council meeting do not,
however, appear to have had the slightest impact on the Presidency's
proposals."[77]

Is it likely that we would have obtained a comprehensive enlargement
agreement with these particular distributional implications in December
2002, had another government than Denmark held the Presidency?
When Denmark took over the Presidency, very few people in leading
positions thought that it was possible to conclude the negotiations
during fall, thus permitting the EU to take in the new members in
May 2004. Even if the negotiations would have progressed during any

---

[77] Ludlow 2004, 245.

Presidency, it is questionable whether the lukewarm enthusiasm for enlargement of some member states, notably the Mediterranean countries, would have sufficed to bring the talks to conclusion.[78] Denmark devoted the lion's share of its political resources to finishing the enlargement negotiations, and took huge political risks for this purpose when negotiating beyond its mandate. In terms of the distributional consequences of this deal, it is likely that a less budget-conscious Presidency would have been more willing to offer sweeter concessions in order to get all candidate countries on board. By the same token, it is likely that governments with stronger interests than Denmark in the reform of the EU's agricultural and regional policy would have exploited the Presidency to steer outcomes in their own favor, possibly at the expense of an early and comprehensive enlargement agreement.

Conclusion

The appointment of the Presidency as EU governments' representative offers a solution to the demands for a Council negotiator *vis-à-vis* third parties. Yet, similar to other cases where negotiation powers are delegated to representatives, the engagement of the Presidency gives rise to a tension between principals and agents. "[R]elationships between representatives and those they represent are mixed-motive in nature. Consequently, some actions in external negotiations will advance shared interests, whereas some will favor the interests of the principal or the representative. The representative may well use her ability to control the process and flows of information to the disadvantage of those she represents, giving rise to the classic principal-agent problem."[79]

This chapter suggests that the position as EU representative grants the Presidency unique opportunities to influence the agreements it negotiates with external parties. The Presidency enjoys access to informational advantages and procedural resources that make it possible to shift outcomes from the natural equilibrium and toward the Presidency's preferences. As the architect of internal compromise, the Presidency gains access to privileged information about state preferences through confidential, bilateral talks. As external negotiator, the Presidency can enter into informal negotiations with third parties beyond the control of other EU governments. The Presidency's position at the nexus of two

---

[78] For instance, the preceding Portuguese and French Presidencies did not put enlargement on the top of their agenda for the six months in office. Bengtsson 2004, ch. 2; Ludlow 2004, ch. 3.

[79] Cutcher-Gershenfeld and Watkins 1999, 36.

interlinked negotiation arenas makes it possible to play off internal and external negotiating parties against each other. Moreover, the Presidency can negotiate external deals that subsequently are presented to EU governments for adoption on a take-it-or-leave-it basis.

The two case studies underline the Presidency's room for maneuver as external negotiator. With little regard to expectations on neutral behavior, the Swedish government exploited the Presidency's informational and procedural resources to negotiate a deal on new transparency rules that went far beyond the Council majority's stand on this issue. The Swedish Presidency initiated informal, bilateral talks with the transparency advocates in the Parliament even before the Council had adopted a common position, and negotiated an agreement that eventually was presented to the other governments as a *fait accompli*. The Danish government mobilized the privileged resources of the Presidency for the purposes of achieving a comprehensive enlargement agreement in Copenhagen, thus achieving Denmark's number one foreign policy objective over the preceding decade. In this process, the Danish Presidency played off its principals in the Council against its counterparts, and negotiated informal and unpopular compromises with the candidate countries that had not been condoned by the other member states. Rather than functioning as a constraint on Presidency behavior, divisions between the member states in the Council provided the Swedish and Danish Presidencies with additional leeway and bargaining strength. Diverging state preferences permitted Sweden and Denmark to interpret the Council's collective position with some flexibility, and strengthened their hand in the negotiations with third parties, by enabling them to justify their demands with reference to internal constraints.

7   Comparative perspectives: formal leadership in multilateral negotiations

Previous chapters have demonstrated how negotiations in the EU lend firm support to the theory of formal leadership. In the EU, the member states have delegated extensive powers of agenda management, brokerage, and representation to the Presidency in response to identifiable collective-action problems. Drawing upon these powers and the Presidency's informational and procedural advantages, EU governments have used the office as a platform for political influence, thus raising the efficiency of negotiations and shaping the distribution of gains from negotiated agreements. Yet what does the EU case actually say about the power of the chair in multilateral negotiations? The EU is sometimes described as *sui generis* – one of a kind – because of attributes that cannot be assumed in all multilateral negotiations, such as the low number of actors, the high level of homogeneity, and the high degree of institutionalized cooperation. To what extent can the conclusions from this particular negotiation context be generalized to multilateral bargaining at large? Is the phenomenon of a negotiation chair that wields power and influences outcomes isolated to the EU or is it a general feature in multilateral bargaining and international cooperation? This chapter addresses these questions by placing the European experience in a comparative perspective. I consider evidence from multilateral negotiations in the areas of security, trade, and environment, drawing mainly on existing secondary accounts.

More specifically, I assess the core hypotheses of the theory of formal leadership in three broad negotiation processes: security negotiations within the CSCE/OSCE, from 1972 up to the early 2000s; trade negotiations within the GATT/WTO, from the Kennedy Round in the 1960s and up to the launch of the Doha Round in 2002; and environmental negotiations within the ambit of the UN, from the talks on the law of the sea in the 1970s, through the negotiation of the ozone agreements in the 1980s, to the conclusion of the climate change convention in the 1990s.

Each of these areas of international cooperation conforms to one of the alternative ways of organizing the chairmanship: rotation between the participating states (CSCE/OSCE), election of chairman from one of the parties (UN conferences), and appointment of supranational official as chairman (GATT/WTO). This careful selection of cases allows us to test the hypothesis that the institutional design of the chairmanship shapes the room for maneuver of negotiation chairs and carries important political consequences. The theory of formal leadership suggests that rotation is likely to create dynamics of diffuse reciprocity, where states refrain from establishing extensive control mechanisms and instead offer each other latitude in the execution of the chairmanship. All parties eventually get their privileged opportunity to shape outcomes and rotation in itself puts a limit on each state's exploitation of the office. By contrast, we would expect the other two institutional models to involve more pronounced concerns with control, with less latitude for chairmen to influence the distributional dimension of negotiated agreements. Unless states wish to grant one of the parties extraordinary means of promoting national interests or give supranational officials special opportunities to pursue organizational interests, they will establish means of *ex ante* or *ex post* control.

This broad comparative outlook generates three conclusions. First, the power of the chair appears to be a general phenomenon in the world of multilateral negotiation. The role of chairmen in EU bargaining is not exceptional. In the security, trade, and environmental negotiations analyzed in this chapter, governmental and supranational chairs fulfill central functions in the negotiations and exert influence over political outcomes. That said, there is notable variation, both as regards the functions delegated to the chairmanship and the capacity of negotiation chairs to exploit the office for private purposes.

Second, the comparative evidence supports the claim that functional demand drives the delegation of tasks and responsibilities to the institution of the chairmanship. The observed variation in powers and responsibilities can be tied to varying functional pressures, and thus explained by the theory of formal leadership. States have not adopted a standardized model for the powers conferred to chairmen in international cooperation, but have tailored the office to match specific functional needs.

Third, the comparative record lends additional support to the argument that negotiation chairs possess privileged resources that enable them to influence outcomes, but are constrained by formal institutional rules. All three areas of cooperation offer examples of formal leaders stepping in to facilitate bargaining and interstate agreement, for instance, by fixing the agenda through a single negotiating text or devising a comprehensive compromise proposal. Yet not all cases provide conclusive evidence of chairmen influencing the distributional dimension of the negotiations. The most powerful explanation of this variation is the institutional design of the chairmanship. As predicted by the theory of formal leadership, states have been more willing to grant extensive discretion to negotiation chairs in the OSCE, where the chairmanship rotates between the parties, than in trade or environmental negotiations.

Formal leadership in the CSCE/OSCE

Three decades of negotiations in the CSCE/OSCE offer fascinating evidence of the power of the chair under varying political and institutional conditions. The Cold War cleavage between the East and the West, and the demand for brokerage in the CSCE, propelled the neutral and non-aligned countries into the chair and gave them a central role in the management of détente. On several occasions, their interventions were crucial for achieving agreement between the US and the USSR. The end of the Cold War and the transformation of the CSCE into a regular international organization, the OSCE, brought a completely new institutional structure, including a new design of the chairmanship. The rotating chairmanship was placed at the center of the new institutional structure and equipped with broad powers of agenda management, brokerage, and representation. During the first decade of negotiations in the OSCE, governments in control of the chairmanship have enjoyed significant discretion and influenced both the efficiency and distributional implications of decision-making in the OSCE.

The CSCE: formal leadership in the shadow of the Cold War

The Conference on Security and Cooperation in Europe was first convened in 1973 and functioned over the next two decades as a forum for East–West dialogue and negotiation. More specifically, the CSCE brought together thirty-five states from Europe and North America for negotiations in three areas: security relations, economic and technological cooperation, and human rights. In the Helsinki Final Act, adopted at the end of the first conference 1973–1975, the participating states committed themselves to a series of follow-up conferences, subsequently held in Belgrade 1977–1978, Madrid 1980–1983, and Vienna 1986–1989. In addition, the CSCE arranged an extraordinary conference on confidence building and disarmament in Stockholm in 1984–1986.

The institutional structure established at the first conference was light and flexible, reflecting the significant degree of mutual distrust between the Warsaw Pact and NATO. No permanent bodies were established, follow-up conferences could only be scheduled through consensus decisions, and *ad hoc* secretariats were set up to perform the necessary service functions at each conference. In practice, CSCE negotiations operated through two parallel structures: one formal and one informal. The mode of negotiation differed between the two systems, as did the design of the chairmanship institution.

Formal negotiations took place in plenary, working bodies, and draft groups, with the requirement of consensus for the adoption of an agreement. In these organs, negotiations were presided over by chairmen who rotated on a daily basis. This extreme design of the chairmanship – unparalleled in the world of multilateral bargaining – is best explained by three considerations.[1] First, equal rotation was seen as a way of preventing the kind of East–West confrontation that could be anticipated if the states were to elect one party's representative as chairman. Since both NATO and the Warsaw Pact wished to keep institutional structures light, the alternative of appointing a supranational chairman was never an option. Second, rotation symbolized the principle of all states' equal standing, even if it was evident that decision-making would be dominated by the Soviet Union and the United States. Third, the choice of *daily* rotation effectively reduced the possibility for the chair to exploit its procedural powers for political ends. The alternation of the chair on a daily basis constituted an instrument of extreme control that permitted the superpowers to agree to an arrangement where negotiations would sometimes be led by their adversary or its cronies.

Yet, even when designed this way, the rotating chairmanship was the object of political strife and controversy. Accounts of CSCE negotiations frequently refer to three episodes at the Madrid conference, when East–West relations were at a low point.[2] In the first case, the Soviet Union provoked a crisis by refusing to allow a stopped clock to be restarted, as this would mean that the chairmanship for particularly sensitive negotiations would shift from Hungary to the Netherlands. In the second case, a Polish chairman caused Western uproar when exploiting questionable procedural caveats, prepared in advance in Warsaw, to prevent thirteen Western representatives from speaking out against the military takeover in Poland. In the third case, a Czechoslovakian chairman sought to end a waiting game initiated by the West, by refusing to step down as prescribed by the principle of daily rotation.

The practice of informal negotiations emerged in response to bargaining impediments in the formal structure. The plenary format left little

---

[1] Sizoo and Jurrjens 1984, 63–64; Lehne 1991, 4; Heraclides 1993a, 18.
[2] See, in particular, Sizoo and Jurrjens 1984, 193–211.

room for constructive negotiation and instead tended to encourage fierce exchanges of declarations between representatives of the two blocs.[3] Furthermore, the design of the chairmanship proved to have predictable effects on the capacity of negotiation chairs to facilitate agreement between the parties. Daily rotation reduced this function to the technical aspects of opening and closing sessions, and did not allow sufficient time for the chair to engage in agenda-management and brokerage activities that could help the parties toward agreement.[4]

In practice, all meaningful negotiation activity took place in informal forums, whose negotiating products were subsequently rubber-stamped at formal meetings.[5] The informal negotiations were structured on the basis of a set of implicit but generally understood and accepted rules. Notably, the negotiations in the informal groups were directed by a permanent chairman, denoted "coordinator," from one of the neutral or non-aligned (NNA) countries.[6] The choice of the NNA countries is best explained by the fact that these states held preferences that were between the competing perspectives of NATO and the Warsaw Pact. By selecting these states as permanent chairs, rather than members of either of the two blocs, the superpowers made sure that the chairmanship would not be systematically exploited in favor of either the West or the East.

Whereas the general conference themes were defined in pre-negotiations between the parties, the chairmanship was responsible for making the agenda negotiable. The NNA countries drafted the overall working program, and each individual chairman determined the order and priority of the items under negotiation in his or her working group.[7] The competing demands of the two blocs created a distinct functional pressure for this kind of agenda management:

East Europeans were always determined to take the easier proposals first so as to establish a large volume of agreed language on different subjects which could then be held up as proof of the success. . . . The West fought against this because its priority was to reach agreement on a small number of proposals important to it in the area of human rights, human contacts and information: it stressed quality rather than quantity. It fell to the co-ordinator to fulfil the important task of steering a path somewhere between these two approaches so that the contact group could get on with its work.[8]

---

[3] Heraclides 1993a, 45–48.
[4] Sizoo and Jurrjens 1984, 63, 157; Lehne 1991, 4.
[5] Sizoo and Jurrjens 1984, 153–175; Heraclides 1993a, 48–50.
[6] The NNA group comprised Austria, Cyprus, Finland, Liechtenstein, Malta, San Marino, Sweden, Switzerland, and Yugoslavia.
[7] Sizoo and Jurrjens 1984, 147, 158.
[8] Sizoo and Jurrjens 1984, 158.

The most central function delegated to the NNA chairmen was brokerage. The CSCE conferences took place in a political climate where the two main negotiating camps had a deep mistrust of the other's intentions and conceived of the negotiations as a struggle to be won or lost. "Until 1988 almost every proposal, phrase, word and at times even commas, however anodyne, would be treated with caution and placed within the wider negotiating gamut, so long as they came from the 'other side'. . . . The inclination of both Eastern and Western delegations was 'zero-sum' and damage control, rather than striving for gains to all sides."[9] The consequence of this inhospitable negotiating environment was a strong demand for third-party intervention.

By contrast, CSCE negotiations did not create a demand for representation by the chairmanship or any other actor. Even if each CSCE conference contained a range of negotiation groups, these bodies were not involved in negotiations with each other. Furthermore, the CSCE was a negotiation process mainly aimed at confidence building and standard setting among the participants – activities for which no external representation was needed. Yet, as we shall see, the development of the CSCE into the OSCE created a demand for both internal and external representation.

Existing research on the CSCE conferences in the 1970s and 1980s unanimously testifies that the chairmanship of the NNA countries was pivotal for bringing negotiations forward and toward agreement. Even though their mandates were only informal in nature, NNA chairmen had access to a range of procedural and informational resources that enabled them to identify and construct viable compromises. The toolbox included the authority to create informal groups, initiate bilateral consultations in order to sound out bottom lines, draft non-papers that could function as single negotiating texts, and construct package deals capable of gaining consensus approval.

The NNA countries had already established themselves as brokers in the 1972 preparatory talks, where they managed to construct an agreement between the East and the West on the negotiation format for the first CSCE conference.[10] At this conference, NNA chairmen were instrumental in paving the way for consensus on the sensitive dossier of human rights, and in developing a formula for the continuation of the CSCE process that could bridge the competing visions of the Soviet Union and the United States.

---

[9] Heraclides 1993b, 24.
[10] Höll 1987; Ghebali 1989, ch. 1; Heraclides 1993a, chs. 2–3.

The initial success was followed by the first and only major failure of the NNA group as brokers, the Belgrade conference of 1977–1978.[11] Despite intensive efforts and a large number of consecutive compromise proposals, the NNA chairs failed to gain the support of the two blocs for their proposals. Both the US and the USSR took an exceedingly confrontational approach, where they focused on the shortcomings of the other party in implementing the provisions of the Helsinki Final Act, especially on human rights. The negotiations ended with the adoption of a four-page document that only contained a general record of the meeting. Observers of this process attribute the failure of the NNA states' brokerage efforts to the actual absence of a zone of agreement.

The Madrid conference of 1980–1983 is generally heralded as the high point of NNA brokerage.[12] The conference was characterized by the continuous worsening of relations between the US and the Soviet Union, with conflict over issues such as the Soviet invasion in Afghanistan, the introduction of martial law in Poland, and the deployment of cruise missiles in Europe. On a number of occasions, leadership efforts by the NNA group saved the entire conference from collapsing. The NNA states were instrumental in finding a way out of an initial stalemate over procedural issues, proposed a temporary adjournment of the conference when negotiations risked falling apart, and presented consecutive package-deal drafts that functioned as single negotiating texts and eventually led to a concluding agreement.

The extraordinary conference in Stockholm in 1984–1986 differed from the three review conferences because of its exclusive focus on military confidence building and disarmament. In these negotiations, the superpowers chose to tackle many key issues in bilateral talks, and the NNA states were not invited to play the same prominent brokerage role as before.[13] The NNA chairmen eased the negotiations by helping the two adversaries to overcome procedural and substantive problems in the first phase of the negotiations, but their contribution was of secondary importance to the overall outcome. The US and the Soviet Union were capable of identifying a zone of agreement on their own, without having to involve NNA chairmen as brokers.

The Vienna conference in 1986–1989 took place in an improved international climate, following the rise to power of Mikhail Gorbachev in the Soviet Union and the progress reached in Stockholm. The

---

[11] Höll 1987; Ghebali 1989, ch. 1; Heraclides 1993a, ch. 5.
[12] Sizoo and Jurrjens 1984; Höll 1987; Neuhold 1987; Ghebali 1989, ch. 1; Heraclides 1993a, ch. 5.
[13] Neuhold 1987; Ghebali 1989, ch. 1; Hampson with Hart 1995, ch. 4.

contribution of the NNA states was most prominent in the area of human rights, where the Soviet position was undergoing change, but not fast enough to prevent conflict on key items. Soviet oscillation between hard and soft positions frustrated Western governments, and it fell to the chairmanship to identify the elusive bottom line of the Soviet delegation. The NNA countries are generally credited with bringing about the initiation of real negotiations in 1987, and devising the draft document around which bargaining converged and the final agreement could be constructed.[14]

This brief review of the CSCE's conferences indicates that NNA chairmen on repeated occasions exerted influence by raising the efficiency of the negotiations. There is less evidence to suggest that these states were simultaneously able to exploit their privileged position to systematically shift substantive outcomes in any particular direction. The absence of a clear distributional effect is best explained by three factors.

First, the NNA chairmen were heavily constrained by the combination of a consensus requirement and highly divergent preferences. Just identifying a zone of agreement was exceedingly difficult, and proved to be impossible on some occasions. Existing research can offer few examples of situations where multiple equilibria seem to have existed, and where the NNA countries were presented with an opportunity to choose one efficient agreement rather than another.[15] Second, the NNA states tended to hold preferences positioned between those of the US and the Soviet Union. As previously noted, this was a prominent reason for the superpowers to grant the NNA states control over the chairmanship. The position of the NNA countries in the distribution of preferences effectively meant that compromise agreements between the US and the Soviet Union would often deliver substantive outcomes favored by the NNA countries. The incentive to exploit the chairmanship for private purposes thus was limited. Third, the NNA states were more concerned with the continuation of the CSCE process, than with the particular substance of agreements produced in these negotiations.[16] The NNA countries could not count on military assistance in the event of an attack from one of the blocs, and were therefore particularly dependent on continued détente. Moreover, the CSCE offered the

---

[14] Ghebali 1989, ch. 1; Lehne 1991; Heraclides 1993a, ch. 7.
[15] One rare example is the negotiations on human rights at the Vienna conference, where NNA chairmen secured support for proposals that clearly were biased in favor of Western and NNA positions. Lehne 1991, 114.
[16] Neuhold 1987; Lehne 1991, 51, 125.

NNA states a chance to participate in the negotiation of security relations in Europe, which would not be the case if this process failed and
was replaced by bilateral East–West dialogue.

The OSCE: formal leadership in the new European security structure

The end of the Cold War fundamentally changed the preconditions for
security cooperation in Europe. Whereas the old ambition of stimulating
détente between NATO and the Warsaw Pact was no longer relevant,
the broad membership still made the CSCE an attractive forum for
security cooperation in the post-Cold War context. Intent on developing
a new role for the CSCE, the participating states negotiated the Charter
of Paris in 1990.[17] This laid down a new institutional structure, and
allowed for an expansion of the CSCE's activities into areas that often
required daily political involvement and operational support, such as the
promotion of free elections, rule of law, market economies, and environmental protection.[18] The decision in 1994 to change the name to
the Organization for Security and Cooperation in Europe reflected the
transformation for the CSCE from a negotiation process into a regular
international organization.

Multilateral negotiations in the OSCE take place in two intergovernmental bodies: meetings of foreign ministers in the Ministerial Council
at least once a year, and meetings of the OSCE ambassadors in the
Permanent Council on a weekly basis. The foreign ministers set long-
term priorities and review progress, whereas the Permanent Council
functions as the real negotiation forum of the organization.

The participating states have chosen to place the Chairman-in-
Office (CiO) at the centre of this decision-making structure. The office
is "vested with overall responsibility for executive action and the coordination of current OSCE activities."[19] The chairmanship rotates on
an annual basis and states are appointed to the office in competition with
each other. Since its creation, the office of the CiO has been given ever
more extensive responsibilities of agenda management, brokerage, and
representation. This growth in powers is directly related to functional
needs arising from the expansion of OSCE activities. "[The powers of
the chairmanship] have developed in a pragmatic and creative way in

---

[17] Lehne 1991; Heraclides 1993b.
[18] The institutional structure defined in the Charter of Paris was subsequently developed
through decisions at a follow-up conference in Helsinki in 1992 and by the new
Ministerial Council at a meeting in Rome in 1993.
[19] OSCE 2000.

parallel to the dramatic expansion of the OSCE's operational activities and the necessities of current action related to the Organization's increased responsibilities."[20]

The conferral of more extensive responsibilities is partly anchored in formal delegation, partly an effect of evolving practices. The OSCE today engages in conflict prevention, crisis management, conflict resolution, post-conflict rehabilitation, and the promotion of democracy, rule of law, and respect for human rights. For these purposes, it utilizes a highly variegated toolbox, including fact-finding visits, semi-permanent missions in troublesome regions, personal representatives in vital issues, *ad hoc* steering groups for specific tasks, and mechanisms for dispute settlement. The CiO is centrally involved in the negotiation and execution of all these activities. "[T]he post of the CiO has developed into the key political leadership of the OSCE, guiding the OSCE bodies and chairing its political organs . . . the CiO has become the 'super-coordinator' and initiator of the OSCE community."[21] In fact, in many ways, the CiO carries more far-reaching political responsibilities than the Presidency in the EU. To compensate for the discontinuity that results from the rotation of the chairmanship, the participating states have strengthened the OSCE Secretariat, and introduced forms of cooperation between consecutive chairmanships.[22]

Through its functions of agenda management, brokerage, and representation, the chairmanship helps the participating states to reach collective goals. At the same time, the procedural and informational resources enjoyed by the CiO permit the government in office to favor certain political outcomes over others. The most notable constraint is the requirement of consensus for decisions in the OSCE's intergovernmental organs.

The function as agenda manager carries a distinct executive profile and includes a range of instruments that enable the CiO to shape the operational activities of the organization. Just like in the EU, each incoming CiO presents a political program for its period at the helm. Yet, in contrast to the EU Presidency, which is dependent on the European Commission for formal agenda setting in large areas of cooperation, the OSCE chairmanship possesses independent powers of initiative. Through this program, the CiO selects areas of activity where

---

[20] Ghebali 2001, 201. See also Bloed 1997; interview, former director of the CSCE Secretariat, 2 May 2003.
[21] Bloed 1997, 46.
[22] Eliasson 1993; Heraclides 1993b, 77; Ghebali 2001; interview, former director of the CSCE Secretariat, 2 May 2003.

it wishes to see particular progress over the next twelve months, thus setting priorities among competing political concerns. Indeed, incoming CiOs generally make a virtue of the element of prioritization in their political programs, which illustrates the extent to which the distributional influence of the chair is seen as an acceptable price for the efficiency it simultaneously produces.[23] Prioritization focuses the organization's resources, while simultaneously permitting the CiO to favor areas of particular national concern. Norms prescribing evenhanded attention to all concerns appear weak or non-existent.

Beyond the political program, the CiO can direct attention to particular issues by convening extraordinary meetings, conferences, and seminars, or appointing personal representatives for prioritized issues.[24] For instance, the Austrian chairmanship in 2000 arranged a special meeting on the domestic problem of trafficking in women, and appointed a former minister to lead an OSCE task force on this topic. Similarly, the Romanian chairmanship in 2001 chose to organize a special conference in Bucharest on the national concern of minority issues.

The CiO functions as the central broker in OSCE negotiations at summits, in the Ministerial Council, and in the Permanent Council. Prominent among the CiO's brokerage instruments is the practice of convening informal meetings in restricted groups in order to sound out concerns and facilitate exchange on controversial points.[25] Once the parties have reached a preliminary agreement, the issue is referred to the appropriate decision-making body for formal decision. The demand for brokerage is considerable, given the requirement of consensus among the fifty-five members. Simultaneously, the consensus rule works to constrain the CiO's capacity to steer negotiations toward outcomes it prefers.[26] One case that illustrates this effect of the consensus requirement was the negotiation of the final declaration of the Vienna Ministerial Council in 2000.[27]

The Austrian chairmanship, supported by other Western governments, sought to include provisions in the ministerial declaration that reviewed Russian commitments on the human rights situation in Chechnya, Georgia, and Moldova. For some time, Russia had complained that the OSCE was paying one-sided and undue attention to human rights problems in the former socialist countries. In Vienna, the Russian

---

[23] For recent examples, see Vollebæk 1998, 6; Dutch Government 2003, 1.
[24] For discussions, see, e.g., Heraclides 1993b, ch. 8; Bloed 1997.
[25] OSCE 2003.
[26] Bloed 1997.
[27] Bloed 2001; Ghebali 2001; Stefan-Bastl 2001.

government went from talk to action, refusing to discuss these issues in the preparations for the meeting, and blocking the adoption of the ministerial declaration. When the Austrian foreign minister nevertheless sought to deliver some form of summary statement, the Russian delegation dismissed this document as out of line with the understanding of all participating states and in violation of the consensus requirement.[28] The Austrian clash with Russia and the constraining effect of the consensus requirement resulted in a noticeably more careful approach on the part of the Romanian, Portuguese, and Dutch chairmanships of 2001–2003.[29]

The CiO has been delegated extensive powers of representation *vis-à-vis* other OSCE bodies, the member states, and international organizations. The representational powers of the CiO do not involve negotiations with third parties, as much as executive foreign policy action on behalf of the OSCE. The authority of the CiO as internal and external representative is regulated in formal provisions, but these tend to be enabling rather than constraining, leaving the chairmanship with important autonomy in its representational duties.

The authority to issue instructions to the OSCE's missions in conflict-laden regions is the CiO's most prominent power as internal representative. The chairmanship communicates with the missions and issues guidelines for their actions, even if the general mandates are decided in the OSCE's intergovernmental decision-making bodies. Diplomacy by the foreign minister of the government in office constitutes the central activity of the CiO as the organization's external representative. According to one estimate, about 80 percent of all international visits conducted by the Romanian foreign minister in 2000 were linked to the country's OSCE chairmanship.[30] In addition, the chairmanship has been equipped with two instruments specifically designed for external representation: personal representatives and *ad hoc* steering groups.[31] Personal representatives are appointed by the CiO and operate under its responsibility, whereas the setting up of steering groups requires consensus support.

The autonomy of the CiO as internal and external representative has been an important source of Russian discontent with the organization.[32] From Moscow's point of view, the CiO enjoys excessive discretion

---

[28] Bloed 2001, 49.
[29] *OSCE Newsletter* 2002; Zellner 2002; Dutch Government 2003.
[30] Bakker 2002, 220.
[31] Heraclides 1993b, 77–80.
[32] Ghebali 2001.

within its powers. Western governments have exploited this discretion to push the issue of human rights, with negative implications for Russia and other former socialist countries. Too often, Russia complains, CiOs have used the office to issue public statements or political directives to OSCE missions that do not reflect the whole spectrum of opinions.

Conclusion: the power of the chair in the CSCE/OSCE

Three decades of negotiations offer important evidence on the sources and effects of formal leadership in the CSCE/OSCE. The end of the Cold War divides this case into two distinct phases and makes it possible to trace how changes in the explanatory variables affect the delegation of powers to the chairmanship and the influence of negotiation chairs on political outcomes.

Cooperation in the CSCE/OSCE provides an excellent illustration of how the functional demands for agenda management, brokerage, and representation can shift over time, with direct and observable consequences in the powers and responsibilities delegated to formal leaders. In the CSCE, fraught with distrust and East–West conflict, brokerage was in strong demand. Similarly, the competing political priorities of the US and the Soviet Union created a need for agenda management. By contrast, there was no identifiable demand for representation *vis-à-vis* other bodies and institutions in this loosely institutionalized process of détente. The end of the Cold War and the transformation of the CSCE into the OSCE fundamentally changed the conditions for cooperation, the ambitions of the regime, and the demand for formal leadership. The powers of the OSCE chairmanship developed in close parallel to the expansion of the organization's activities. Brokerage remained important, but the real growth in responsibilities took place in the areas of agenda management and representation, where the chairmanship gained extensive executive powers – matching or even surpassing those of the EU Presidency.

In both the CSCE and the OSCE, the chairmanship used its powers and resources for collective gain, raising the efficiency of cooperation. Existing evidence underlines the pivotal influence of the NNA countries in the brokering of East–West compromises. Similarly, the tasks performed by the OSCE chairmanship are vital for the functioning of the regime. However, when we turn to the distributional effects of these interventions, the evidence reveals important differences between the CSCE and the OSCE. The chairmen of CSCE negotiations affected the substantive content of policy outcomes to a lesser extent than their successors in the OSCE. This pattern can be explained by variation in the factors privileged by the theory of formal leadership, especially the institutional design of the chairmanship.

In the CSCE, the formal chairmanship was designed to minimize the risk of exploitation for private gain. Whereas, theoretically, the rotation of the chairmanship could have stimulated dynamics of diffuse reciprocity, the alternation of the chairmanship on a daily basis, in effect, constituted an extreme form of control. But daily rotation hurt the chairmanship's ability to offer constructive brokerage as well, forcing the parties into an institutionalized structure of informal negotiations. Engaging in *ex ante* control, the superpowers selected the NNA countries as informal negotiation chairs. Relatively speaking, this group of states held more centrist preferences, and thus had few incentives to seek outcomes that would systematically favor either the East or the West. The requirement of consensus functioned as a form of *ex post* control, which proved particularly constraining when combined with the strongly diverging preferences of the two political blocs. In the OSCE, independent executive powers grant the governments in control of the chairmanship notable discretion in agenda management and representation, whereas the consensus rule still exerts a constraining effect on the room for maneuver in brokerage. The rotation of the chairmanship makes the varying emphasis on competing political concerns broadly acceptable to the parties, even if Russia considers itself a victim of successive campaigns by Western governments.

Formal leadership in the GATT/WTO

The global trade regime evolved from 1948 to 1994 through eight rounds of negotiations, where the participating states broadened and deepened their commitments within the General Agreement on Tariffs and Trade. The conclusion of the Uruguay Round in 1994 transformed the GATT into a proper international organization: the World Trade Organization. To a significant extent, the WTO extends negotiation and decision-making practices that have evolved gradually over five decades. Existing evidence indicates that the director general of the GATT/WTO, as chairman of the central negotiation forum, has played a key role as broker in successive trade rounds, developing single negotiation texts and engineering agreement.

The demand for formal leadership in trade negotiations

Trade round negotiations generally take place in three intergovernmental forums: ministerial conferences, the Trade Negotiations Committee

(TNC), and specialized negotiating groups.[33] The contracting parties have chosen to organize the chairmanship differently in these arenas – a feature which sets trade negotiations apart from most multilateral regimes.

Ministerial conferences are convened to initiate, review, and conclude negotiation rounds. In theory, these conferences should be sufficiently well prepared for the ministers to be able to rubber-stamp agreements prepared in pre-negotiations. In practice, however, ministerial conferences often have been devoted to last-minute negotiations on controversial issues. These meetings are chaired by the minister of the host government, who has the overall coordinating responsibility for the conference. Since little negotiation actually occurs in plenary, the role of the conference chairman tends to be one of order and procedure. Instead, most negotiation activity takes place in the working groups set up specifically for the conference. These groups are chaired by ministers appointed by the conference chairman and the director general of the GATT/WTO, in consultation with a restricted group of key parties.

The TNC is composed of the ambassadors to the GATT/WTO, and traditionally has functioned as the central coordinating body of trade rounds. The TNC decides the structure of negotiations through the creation of subsidiary working bodies, and monitors the development of the negotiations. It regularly meets throughout a trade round, and tends to constitute the forum where political trade-offs are identified and package deals stitched together. The chairmanship of this body has been delegated to the director general of the GATT/WTO. Hence, the TNC was headed by Eric Wyndham White during the Kennedy Round, Olivier Long during the Tokyo Round, Arthur Dunkel and Peter Sutherland during the Uruguay Round, and Mike Moore and Supachai Panatchpakdi during the Doha Round.

The specialized negotiating groups address specific trade rules. These groups are organized along issue divisions and comprised of state experts. Negotiations in these specialized groups tend to be very technical and complex. Formally, each group elects its own chairman among the parties. In practice, however, chairmen are selected following informal consultations between the participating states, with careful regard to

---

[33] In addition, the GATT/WTO maintains an organizational structure for everyday decision-making in between trade rounds. The chairmanship arrangements in these bodies closely resemble those set up specifically for trade rounds. Whereas each council, committee, or body formally elects its own chairman from among the parties for a period of one year, WTO rules prescribe careful regard to the balance between developed and developing countries, as well as the balance between alternative regional groupings among the developing countries.

regional power balances. In the 1950s and 1960s, the industrialized countries retained firm control over the chairmanship of all negotiating groups. With the Uruguay Round, this exclusive privilege gave way to an informal quota system, nowadays formally established, where the chairmanship of the various groups is divided between industrialized countries and developing countries.[34] In addition, the developing countries have established a quota system within their own group, rotating the chairmanships between the main regional groupings. This power-balancing system is coupled with an informal practice of not appointing states with strong interests in an issue, such as the EU and the US on agriculture, to the chairmanship of that particular negotiating group.[35]

The chairmen of trade negotiations have been engaged to perform functions of agenda management and brokerage, whereas their representational duties are highly limited. Partly, the demand for agenda management by the chairmanship is reduced by informal practices that give the US and the EU joint control over the agenda. Trade rounds generally come about on the initiative of these two parties, which also decide the areas of negotiation and fix the mandates of the negotiation groups.[36] Even if all states formally have the same right to propose negotiation themes, the US and the EU have tended to dictate the agenda. Once a trade round has been launched, however, the chairmen of the individual negotiation bodies become involved in the management of the agenda. Their formal powers include standard procedural responsibilities, such as opening and closing meetings, distributing the right to speak, deciding the order of items on the meeting agenda, and summarizing the outcome of negotiations. Yet, in addition, GATT/WTO chairs can draw on a range of informal practices, enabling them to control the process and shape the agenda.[37] The presence of large numbers of competing proposals tends to create a demand for interventions aimed at creating a negotiable agenda. GATT/WTO chairmen typically seek to improve the chances of productive negotiations by keeping sensitive issues off the agenda and placing less conflict-ridden issues at the forefront of the agenda, thus creating momentum in the negotiations.

The large number of negotiating parties, the competing interests of the two dominant trading powers, and the consensus requirement together create a strong demand for brokerage. This explains why GATT/WTO chairmen in general, and the chairman of the TNC in particular,

---

[34] Sjöstedt 1994, 62.
[35] Interview, Swedish government representative, 22 May 2003.
[36] Winham 1992, 54–55; Sjöstedt 1994, 54–55.
[37] Odell 2005; interview, Swedish government official, 22 May 2003.

have been given a central role in this area.[38] The horizontal perspective of the TNC makes the director general well placed to function as broker and package-deal engineer. In his mediation activities, the director general enjoys access to particular procedural and informational resources. The director general may convene so-called Green Room meetings – informal negotiation sessions between a restricted number of key parties under the chairmanship of the director general.[39] Participation in the Green Room varies by issue, but has increased over time, from less than eight delegations during the Tokyo Round to twenty or more delegations during the Doha Round. Once a deal has been reached in the Green Room, it is submitted to all parties for acceptance, which usually involves few problems, since the states with the most intense interests in an issue should have been invited to the informal negotiations. Furthermore, the director general can initiate bilateral consultations with recalcitrant parties, in order to sound out concerns, identify bottom lines, and test potential compromise solutions. Finally, the GATT/WTO Secretariat assists the chairmanship by providing both privileged information about the parties' positions and potential bottom lines, and technical expertise in the often highly complex dossiers under negotiation.[40]

The representational function of GATT/WTO chairmen is limited or even non-existent. The various bodies do not engage in negotiations with each other, and are therefore not in need of chairmen with representational duties. Even if GATT/WTO chairmen possess certain reporting functions within the internal negotiation machinery, these do not comprise the power to speak or negotiate on behalf of others. Rather, the chairmen of the specialized negotiation groups forward reports to the TNC, where state representatives subsequently attempt to hammer out cross-cutting package deals. In its relations with non-members and other international organizations, the GATT/WTO is represented by the director general, acting in his capacity as head of the Secretariat, rather than as chairman of the TNC.

The supply of formal leadership in trade negotiations

Existing research on the Kennedy, Tokyo, Uruguay, and Doha Rounds speaks of the political importance of formal leadership in trade negotiations, especially through the brokerage efforts of the TNC chairman.

---

[38] Odell 2005.
[39] E.g., Hampson with Hart 1995; 191–192; Schott and Watal 2000, 285–286; Hoekman and Kostecki 2001, 60–61; Moore 2003, 128–129.
[40] Hoekman and Kostecki 2001, 54–55; Sjöstedt 2002, 150.

Maneuvering in a strategic context shaped by US and EU preferences, successive director generals have undertaken informal consultations, identified resistance points, constructed compromise texts, and engineered agreement on contentious trade issues. These activities have raised the efficiency of the negotiations, but there is little evidence of systematic effects on distributional outcomes.

In the Kennedy Round (1964–1967), Director General Wyndham White made pivotal contributions to the negotiations, characterized by US–EC confrontation.[41] In his efforts to achieve progress and guide the negotiations toward conclusion, Wyndham White effectively used the chairman's arsenal of procedural and informational resources. "The GATT Secretariat was an excellent example of organizational mediation in the Kennedy Round. One reason was because the top leadership at the GATT Secretariat set about quite consciously to force an instrument that could service multilateral negotiations. This plan involved both technical and political components."[42] The TNC chairman helped the parties out of deadlocked negotiations by proposing a reorganization of the talks into specific working groups. The GATT Secretariat collected and communicated information on domestic political constraints and resistance points that helped the parties to escape negotiation failure and to identify a zone of agreement. When negotiations stalled from lack of realistic proposals, Wyndham White took initiatives in the formal and informal groups to restart the talks. In sum, "[t]he political function of the Secretariat at the Kennedy Round was essential to communicating structural problems to the adversaries and to engage in 'trouble-shooting.' . . . Trouble-shooting by the mediator at the Kennedy Round entailed monitoring the process of consensus building to guard against bottlenecks and any de-escalation of concessions."[43]

Just like the Kennedy Round, the Tokyo Round (1973–1979) revolved around the US–EC relationship. Negotiations were pyramidal: everything hinged on then two main adversaries reaching an agreement, which would then extend to the other parties. Yet, unlike in the Kennedy Round, the GATT director general in these negotiations, Olivier Long, is not given a prominent role in accounts of the Tokyo Round. This is partly explained by the absence of a zone of agreement during the first part of the negotiations, rendering third-party brokerage futile, and a readily identifiable zone of agreement during the latter part of the

---

[41] Preeg 1970; Winham 1979.
[42] Winham 1979, 197.
[43] Winham 1979, 197–198.

negotiations, making third-party brokerage redundant.[44] Another explanation, compatible with the first, is Long's personal preference for the US and the EU to settle their differences in informal bilateral negotiations, without interventions from the director general.[45] Needless to say, Long could only afford this approach if the two main parties were capable of identifying a zone of agreement on their own. Instead, analyses of the negotiations point to the leadership exercised by the US trade representative Robert Strauss.[46] The negotiations began in 1973, but real progress was only achieved after the election of Jimmy Carter as US president in 1976. The change in administration led to a shift in US preferences and the opening of a zone of agreement between the two adversaries. Strauss was the leading communicator of the new American approach, but also initiated bilateral or multilateral encounters between the dominant trading powers, which helped remove logjams and led to crucial political trade-offs.

With the Uruguay Round (1986–1994), the character of global trade negotiations underwent important changes. Compared to previous rounds, the Uruguay Round was considerably more complex, involving more issues and parties. The magnitude of the agenda brought a high degree of compartmentalization to the negotiations, which first were divided across fifteen specialized groups. Even if the US and the EC remained the most central actors, more parties were closely involved in the negotiations, not least the developing countries, which led to a shift from pyramidal negotiations to coalition negotiations.[47] Accounts of the Uruguay Round generally attribute the influential role of TNC chairman Arthur Dunkel to this complexity and the demand it created for agenda management and brokerage.[48]

While playing a central part in the negotiations from the start of the round in 1986, Dunkel's contribution was particularly important on two occasions, when it saved the negotiations from collapse. At the mid-term review in Montreal in December 1988, divisions between the US and the EC on agricultural liberalization caused a breakdown of the ministerial conference. Strengthened by a ministerial mandate to suggest ways forward, over the next four months Dunkel engaged in intense discussions with the parties, meeting bilaterally in the capitals or minilaterally

---

[44] Winham 1986.
[45] Hampson with Hart 1995, 191.
[46] See, especially, Winham 1986.
[47] Winham 1992, 54–55; Sjöstedt 1994.
[48] Sjöstedt 1994; Underdal 1994; Hampson with Hart 1995, chs. 7–8; Paemen and Bensch 1995.

in the Green Room. In April 1988, Dunkel felt confident that the deadlock could be broken and convened the TNC, which approved the mid-term review package. Yet the restarted negotiations soon ran into new problems and produced the second major breakdown of the Uruguay Round, this time at the ministerial conference in Brussels in December 1990, which had been scheduled to conclude the negotiations. As in 1988, agriculture constituted the major stumbling block.

Again, Dunkel was charged with undertaking intensive consultations and reconvening the process in his capacity as TNC chairman. To create a negotiation structure where political trade-offs more easily could be identified, Dunkel reduced the number of specialized groups from fifteen to eight, and eventually to four. Furthermore, the TNC chairman engaged in consultations with the key delegations and the chairs of the specialized negotiation groups, on the basis of which he developed a single negotiating text. For the remainder of the Uruguay Round, the negotiations centered on the so-called Dunkel draft and revised versions of this text, which eventually formed the backbone of the final act. Dunkel himself was intimately involved in the molding of this text into an endorsable document, initiating informal consultations, sounding out concerns, and revising paragraphs. Dunkel's brokerage efforts provided the necessary platform for his successor Peter Sutherland to pressure the parties to an eventual agreement in December 1993.

The launch of the Doha Round provides a final illustration of the supply of formal leadership in trade negotiations. The original intention had been to launch the new trade round in Seattle in late 1999, but the ministerial conference collapsed. This failure was followed by a second attempt in Doha in November 2001, when the impasse was broken and negotiations initiated. Comparative analysis of these two cases suggests that shifts in the preferences of the major players and in the supply of brokerage constitute the decisive factors explaining the variation in outcomes.[49] Since the TNC is first convened once a trade round has been initiated, the major responsibility for brokering an agreement rested with the chair of the WTO General Council, rather than the director general and future TNC chairman, Mike Moore.

The Seattle negotiations were marked by the strikingly divergent positions of the US and the EU, which were unable to agree on a negotiation platform before the meeting and failed to achieve approximation at the actual conference. It is uncertain whether skillful brokerage could have bridged this gap and unveiled a previously unrecognized

---

[49] Odell 2003; interview, Swedish government official, 22 May 2003.

zone of agreement. Yet it is certain that the mediation efforts undertaken by the chair of the General Council, Ali Mchumo of Tanzania, did little to help – a paradoxical illustration of the chair's importance for the efficiency of multilateral negotiations. In the lead-up to Seattle, Mchumo managed to encourage rather than overcome conflict, when presenting a compilation of competing positions as the basis for negotiation. Instead of producing a single negotiating text, Mchumo included rival texts advanced by contending groups, which exacerbated the stand-off and proved counterproductive.

Key factors changed between Seattle and Doha, making agreement possible. The EU and the new US administration stepped back from some of their previous demands, as did the increasingly influential group of developing countries. For most parties, the alternative of a second failure and possible deathblow to the WTO was less attractive than the deals negotiations potentially could produce. Simultaneously, the chair of the General Council, Stuart Harbinson of Hong Kong, together with Director General Mike Moore, engaged in intense brokerage efforts, meeting informally with delegations, sounding out concerns and testing resistance points. In September 2001, Harbinson presented a true single negotiating text – his best approximation of what could be achieved in Doha. This text was subsequently revised in response to reactions from the parties, and eventually formed the backbone of the Doha ministerial declaration, whose structure and language in many respects was identical to Harbinson's draft.

Conclusion: the power of the chair in the GATT/WTO

Negotiations in the GATT/WTO present us with quite stable patterns over successive negotiation rounds. The evidence is broadly conformant with the expectations generated by the theory of formal leadership.

The chairmanship of the various negotiation bodies in the GATT/WTO has been delegated basic responsibilities of agenda management and extensive informal powers of brokerage, but no specific role in representation. This pattern reflects variation in functional demands in the global trade regime. Whereas the US and the EU engage in pre-negotiations that define the general areas of negotiation, GATT/WTO chairmen carry the responsibility for preparing negotiable agendas within their respective groups. The competing interests of the main parties to trade negotiations – the US, the EU, and since the 1980s, the developing countries – have created a strong demand for third-party intervention and led the parties to engage GATT/WTO chairmen as brokers. By contrast, the representational responsibilities are highly limited, reflecting the absence of internal bargaining between negotiating groups and the fulfillment of certain external representation tasks by the director general of the organization.

Accounts of the four most recent negotiation rounds paint a very similar picture of the influence exerted by GATT/WTO chairmen over the efficiency and distributional effects of these trade talks. Brokerage by the chairman of the TNC, and on one occasion by the chair of the General Council, has been pivotal in stitching together package agreements that can secure unanimous adoption by the parties. The director general has usually made effective use of the privileged resources of the TNC chairmanship, calling informal negotiation sessions in the Green Room, conducting bilateral talks to unveil bottom lines, and developing single negotiating texts around which bargaining can converge. The one case where such influence is not discernible – the Tokyo Round – is best explained by the futility of brokerage during the first phase of the negotiations, and the fact that brokerage became redundant once the Carter administration had assumed office.

Existing accounts further testify to the absence of clear effects on the distributional dimension of the negotiated trade agreements. The cleavage between the US and the EU, coupled with the requirement of consensus, has significantly limited the discretion of GATT/WTO chairmen. Yet equally important is the institutional design of the chairmanship. In those organs where state representatives are elected to the chairmanship, the parties have been careful to introduce informal power-balancing practices and consciously avoid appointing states with particularly strong interests in the issues under negotiation, thus reducing the risk of exploitation. Whereas the parties have not established unusually intrusive control mechanisms *vis-à-vis* the chairman of the TNC, as the supranational design of this office would lead us to expect, the risk of systematic effects on distributional outcome still appears relatively small, potentially explaining the absence of control instruments. Just like the strongest preference of the European Commission is deeper integration, the overarching objective of the GATT/WTO Secretariat is "more free trade." For the TNC chairman, this goal translates into a preoccupation with process – keeping negotiation rounds on track – whereas the particular distributional implications of liberalization for the EU, the US, or developing countries is accorded less weight.

Formal leadership in UN environmental negotiations

Three of the most central environmental negotiations over the last thirty years are the negotiations on the law of the sea (1973–1982), the ozone convention and protocol (1982–1987), and the climate change convention (1991–1992). In all cases, the negotiations were led by chairmen drawn from the participating states. Existing accounts point to the central importance of these chairmen as brokers in the three negotiation processes. Making effective use of the control over procedure and the access to privileged information, the conference chairs created negotiation conditions conducive to agreement and developed single negotiating texts. At the same time, the combination of widely diverging state preferences and the requirement of consensus restricted the chairs' room for maneuver and capacity to favor certain outcomes rather than others.

Formal leadership in the law of the sea negotiations

The most central environmental negotiation of the 1970s and early 1980s was the Third United Nations Conference on the Law of the Sea (UNCLOS III), which followed up on previous efforts to regulate the exploitation of seas and seabeds. The LOS conference was convened in 1973, and over the next decade it met in eleven official sessions, before the new convention was adopted in 1982. The formal negotiation structure of the conference consisted of the plenary, four committees, and subsidiary negotiation groups. The chairmanship was organized in the same way at all three levels. Negotiation chairs were drawn from the group of state representatives and elected for the duration of the conference. Following the informal principle of geographical balance, the posts were divided between the main regional groupings. The representative of Sri Lanka headed the conference until his death in 1980, when the representative of Singapore took over the presidency. The committees were chaired by the representatives of Cameroon, Venezuela, Bulgaria, and Canada. Similarly, the chairmanship of the subsidiary negotiation groups was distributed between the different regional groupings in a roughly even way. The states with the most intense and extreme interests in the negotiations were not appointed to chair any of the formal negotiation groups.[50]

The chairmen of the LOS negotiations were engaged to perform extensive agenda-management and brokerage activities, in response to clear and identifiable functional demands in the negotiation process. At the outset, no powers beyond the standard procedural responsibilities had been delegated to the chairmen of the various negotiation organs. Yet, over the course of the negotiations, the parties endowed

---

[50] Koh and Jayakumar 1985.

the negotiation chairs with more substantive political responsibilities, notably, the power to draft a single negotiation text and broker agreement around revised versions of this text. Existing accounts of these negotiations unanimously emphasize the contribution of the conference chairs as a crucial factor in the process toward agreement.[51]

The functional demand for agenda management stemmed primarily from the absence of a preparatory negotiation text.[52] The United Nations Sea-Bed Committee, charged with preparing the conference, had not been able to agree on a joint document. Instead, the committee submitted a report consisting of hundreds of individual proposals and draft articles. The complexity increased further when new proposals and documents were presented at the second session of the conference, when negotiations on substantive matters were scheduled to begin. The lack of a single preparatory text had clear adverse effects on the negotiations, which did not get off the ground. At the third session of the conference, the parties delegated to the committee chairmen the task of developing single negotiating texts within their respective domains. Two participants in the negotiations explicitly point to agenda failure as the explanation for why the negotiating parties surrendered their own agenda-setting powers:

> An intriguing question is: what is the rationale underlying the willingness of the majority of the delegations to confer such an important task on three individuals. We consider this to be an intriguing question because the three Chairmen were representatives of States each having its own national interests. Furthermore, despite the caveat that the text would be informal and that it would be a negotiating and not a negotiated text, most delegations anticipated that the text would have a special significance. Perhaps the main explanation was the sheer frustration of most delegations over the cumbersome and unproductive procedures then operating.[53]

The single negotiating text was presented at the end of the third session and accepted as the basis for the negotiations. With the tabling of this text, the function of the conference chairmen shifted from that of developing a negotiable agenda to that of brokering agreement on the basis of this document. At the fourth session of conference, the parties conferred the power to revise the original text to the conference president and the committee chairmen. The single negotiating text underwent a total of seven revisions during the remainder of the LOS

---

[51] Sebenius 1984; Koh and Jayakumar 1985; Antrim and Sebenius 1992.
[52] Koh and Jayakumar 1985; Antrim and Sebenius 1992.
[53] Koh and Jayakumar 1985, 115–116. The chairmen referred to are those of the three specialized committees, dealing with the substantive work of the negotiations.

conference.[54] The revision process consisted of a number of stages, where the negotiation chairs first collected responses in formal meetings, informal negotiations, and bilateral consultations, before revising the text in the group of chairmen. The conference president and the committee chairmen emerged as central political actors, courted and cajoled by delegations wishing to affect the process of text revision. As Lance Antrim and James Sebenius explain: "Responsibility for issuing new versions of the negotiating text added a significant new power to the limited authority of the presiding officer. The authority to revise the draft text was, in effect, the power to define the issues to be addressed in the negotiation process."[55]

Existing research on the LOS negotiations specifically points to the brokerage efforts of Ambassador Tommy Koh of Singapore, first as chairman of the negotiation group on financial arrangements, and then as president of the overall conference from March 1981 until its conclusion.[56] Before the negotiating group on financial issues was created by the conference chairmanship in 1978, no progress had been achieved in this area. The negotiations were characterized by extreme proposals, an adversarial air of mutual suspicion, and ideological clashes on the merits of regulation versus market forces. The convergence of state positions on an acceptable text over the next three years is generally attributed to Koh's brokerage strategies. Making effective use of his procedural arsenal, Koh established his own informal secretariat charged with collecting information and drafting new proposals, hot-housed the talks by progressively restricting the size of the negotiating group, created a broadly accepted formula for the negotiations by incorporating a financial model developed by US researchers, and linked the two main issues in the negotiations to each other, thus creating a potential zone of agreement.

There is less evidence to suggest that the influential chairmen of the conference exploited their position to move the negotiations toward a particular distributional outcome. There are several explanations for this, largely conformant with the theory of formal leadership. First, the states whose representatives were appointed to chair the main negotiation forums held relatively weak and central preferences, which gave these chairmen few incentives to systematically favor certain outcomes. Second, the four main negotiation chairs – representing four different

---

[54] Antrim and Sebenius 1992, 101.
[55] Antrim and Sebenius 1992, 101.
[56] Raiffa 1982, ch. 18; Sebenius 1984; Antrim and Sebenius 1992; Rubin 1993.

regional groupings – drafted the single negotiating text together, thus reducing the room for an individual chair to favor specific regional interests. Third, it was difficult to identify a zone of agreement in the first place, never mind selecting one efficient outcome over another. In fact, it proved impossible in the end to get all parties on board, with the effect that some parties refrained from adopting the convention. Fourth and finally, in those few cases where negotiation chairs sought to steer the negotiations to their own advantage, the aggrieved parties used the "nuclear option" of threatening to leave the negotiations and to reduce the powers of the conference chairs.[57]

Formal leadership in the ozone negotiations

The most comprehensive environmental negotiation of the 1980s was the talks leading to the adoption of the Vienna Convention for the Protection of the Ozone Layer in 1985 and the Montreal Protocol on Substances that Deplete the Ozone Layer in 1987. The negotiations took place within the ambit of the United Nations Environmental Programme (UNEP), where an *ad hoc* working group of legal and technical experts was set up in 1982 with the mandate of preparing an ozone convention. After three years of negotiations, this group reached an agreement on a framework convention. Following the adoption of the convention, the parties initiated negotiations on a protocol that would lay down specific obligations with legally binding targets and control measures. In September 1987, the Montreal Protocol was signed by twenty-five states, including all the major producers of chloro-fluorocarbons (CFCs).

The structure of the two rounds conformed to a format generally used by the UNEP in treaty negotiations.[58] The work in the negotiating group began with an inventory of the issues under debate and an exchange of proposals and ideas. On this basis, the UNEP Secretariat prepared a draft text, which then was negotiated by the parties with the aim of reaching consensus on as many parts as possible. The process culminated with a diplomatic conference, where ministers negotiated the outstanding issues and adopted the final text. The formal control of the

---

[57] The chairman from Cameroon created a crisis in 1977 when altering a compromise text in favor of the developing countries. The US and other industrialized countries declared the text unacceptable and only returned to the negotiations once changes in the text and in the powers of the committee chairmen had been agreed. See Koh and Jayakumar 1985, 64–65; Antrim and Sebenius 1992, 104.

[58] Széll 1993, 40–43.

proceedings rested with the chair, elected among state representatives for the period leading up to the diplomatic conference, when a representative of the host country held the chairmanship. In the ozone negotiations, Austrian diplomat Winfried Lang was appointed to chair the Vienna conference in 1985, and subsequently kept this position until the conclusion of the negotiations in Montreal in 1987. The chairman was supported by a bureau, consisting of two vice-chairs and a *rapporteur*, elected to ensure a balanced geographical distribution.

Accounts of the ozone negotiations testify to a demand by the parties for agenda management and brokerage, supplied jointly by the chairmanship and UNEP executive director Mustafa Tolba.[59] In addition, the US and several smaller states – New Zealand and the Nordic countries – pushed the negotiations forward and helped the parties transcend bargaining impasses at crucial stages of the process.

The negotiations on the Vienna Convention were heavily shaped by the diverging preferences of two groups of industrialized countries: the Toronto Group, consisting of Canada, the United States, Sweden, Finland, Norway, and Australia, advocating large-scale reductions of ozone-harming substances; and the EC, opposing production cuts in the present while envisaging limits in the future. Whereas the parties could agree on the need for a convention, they presented competing proposals on the precise obligations. The chairman of the Vienna conference sought to achieve approximation through informal consultations, the creation of small drafting groups, and revisions designed to make the obligations more flexible.[60] In the end, however, Lang was forced to recognize that agreement on the precise commitments was beyond reach, placing the bulk of the blame on EC reluctance.

The decision to initiate a second round of negotiations, for the purpose of developing specific obligations in a protocol, was the result of an initiative from the Toronto Group. Yet this decision did not reflect an actual convergence in the positions of the two camps. Little progress was achieved at the first and second negotiating sessions in December 1986 and February 1987.[61] As US chief negotiator Richard Benedick testifies: "The negotiations for the Montreal Protocol opened chaotically with several conflicting proposals on the table."[62] The Toronto Group and the EC stuck to their original positions, and efforts by chairman Lang to

---

[59] Benedick 1991, chs. 6, 7; Széll 1993; Hampson with Hart 1995, ch. 9; Tolba 1998, ch. 5; Wettestad 2002.
[60] Széll 1993, 42; Tolba 1998, 61.
[61] Benedick 1991, 68–71; Hampson with Hart 1995, 261–262; Tolba 1998, 68–70.
[62] Benedick 1993, 239.

focus the negotiations through a paper on control measures did not succeed in producing convergence between the parties.

The third session produced a breakthrough in the negotiations, following joint brokerage efforts by the UNEP executive director and the conference chairman.[63] For the first time in the negotiations, Tolba and Lang organized small closed meetings in a group of key representatives, called "Friends of the Chairman." Membership in this informal negotiating group reflected a combination of a country's weight in the CFC market, its interest in the ozone issue, and geographical balance. The format of this group had its desired effect: "Working in secrecy on an unofficial text enabled representatives to negotiate with more flexibility, since they did not in this process commit their governments to any particular formulation."[64] The group managed to produce a single negotiating text, labeled Tolba's personal text, which was greeted with considerable support when presented to the broader group of negotiating parties.

Tolba's text became the basis for the remainder of the negotiations, even if important disagreements remained. When the parties convened in Montreal, several issues were still outstanding. The Friends of the Chairman negotiated in closed, informal sessions, directed by Tolba and Lang, but had not been able to agree on a protocol when the diplomatic conference opened. To prevent ministers from establishing positions they would be unable to surrender at a later point, Lang adjourned the official plenary meeting immediately after his own and Tolba's opening statements, instead convening the informal negotiating group.[65] On the second day of suspended official proceedings, but fierce informal negotiations, the US and the EC eventually reached the compromise that delivered the new treaty.

The ozone negotiations point to the complementarity of alternative leaders in multilateral bargaining. Multiple competing proposals and the absence of an observable zone of agreement created a strong demand for agenda management and brokerage. These services were provided jointly by the UNEP Secretariat and the chairman. Existing accounts suggest that Tolba was pivotal in the forging of a single negotiating text and in moving the discussions forward through the invention of novel solutions to seemingly intractable problems. Lang, for his part, exploited the procedural instruments of the chairman to create

[63] Benedick 1991, 71–72; Hampson with Hart 1995, 262–263; Tolba 1998, 70–71.
[64] Benedick 1993, 72.
[65] Tolba 1998, 72.

framework conditions conducive to constructive negotiations, and played an active part next to Tolba in the hammering out of compromises at the end stage. While providing extensive evidence of the efficiency-enhancing effects of these interventions, accounts of these negotiations do not point to systematic distributional effects. This may be explained by the limited room for choice between multiple equilibria, given the competing perspectives of the US and the EU and the requirement of unanimity. But, in addition, neither Tolba nor Lang represented a party with strong distributional interests in the negotiations, the UNEP Secretariat was mainly concerned with the reaching of an agreement, and Austria was standing outside the two contending camps.

Formal leadership in the climate change negotiations

The negotiations leading to the United Nations Framework Convention on Climate Change (UNFCCC) in 1992 dominated global environmental policy-making in the early 1990s. The negotiations in the Intergovernmental Negotiating Committee (INC) commenced in February 1991 and were conducted under the auspices of the UN General Assembly. The INC held a total of six negotiation rounds over 16 months, before the UNFCCC was adopted unanimously by the participating states in May 1992 and referred to the Earth summit in Rio de Janeiro for signature.

The negotiations were structured in a plenary and two working groups, whose chairmen were state representatives elected for the duration of the negotiations. French representative Jean Ripert was elected chairman of the general negotiating group. Next to Ripert, the bureau consisted of four vice-chairs, drawn from four different regional groups in an effort to achieve geographical balance. At the final stages of the negotiations, Ripert extended the bureau on several occasions and developed this body into a proper negotiation forum. The conflict between industrialized and developing countries on climate change translated into an arrangement of dual chairs for the two workshops, where the first was co-chaired by the representatives of Japan and Mexico and the second by the representatives of Canada and Vanuatu. The chairs were assisted by an *ad hoc* secretariat set up specifically for the negotiations. The INC Secretariat initially sought an independent role and presented a preliminary negotiating text, but met with state disapproval and later confined itself to supporting the chairs through information on government positions and preferences.[66]

---

[66] Djoghlaf 1994, 103–104.

Broad disagreements between industrialized and developing countries, as well as among the industrialized states, translated into a distinct demand for agenda management and brokerage. Accounts of the negotiations indicate that Ripert and the chairs of the working groups acted on this demand, providing single negotiating texts, convening informal negotiation forums, and conducting bilateral consultations.[67]

The initiation of the negotiations in February 1991 was dominated by conflict over procedural questions, such as the selection of chairs, the size of the bureau, and the establishment of working groups, which functioned as a surrogate for real bargaining in the divisive substantive issues. At the second session, substantive negotiations finally got under way. Working group I focused on the principles for a climate change convention, minimum commitments, as well as technology transfer and financial assistance. Working group II dealt with legal and institutional mechanisms related to decision-making, scientific cooperation, and financial and technological cooperation. In working group II, the parties sought to create a firmer basis for the negotiations by authorizing the two co-chairs to prepare a single negotiating text on the basis of existing submissions. Working group I followed this example at the second session, once it became clear that compilations of competing proposals did not provide a sound basis for bargaining, whereas the negotiations in working group II advanced well, guided by a single negotiating text that "helped to explore various concepts and options, concretize discussions, and elicit specific proposals from delegations for possible draft articles. Although discussions were not intended to be a drafting exercise, they did, in fact become that, with line-by-line reviews of the text."[68]

The fourth negotiating session produced minimal progress, but intensive negotiations finally got under way with the fifth session. The working-group co-chairs managed to accelerate the negotiations by encouraging the formation of specific contact groups. Yet the differences between the parties remained strong on several core issues, and the session ended with the distribution of a new version of the single negotiating text, saturated with bracketed text and alternative formulations. The requirement of consensus gave all participating states a veto, and this was reflected in the slow progress of the negotiations.[69]

---

[67] Benedick 1993; Mintzer and Leonard 1994; Hampson with Hart 1995, ch. 11.
[68] Hampson with Hart 1995, 320.
[69] Bodansky 2001, 31–34.

Existing accounts unanimously point to the intervention of conference chairman Ripert after the fifth session as the turning point in the negotiations.[70] Recognizing the difficulties involved in negotiating an agreement among all participating states on the basis of the existing consolidated draft, Ripert convened an informal meeting of a group of about twenty key delegations, denoted the "expanded bureau." This group achieved progress on certain key issues. More importantly, however, it authorized Ripert to develop his own compromise text, devoid of brackets and options, for the concluding session. Following informal, bilateral consultations with the key bargaining parties, Ripert prepared a draft convention that constituted his best approximation of a potential agreement.

The parties welcomed Ripert's draft convention as a balanced compromise product, and adopted it as the basis of negotiation. At the concluding session, the chairmanship restructured the formal negotiations in three "cluster groups," each of which reviewed specific portions of the draft text. Simultaneously, Ripert engaged in informal, bilateral consultations with key parties, which helped settle outstanding differences between industrialized and developing countries on a number of matters, notably the objectives and principles of the convention. Once the review work in the cluster groups had been concluded, the chair met in closed sessions with the expanded bureau to prepare a revised text. The parties eventually reached an agreement on a text broadly reflecting Ripert's draft convention. The UNFCCC was adopted by consensus and signed by nearly all UN member states at the Earth summit in Rio de Janeiro.

The climate change negotiations provide an excellent illustration of the causal processes by which chairmen are attributed a central function in multilateral negotiations and can help states toward efficient agreements. In these negotiations, the parties held widely divergent preferences and showed a reluctance to compromise and achieve approximation on their own. The absence of an identifiable zone of agreement created a strong demand for single negotiating texts, informal consultations, and third-party brokerage. Gradually, the participating states conferred more extensive powers on the chairs of the working groups and the conference chairman. Once he had been given the power to develop a draft convention, Ripert took much-needed initiatives that succeeded in propelling the negotiations toward agreement. Existing

---

[70] Bodansky 1994; Borione and Ripert 1994; Djoghlaf 1994; Dowdeswell and Kinley 1994; Hampson with Hart 1995, 329–332, 408.

accounts unanimously underline the importance of Ripert's procedural maneuvering and draft convention for the deal that eventually came about. By contrast, there is less evidence to suggest that the chairmen of the negotiations enjoyed the room for maneuver required to affect distributional outcomes. The system of co-chairs constituted an instrument of mutual control, enabling industrialized and developing countries to keep a check on each other. Furthermore, the combination of diverging preferences and the consensus rule reduced the zone of agreement and the chairmen's possibilities to choose from alternative equilibria.

Conclusion: the power of the chair at UN environmental conferences

The negotiations on the law of the sea, the ozone accords, and the climate change convention display important similarities with regard to the role and influence of negotiation chairs. The theory of formal leadership can help us understand these patterns.

The format of large multilateral conferences on divisive environmental issues created strong functional pressures for agenda management and brokerage by conference chairs, but no demand for representation *vis-à-vis* other international actors. The combination of broad conference mandates and equal agenda-setting rights for all parties produced overcrowded negotiation agendas, swamped by competing proposals. In all cases, the risk of agenda failure led the participating states to endow the conference chairmanship with important agenda-management powers, especially the authority to structure the negotiations through the development of single negotiating texts. Yet the most central function of the chairmanship in these three environmental negotiations was brokerage. The large number of participants, the broad spectrum of preferences, and the requirement of consensus made it exceedingly difficult for the parties to identify a zone of agreement on their own. The engagement of the conference chairmen as brokers was the parties' favored solution to escape deadlock and produce progress.

The three cases generate consistent observations on the influence of negotiation chairs. Existing accounts testify to positive effects on the efficiency of the negotiations, while offering little evidence of outcomes systematically being biased in particular distributional directions. As agenda managers and brokers, the conference chairs transformed the wealth of competing proposals into negotiable core texts, created negotiation conditions conducive for compromises and concessions, encouraged the parties to unveil their bottom lines in confidential talks, discovered issue-linkages, and engineered package agreements. This observation is supported by the findings in a recent comparative volume, which concludes that the involvement of negotiation chairs tends to produce better and more effective environmental agreements.[71] The absence of evidence on distributional influence is best explained by the decision rule, the preference distribution, and the institutional design of the chairmanship. The same unfavorable conditions that created a pressure for brokerage – highly divergent preferences and the demanding requirement of consensus – also made it exceedingly difficult for formal leaders to steer the negotiations toward outcomes they privately preferred. Merely identifying a zone of agreement posed a challenge, and the possibility to select one efficient outcome rather than another oftentimes did not exist. The institutional design of the chairmanship simultaneously worked to limit the likelihood of exploitation. Typically, the overall conference chairman was selected from a country with weak preferences in the negotiations. In addition, the chairmanships of subsidiary bodies were either distributed to ensure regional power balance, or divided between two co-chairs that represented alternative interest constellations.

Conclusion

Is the EU the only international organization with negotiation chairs that wield power and influence outcomes or is it a general phenomenon in international cooperation? This chapter has considered evidence from multilateral negotiations in the areas of security, trade, and environment. It generates a distinct answer to this question: the influence that the EU Presidency has is not an exceptional phenomenon, only a particularly illustrative example of the power of the chair. The three areas of multilateral cooperation explored in this chapter demonstrate that states commonly delegate important political functions to the chairmanship, and that negotiation chairs frequently use their privileged resources to influence the efficiency and distributional implications of negotiated outcomes. At the same time, this chapter presents us with notable variation across the three cases in the kinds of powers delegated to the chairmanship and the form of influence exerted by negotiation chairs.

The comparative evidence endorses the argument that states empower formal leaders to overcome bargaining problems that prevent efficient exchange and collective gain. States have not adopted a standardized model of delegation, but have custom-fitted the powers of the chairmanship to the requirements of efficient international cooperation. Where

---

[71] Miles *et al.* 2002.

clear and identifiable functional demands for agenda management, brokerage, or representation exist, states have conferred such powers on the chairmanship. By the same token, states have abstained from delegating responsibilities to the chairmanship where functional needs are absent.

The comparative record further speaks to the chairmanship as a powerful position in multilateral negotiations, enabling the actors in control of this position to influence the efficiency, and to a lesser extent the distributional implications, of international cooperation. In the three areas of negotiation covered in this chapter, the functions of agenda management and brokerage constituted the most pronounced channels of influence. Making effective use of informational and procedural power resources, negotiation chairs in all three areas helped states toward agreements they otherwise might not have reached. Yet, with the exception of the OSCE, the influence of negotiation chairs was limited to effects on the efficiency of interstate bargaining. The capacity of negotiation chairs to influence the distribution of gains from agreements was constrained by the prevalent combination of highly divergent preferences and the requirement of consensus decision-making. In addition, the comparison confirms the importance of the institutional design of the chairmanship for the likelihood of exploitation and systematic effects on distributional outcomes.

8 Conclusion

The chairmanship is a generic feature of political decision-making, whether at local, national, or international level. In city councils, parliamentary committees, and multilateral institutions, chairmen facilitate and influence decision-making by managing the agenda, brokering agreement, and representing the decision body *vis-à-vis* external parties. In many cases, the institution of the chairmanship is itself an object of contention. Political parties compete for formal control of legislative committees, and states struggle over the right to appoint the chairmen of multilateral conferences and international organizations. Indeed, this phenomenon extends beyond the political domain, to decision-making in other areas of social organization, from company boards to university departments and local associations.

Yet, so far, political scientists have been slow to ask and answer the kind of questions motivated by these observations. Influenced by the game-theoretical heritage of the field, students of negotiation and decision-making have tended to treat bargaining parties as functionally and formally equivalent, thus leaving little theoretical space for formal leaders with asymmetrical control over the nature of the game. In this book, I have sought to remedy this lack of attention to formal leadership in existing research. Developing and testing a rationalist theory of formal leadership, this book offers answers to three questions of general interest: Why is the institution of the chairmanship a universal feature of political decision bodies? What are the power resources of formal leaders? When, why, and how do negotiation chairs wield influence over political outcomes?

The theory explains the delegation of process powers to the chairmanship as a functional response to collective-action problems in decentralized bargaining, identifies asymmetrical access to information and asymmetrical control over negotiation procedure as the most central power resources of formal leaders, and suggests that opportunistic chairs will use these privileged resources for both collective and private gain. Empirically, I have assessed the explanatory power of this theory through an in-depth study of negotiations in the EU, as well as comparative observations from international regimes in the areas of trade, security, and environment. The evidence strongly supports an understanding of the chairmanship as a power platform in multilateral decision-making, enabling formal leaders to shape the outcomes of international negotiations.

This concluding chapter summarizes the book's empirical findings, identifies its implications for the study of EU politics, and isolates its consequences for theories of international negotiation and cooperation.

Summary of the empirical findings

The empirical examination of the EU Presidency generated evidence on the demand for, and supply of, formal leadership in the EU. This section summarizes the principal empirical conclusions on each of these issues. In addition, it provides a preliminary assessment of the explanatory power of sociological institutionalism, which offers contending hypotheses on the key analytical concerns of this book. The reliability of these findings is secured by the methodological strategy of the study, involving a historical mapping of the development of the office of the Presidency across three parallel negotiation arenas, as well as an assessment of the influence of individual Presidencies through a set of six carefully chosen case studies, offering process tracing and counterfactual analysis.

The demand for formal leadership

In Chapter 3, I set out to test the functionalist claim about the origin of the chairmanship as an institutional form in negotiation and decision-making. According to the theory of formal leadership, we would expect states to confer powers of process control to the chairmanship in response to three collection-action problems in decentralized bargaining: agenda failure, negotiation failure, and representation failure. The process powers delegated to the chairmanship were hypothesized to consist of functions of agenda management, brokerage, and representation. The theory thus generated the expectation that variation in collective-action problems over time or across negotiation contexts would explain the extent to which states empower the chairmanship with these forms of process powers. At the same time, this hypothesis was coupled with an important caveat: the chairmanship is not the only institution that can perform such functions. This suggests that the identified collective-action problems constitute necessary, but not sufficient, reasons for delegation.

The historical evidence strongly supports such a functionalist interpretation of the EU Presidency's evolution from the 1950s until the early 2000s. When first established in 1957, the office of the Presidency was only equipped with weak process functions. Today, the institution enjoys far-reaching powers of agenda management, brokerage, and representation, making it a central and contested part of the political life of the Union. Existing primary and secondary sources suggest that this transformation of the Presidency reflects rational institutional adaptation on the part of European governments in response to actual, or anticipated, collective-action problems in EU cooperation. The member states have continuously adjusted and extended the functions of the Presidency, in search of more efficient methods of decision-making. Even if other EU institutions and actors have at times been chosen to perform similar process functions, each decision to confer powers of agenda management, brokerage, and representation to the Presidency can be linked to considerations of efficiency in EU bargaining.

In the original design of the EC, the Presidency was only entrusted with limited procedural tasks in the *management of the agenda*, whereas the Commission enjoyed exclusive authority to set the Community's legislative agenda. Existing historical accounts point to two parallel developments that propelled the Presidency into a more pronounced agenda-management role. First, the Commission's control over the substantive agenda weakened from the mid-1960s onwards. Second, the scope and intensity of EC policy-making increased in the late 1960s, leading to a fragmentation of Council business. In the years that followed, consecutive rounds of adaptation in institutional practices reinforced the Presidency's function as agenda manager. In the 1970s, when the member states created new negotiation forums outside the traditional Council machinery, through the establishment of the EPC and the European Council, they eschewed the services of the Commission and placed the Presidency in control of both the procedural preparation and the substantive setting of the agenda. The expansion of EU cooperation in the 1980s and early 1990s challenged the coherence of the Council's agenda and brought renewed initiatives to strengthen the Presidency. Most notably, the Presidency gained the explicit authority to prioritize among competing policy concerns through the formulation of a comprehensive work program.

In the early years of EC cooperation, the member governments mainly relied on the Commission for the *brokering of compromises*. Yet, increasingly aware and sceptical of the Commission's supranational agenda, member states began to depend more heavily on the Presidency as their preferred broker from the mid-1960s and onwards. In the EPC and the

European Council, the decision to exclude the Commission from the institutional framework left the Presidency without a competitor. The evidence suggests that the demand for the brokerage services of the Presidency was mainly driven by two developments. First, the growing complexity of EU decision-making made it relatively more difficult for the parties to identify potential agreements. Successive waves of enlargement expanded the number of bargaining parties, and the growth in policy areas created a pressure for cross-cutting package deals. The Presidency's position as a link between the multiple bargaining arenas in the Council offered unique possibilities for it to channel information, identify trade-offs, and construct package deals. Second, institutional reforms, especially the introduction of majority voting, created a demand for more active coalition-building efforts on the part of the Presidency. To facilitate brokerage, EU governments equipped the office with specific mediation instruments, notably, the practice of bilateral confessionals at which member states offer the Presidency privileged information about national bottom lines.

While only possessing insignificant powers of *representation* when first created, from the early 1970s onwards the Presidency acquired more encompassing responsibilities as both an external and internal representative. The empirical evidence unequivocally points to functional demands for an institutional solution to the problem of representation as the driving force behind these developments. The evolution of the Presidency as external representative went hand in hand with the EU's increasing involvement in world politics and growing foreign policy ambitions. When EC governments launched the EPC in the 1970s, they granted the Presidency the power to speak on their behalf in EPC dialogue and in the UN General Assembly. In the early 1980s, the Presidency gained the authority to meet with third parties, in response to calls for more developed contact channels. Finally, in the 1990s, the Presidency was delegated new executive authority in foreign policy and the power to negotiate international agreements on behalf of EU governments. The evolution of the Presidency as the Council's internal representative closely reflects the European Parliament's development into an important interlocutor in the EU's budgetary and legislative procedures. When the Parliament was given an important role in the adoption of the EC budget in the 1970s, the Council required a representative in the inter-institutional negotiations, and the member states chose to appoint the Presidency as their intermediary. By the same token, the rise of the Parliament as a key player in the adoption of legislation in the late 1980s and 1990s, especially through the introduction and extension of the co-decision procedure, led the member states to delegate powers of representation and negotiation to the Presidency.

Having summarized the book's argument about the evolution of the Presidency office, it is imperative to spell out what it does not claim. Functionalist explanations of institutional selection and development are frequently subject to straw-man criticism. First, the argument should not be misunderstood as a claim that the Presidency is the only solution to leadership problems in the EU, historically and today. As the chapter on the evolution of the Presidency illustrates, the member states have chosen between a set of alternative, institutional solutions when responding to collective-action problems in EU cooperation. Second, the book does not claim that the Presidency institution at all times meets the demand for leadership. Rather, it shows that the rationale for additional delegation of process powers to the Presidency has generally been the inability of the institution in its existing format to adequately address agenda failure, negotiation failure, and representation failure. In conclusion, the book's take-home message on the issue of institutional development is that the Presidency has gained its powers as a result of state concerns with negotiation efficiency – not that this institution in any way would be intrinsically efficient.

The supply of formal leadership

In Chapters 4 to 6, the attention turned to the influence of individual Presidencies in EU negotiations, measured along the dimensions of efficiency and distribution. According to the theory of formal leadership, we would expect the delegation of process functions to the chairmanship to ameliorate collective-action problems in decentralized bargaining, while simultaneously creating an exclusive power platform, from which governments in office can pursue private interests as well. More specifically, I posited that the office of the chairmanship offers the incumbent two important sets of power resources: asymmetrical access to information and asymmetrical control over negotiation procedure. Furthermore, I hypothesized that the capacity of chairmen to influence the outcomes of negotiations would be conditioned by the formal institutional environment in which they operate.

The six case studies provide comprehensive empirical evidence in favor of the Presidency office as a platform for political influence. While performing functions that enhance the efficiency of EU negotiations, Presidency governments have simultaneously exploited the chairmanship for national political purposes, wielding its privileged power resources for their private gain. Making effective use of their asymmetrical control over information and procedure, the Danish, Finnish, French, German, and Swedish Presidencies in the late 1990s and early 2000s succeeded in shifting outcomes in their own favor in the areas of enlargement, institutional reform, environmental policy, budgetary policy, and foreign policy. At the same time, the case studies point to the conditionality of Presidency influence. Agenda-setting rules shape the extent to which Presidencies can independently launch new policy initiatives, or must rely on close cooperation with the Commission. Decision rules affect the capacity of Presidencies to shape distributional outcomes by limiting or expanding the zone of agreement. Taken together, the six case studies grant support to the proposition that rotation as a design principle produces a system of diffuse reciprocity, where states take turns in providing the services and enjoying the benefits of the chairmanship.

The *management of the agenda* permits EU Presidencies to assign priority to competing political concerns. The cases selected from the Finnish and German Presidencies in 1999 demonstrate that influence over the agenda both takes the shape of traditional agenda setting and includes forms of non-decision-making. EU Presidencies call attention to prioritized concerns by including them in the official Presidency program and scheduling informal meetings. They place new issues on the formal agenda either directly, where the member states share the power of initiative, or indirectly, where the Commission holds this right and can be convinced to present Presidency initiatives as its own. But Presidencies also exploit the exclusive control over the agenda to downplay, or even exclude, controversial issues.

The Finnish campaign to establish a Northern Dimension in the EU's foreign policy shows how access to the power resources of the chairmanship may be used to launch new policy initiatives. Finland kicked off the campaign for the Northern Dimension in 1997, with the intention of consolidating and institutionalizing this policy initiative during its Presidency in 1999. Once in control of the chairmanship, the Finnish government made extensive use of the procedural instruments at its disposal. Finland anchored the initiative in the Presidency program, placed it on the agenda of formal and informal meetings, courted the Commission to secure the supranational executive's support in implementation, arranged a ministerial conference specifically devoted to the issue, and engineered support for a European Council decision on a policy action plan. The Finnish campaign was central to the institutionalization of the Northern Dimension, even if the requirement of unanimous approval forced the Finnish government to dilute the contents of the initiative.

The German government's removal of the nationally sensitive direct-ive on car recycling from the Council's agenda illustrates the Presi-dency's ability to engage in non-decision-making. At its first meeting in charge of the Environmental Council, the German Presidency ex-ploited the prerogatives of the chairmanship by unilaterally deciding to drop the issue from the agenda and force a postponement of the deci-sion. During the spring of 1999, Germany successfully used the time it had gained to lobby the UK and Spain, thus building a blocking minor-ity in the Council. At the final meeting of the Environmental Council, the German Presidency could conclude that the proposed directive no longer enjoyed the support required for adoption. The directive eventu-ally was adopted more than a year later, on terms more favorable to the German car industry than had initially been the case.

The *brokering of intergovernmental agreements* permits EU Presidencies to select from multiple equilibria and steer negotiations toward out-comes they privately prefer. The cases drawn from the German and French Presidencies in 1999 and 2000 demonstrate how institutional practices specifically developed to aid the Presidency in its function as broker are used for both collective and private gain. Presidencies exploit the privileged information about state preferences obtained through bilateral confessionals and *tours des capitales* to extract concessions from adversaries. They use the brokerage mandate to devise single negotiating texts that keep desired components on the negotiation table and sensi-tive options away from it. They speed up negotiations and improve the chances of agreement on nationally prioritized issues through decisions on the frequency and format of bargaining sessions. As a consequence, it is exceedingly difficult for the Council to arrive at decisions that go against the explicit desires of the Presidency.

The German Presidency made full use of its brokerage resources when forging a package agreement on the Agenda 2000 reforms which were acceptable to all parties but which also safeguarded central German interests. To create favorable conditions for a deal, the Presidency in-tensified the meeting schedule, moved the dossier to the top of meeting agendas, and called informal negotiation sessions. In order to focus and steer the negotiations, the Presidency adopted a specific brokerage formula that effectively constituted a single negotiating text. Issues of contention were unlocked through a combination of bilateral confes-sionals that unveiled the parties' bottom lines, and follow-up papers that outlined new compromise alternatives. The final deal corres-ponded closely to the German positions on agricultural reform and budget discipline. By contrast, Germany only partially reached the goal of reducing its net contribution to the EU budget, which is best explained by the veto power conferred on the net beneficiaries by the requirement of unanimity.

The French Presidency's handling of the IGC 2000 negotiations points to the same opportunities and constraints for the Presidency as broker. To facilitate the reaching of an agreement by December 2000, France intensified the meeting schedule, moved the IGC to the top of Council agendas, and structured the negotiations to solve the easiest questions first and save the thorny matters for the European Council summit in Nice. Confessionals and *tours des capitales* served to elicit privileged information about national resistance points, which was subsequently used to draft revised versions of the Presidency's single negotiating text. On the eve of the Nice summit, the Presidency distributed institutional side payments. Throughout the negotiations, the French government scrupulously exploited the chairmanship to favor national objectives, which resulted in much negative publicity. Yet, if we assess the substantive outcome of the negotiations, France was remarkably successful in protecting its vital interests.

The function as *representative in internal and external bargaining* grants Presidencies the opportunity to influence the terms of agreements EU governments negotiate with third parties. The Swedish and Danish Presidencies in 2001 and 2002 offer cases that well illustrate how the discretion as representative simultaneously can be used to favor collective and private interests. Privileged by informational and procedural asymmetries, and relieved of intrusive control mechanisms, Presidencies attempt to steer negotiations toward their ideal outcome. Typically, Presidencies exploit their unique position at the interface between internal and external negotiations to play off recalcitrant parties against each other, channel preference information in strategic ways, initiate informal negotiations beyond the control of member governments, and negotiate *fait accompli* agreements.

The Swedish Presidency's negotiations with the European Parliament on new transparency rules for the EU institutions well illustrate the Presidency's discretion as Council representative in legislative bargaining. Whereas the large majority of member states wished to uphold confidentiality, Sweden belonged to the minority of states desiring far-reaching transparency reforms. Despite this problematic position, the Swedish Presidency managed to engineer an agreement close to its preferred outcome. Exploiting its procedural prerogatives, the Presidency initiated informal negotiations with the Parliament's representatives even before the Council had come to an internal position. In order to achieve a solution that met the interests of the Council minority, Sweden played off the secrecy hawks in the Council against the transparency extremists in the Parliament. The deal negotiated with the Parliament met with strong objections when presented to the Council, but the secrecy-oriented states could do little but approve the agreement, given the scheduled deadline of the negotiations. The success of the Swedish strategy was dependent on the use of majority voting, and would not have succeeded if unanimity had been required.

The Danish Presidency's conclusion of the accession negotiations in 2002 testifies to a similar room for maneuver in the function as external representative. Whereas a broad and swift enlargement of the EU had been Denmark's top priority for over a decade, several other governments were more skeptical of the benefits of this "big bang" strategy. Once in office, the Danish government used the procedural powers of the Presidency to put other urgent concerns on the back burner and focus the EU's negotiation resources on the enlargement dossier. Denmark reserved the summits of the European Council for enlargement negotiations, transformed Council meetings into accession negotiation sessions, and engaged in bilateral consultations with both member states and candidate countries. The simultaneous access to internal and external bargaining arenas was skillfully utilized to play off the most recalcitrant parties on both sides against each other. At the concluding summit in Copenhagen, the Danish Presidency exploited its discretion by offering concessions that had not been condoned by the Council, but that the Presidency correctly judged would be accepted by reluctant EU members, when presented as a *fait accompli*.

In sum, the six case studies demonstrate that EU Presidencies generally employ the privileged position of the chairmanship to advance both collective and national interests. This conclusion motivates four additional comments.

First, the systematic selection of cases where Presidencies hold extreme preferences in the issues under negotiation generates specific expectations about Presidency influence in the broader universe of cases. Selection on this principle carried distinct methodological advantages, by making it possible to empirically trace the process through which Presidencies move outcomes from the expected equilibrium and toward their own position at the end of the preference spectrum. Yet it simultaneously grants these cases least-likely qualities, since it is relatively more difficult for Presidencies in outlier positions to achieve their most preferred outcome, compared to Presidencies that hold central preferences, which only need to secure an agreement close to the expected equilibrium. We would therefore expect it to be relatively easier for Presidencies to reach their most preferred distributional outcomes in the large number of cases where the government at the helm does not seek extreme negotiation results.

Second, these cases offer little support for the proposition that large member states are more prone to abuse the office for national purposes than small member states, as is often suggested in the existing literature on the EU Presidency. Instead, this set of six case studies demonstrates that national governments, irrespective of structural power capabilities, seek to exploit the privileged power resources of the chairmanship. The opportunism of governments in international cooperation is not a product of state size, even if variation in structural power may influence the ease with which private gains are realized. To be sure, comparative analyses of Presidencies will find variation in the ways governments organize and conduct their periods at the helm. Yet the message of this book is that Presidencies display far more commonalities than differences, because of roughly similar incentives, opportunities, and constraints in the strategic context of EU decision-making.

Third, these six cases call into question the distinction between high- and low-profile dossiers, and the associated notion that Presidency influence would be more or less likely in either category of cases. The selection of cases involves dossiers generally considered to be of great political weight – the IGC 2000, the Agenda 2000 reform package, and the enlargement negotiations – and dossiers of a more routine character – the Northern Dimension initiative, the car recycling directive, and the regulation on public access to EU documents. Part of the explanation for the lack of a systematic pattern across dossiers rests with the limited analytical value of the high–low distinction. What constitutes a high-profile dossier to one member state, because of its salience in domestic politics, may be a low-profile dossier to another member state.

Fourth, the criteria for the selection of cases indirectly restrict the generalizability of the book's findings to negotiations where the government in the chair prefers certain political outcomes before others. The six cases exclusively involve dossiers where the Presidencies in question possess distinct and known preferences, rather than diffuse, unknown, or non-existing preferences. In principle, this means that the claims of this book must be limited to the universe of cases where Presidency governments indeed have an interest in the substantive political outcome of the dossiers under negotiation. Only then can we expect the Presidency government to mobilize the resources of the office to skew outcomes in its own favor. While certainly a limitation in the scope of generalization, it is less consequential for the theoretical concerns political scientists generally care about. After all, we tend to be more interested in the question of whether political actors – be they states, supranational institutions, government agencies, or non-governmental organizations (NGOs) – are capable of achieving the outcomes they desire in issues they care about, than if they impact on issues to which they are indifferent.

Sociological institutionalism: assessing the alternative approach

As explained in Chapter 2, sociological institutionalism today constitutes the primary theoretical alternative to rational choice institutionalism on the emergence, development, and consequences of political institutions broadly interpreted. Even if sociological institutionalists so far have not presented a coherent account of formal leadership comparable to the rationalist argument I advance, this approach generates expectations that can be formulated as competing hypotheses. It is now time to revisit these hypotheses in light of the empirical evidence. While we should bear in mind that this study was not designed to systematically test these contending claims, the findings nevertheless suggest that the causal mechanisms privileged by sociological institutionalism generally play a secondary role in explaining the sources and effects of formal leadership in the EU. The assessment is structured in three parts, each evaluating one of the core claims in the sociological alternative.

First, sociological institutionalists conceive of institutional development as a process where low priority is given to concerns of efficiency, relative to concerns of legitimacy. The organizational models that states adopt are usually not chosen because of their expected efficiency in any given context, but because they reflect broader social conceptions of what constitutes legitimate and appropriate institutional design. By the same token, sociological institutionalists reject rationalist claims about efficient institutional adaptation, emphasizing instead the stickiness of institutional models and the slow pace of adjustment to changing functional demands.

With one exception, the empirical evidence on this point should be disappointing to sociological institutionalists. When creating the Presidency office of the ECSC, the founding governments did not adopt chairmanship arrangements familiar from other, newly established, Western European institutions in which they participated, such as NATO, the OEEC, and the Council of Europe, but instead engaged in institutional innovation. When the nature of the EC as a decision-making system shifted over time, giving rise to new functional demands, the member states adjusted the powers of the Presidency accordingly.

The extension of the Presidency's functions of agenda management, brokerage, and representation was deliberate and continuous, with few signs of extended and unaddressed gaps between needs and demands. The model of the rotating Presidency was not taken for granted, but re-evaluated at regular intervals and only retained after careful consideration of available alternatives. Furthermore, the international comparison reveals that states have refrained from adopting standardized organizational models, instead tailoring the chairmanship to the specific political conditions and functional demands in a given empirical context.

The exception to this pattern is the process of institutional mimicking that appears to be at play in the routine inclusion of the chairmanship in the design of decision-making bodies. In none of the negotiations surveyed in this book did the parties appear to consider refraining from instituting a chairmanship. The chairmanship today constitutes one of few institutional features that can be considered to be a standard component in political decision-making, whether at local, national, or international level. That is not to say that the routine inclusion of this institutional feature is divorced from considerations of efficiency. Rather, it is likely that this pattern of institutional isomorphism reflects the historically internalized lesson that negotiations in the absence of a chairman cannot be recommended for any decision-making body.

Second, sociological institutionalists advance competing claims about political power resources, rejecting the rationalist emphasis on informational advantages and formal prerogatives. Instead, they tend to stress the legitimacy of an actor's claim to authority, and the ability to persuade through good and normatively appropriate arguments. This perspective resonates with large parts of the literature on mediation, which stresses the importance of legitimacy for success in brokerage.

The assessment of this hypothesis is not unproblematic, mainly because of the hazards involved in measuring legitimacy. Yet, as far as they permit such a test, the case studies in this book suggest that legitimacy and good arguments do not constitute prerequisites for the Presidency influence. In several of the cases, the Presidencies attracted significant criticism for the way they handled the negotiations, attempting to favor outcomes close to their own preferences. Yet in none of the cases were the challenges to the Presidency's authority, and the well-known partiality of its conduct, sufficient to prevent the government at the helm from influencing outcomes. Other states' acceptance of this behavior appears to have been less a product of their respect for the office of the Presidency, than the result of Presidencies' privileged control over the procedural resources required to undo the outcome. Whereas the French

Presidency's crude favoring of national objectives in the IGC 2000 is the quintessential example, the same holds true for the other cases as well. Even if Presidencies tactically sought to frame their proposals in ways that made them seem less overtly nationalistic and thus more appetizing for other member states, there is little to suggest that the proposals were accepted as a result of this framing exercise.

Third, sociological institutionalists conceive of informal norms of appropriate behavior as the primary constraint on actor behavior, and challenge the emphasis of rational choice institutionalists on formal rules. According to this perspective, norms spread through processes of socialization and internalization, and actors conform to norms, not on the basis of cost-benefit calculations, but because they wish to do the right thing. In the context of EU negotiations, sociologically informed accounts in existing literature generate the expectation that the norm of the honest broker would exert an important constraining effect on EU Presidencies.

The case studies provide striking evidence on the role of norms in EU negotiations, mainly challenging the expectations of sociological institutionalism. The six negotiations suggest that EU governments are well aware of the norm of neutrality, but do not let their behavior be guided by this expectation when important national interests are at stake. Whereas Presidency representatives often make a virtue of their adherence to this norm in interviews and official documents, as well as defend themselves against allegations of partisan behavior, talk and action tend to be de-coupled.[1] Lip service rather than norm conformance characterizes the cases in this book, with the exception of Finland's campaign for the Northern Dimension, which was carefully planned so as not to evoke accusations of exploitation. Yet, even in this case, there is much to suggest that the Finnish government's adaptation to this norm was based on a consequentialist cost-benefit calculation, where norm conformance in the present was viewed as holding the promise of rewards in the future.

Implications for the study of EU politics

The theoretical and empirical argument advanced in this book generates implications and provides insights that open up for a more advanced understanding of politics in the EU. In this section, I explain how the book challenges prevailing conceptions of efficiency and distribution in

---

[1] Brunsson 1989.

EU negotiations, and can help us understand the sources and potential effects of existing treaty proposals to modify the Presidency office.

Efficiency and distribution in EU negotiations

The argument in this book speaks to the ongoing debate in EU studies on the influence of supranational institutions versus national governments. Contributions emphasizing supranational entrepreneurship typically highlight scarcities of information and ideas in EU negotiations, and suggest that the Commission can help national governments to overcome these bottlenecks, simultaneously influencing outcomes in the direction of "more Europe."[2] By contrast, intergovernmentalist analyses typically present EU bargaining as a process where the member states themselves are fully capable of removing bargaining impediments that prevent efficient exchange. As Andrew Moravcsik concludes: "[S]upranational intervention, far from being a necessary condition for efficient interstate negotiation in the EC, is generally late, redundant, futile, and sometimes even counterproductive."[3] Distributional outcomes, in this perspective, reflect the relative bargaining power of governments, understood as the pattern of asymmetric interdependence, or the respective parties' best alternative to a negotiated agreement (BATNA). The better the backup alternative, the less dependent a state will be on a negotiated agreement, and the less willing it will be to offer concessions.

This book lends support to the intergovernmentalist claim about negotiation efficiency, by specifying what is probably the most important institutional mechanism through which governments reach bargains without supranational intervention. Through the rotating Presidency, governments take turns in providing the efficiency-enhancing functions of agenda management, brokerage, and representation, reducing the demand for supranational entrepreneurship. This helps to explain why agenda failure, negotiation failure, and representation failure are reasonably rare occurrences in EU politics.

The historical record demonstrates that EU governments have developed the Presidency office to address actual or anticipated collective-action problems in EU cooperation. In this process, delegation to the Commission has constituted an alternative institutional solution. Yet, aware of the Commission's political agenda, EU governments in many cases have eschewed the services of the supranational executive, and

---

[2] Sandholtz and Zysman 1989; Garrett and Weingast 1993; Stone Sweet and Sandholtz 1997.
[3] Moravcsik 1999a, 269–270. See also Garrett 1992; Moravcsik 1998.

instead chosen to boost the authority of the rotating Presidency, thus retaining control over outcomes among themselves. Likewise, the case studies in this book confirm that Presidencies do raise the efficiency of cooperation through the functions they perform and the interventions they conduct.

Indeed, if we revisit empirical analyses of intergovernmental conferences during the last fifteen years, we find that Presidencies' brokerage efforts often are identified as pivotal for the conclusion of efficient agreements, but that these observations so far have not been integrated into a theoretically coherent argument about formal leadership. Studies on the negotiations leading to the Maastricht Treaty in 1991 identify the Luxembourg Presidency as an important entrepreneur, sorting through hundreds of national proposals and managing the negotiations through a single negotiating text.[4] Analyses of the IGC in 1996–1997, resulting in the Amsterdam Treaty, highlight the contributions of the Irish and Dutch Presidencies, which composed consecutive draft treaties, designed to capture the zone of agreement.[5] Accounts of the IGC in 2000, other than Chapter 6 in this book, emphasize the French Presidency's essential role in nudging the parties toward an agreement through a strong hand on the negotiations.[6] Finally, recent research credits the Irish Presidency of the first half of 2004 for bridging divisions among the Member States on the shape of the 2004 EU Constitutional Treaty, through the traditional combination of bilateral confessionals and compromise proposals.[7]

This argument should not be misunderstood as an unconditional claim about the virtuous effects of the Presidency on the efficiency of European cooperation. Rather, it is subject to two caveats. First, the Presidency's brokerage efforts may be superfluous, to the extent that the bargaining parties themselves can identify a viable compromise, or redundant, if preferences are sufficiently divergent to prevent a zone of agreement from arising. Second, the individuals that perform Presidency functions on behalf of their national governments may be more or less apt for these duties. Like other institutional platforms, the office of the Presidency office can offer individuals opportunities for influence, but cannot guarantee that these individuals at all times act skillfully on these opportunities.[8]

---

[4] Moravcsik 1998, ch. 6.
[5] Moravcsik and Nicolaïdis 1999; Svensson 2000; Stubb 2002.
[6] Schout and Vanhoonacker 2001.
[7] Dür and Mateo 2004; Crum 2006.
[8] For a recent attempt to theorize leadership in international politics with reference to individuals' personal capabilities, see Hermann et al. 2001.

On the distribution of benefits from European cooperation, this book presents a challenge to intergovernmentalist bargaining analysis. Whereas patterns of asymmetric interdependence are clearly fundamental for understanding who concedes and why in EU negotiations, they do not provide the full story about the division of gains. As demonstrated in the case studies, the very same resources that permit Presidencies to raise the efficiency of EU negotiations simultaneously enable them to exert extra leverage over outcomes. Where the zone of agreement permits Presidencies to select among multiple equilibria, we would expect outcomes to be biased in favor of the incumbent's national political objectives.

The negotiations leading to the Nice Treaty and new EU transparency rules provide illustrative examples of the limits of asymmetric interdependence as a predictor of bargaining power. In the IGC negotiations, a consideration of asymmetric interdependence would lead us to expect great French willingness to compromise on the size of the Commission and the weighing of votes in the Council, since these were issues where France held relatively more intense interests and faced relatively worse backup alternatives than the other member states. If France could not convince the other governments to move away from the status quo, she would fail to obtain the much-wanted reduction of the Commission's size and formal vote parity with Germany. Yet, rather than offering disproportionate concessions in order to reach these goals, the French government exploited the power resources of the Presidency to steer the outcome in its favor. In the negotiations on new transparency rules, the Swedish government similarly constituted the state with the most intense interest in a policy change, given the threat of existing EU rules to Sweden's freedom of information act. But, instead of making extraordinary concessions in order to win over status quo-oriented member states, the Swedish government used its privileged position to negotiate a favorable deal with the Parliament.

Recent theoretical and comparative research suggests that Presidencies' distributional influence generates interesting knock-on effects for the policy mix at the European level. The rotation of the privileged opportunity to set the agenda, broker compromises, and negotiate external deals leads to a broader and more varied combination of policy than would have been the case under another chairmanship model.[9] Slightly simplified, the combined effect of this system is a parallel – if somewhat

---

[9] Kollman 2003.

irregular – advancement of policy across several fronts.[10] In the EU's relations to neighboring regions, for instance, Spanish and French Presidencies consistently promote cooperation in the Mediterranean, whereas the Nordic member states use their periods at the helm to favor cooperation in the Baltic Sea region. By the same token, left-wing governments have tended to use the Presidency for the purposes of strengthening the EU's social dimension, whereas liberal or right-wing governments have emphasized economic liberalization and competitiveness. Finally, certain member states have utilized the period at the helm to push for a deepening of the EU through institutional reform, whereas others have prioritized progress in enlargement negotiations.

This book suggests that the key to understanding the acceptability of these distributional consequences rests with the rotation of the Presidency office. Rotation of the chairmanship avoids the concentration of formal power in one member state or supranational institution, by granting each government, in turn, a privileged opportunity to influence the outcomes in European cooperation. This system rests on a long shadow of the future, where the gains from the Presidency position are temporally structured and distributed between the member states. Governments accept the exploitation of the Presidency in the present because they will get their opportunity in the future. As one close observer of the Council notes: "[M]ember states seem to use the Council Presidency to promote their own domestic policy priorities, but this is not necessarily negative and is probably a recognized and accepted practice by all member states."[11]

This argument may be challenged on several grounds. National elections lead governments in the member states to shift between the moments when they must accept exploitation and can collect gains. Furthermore, the EU's policy agenda changes over time, with the effect that Presidencies get to handle issues of varying political weight and salience. For both of these reasons, EU governments should be hesitant to accept the distributional effects of the Presidency office. Yet what these challenges overlook is the relative attractiveness of diffuse reciprocity within a rotating Presidency model, compared to alternative institutional solutions. Whereas rotation cannot guarantee evenly balanced and valued opportunities for exploitation across Presidencies, it diffuses the power that otherwise would be placed in the hands of a supranational institution or a single government. The fact that power

---

[10] The examples below are drawn from Elgström 2003b and summarized in Elgström and Tallberg 2003.
[11] Sherrington 2000, 166.

sharing and power diffusion go hand in hand remains one of the continuing attractions of a rotating Presidency, despite calls for reform.

A European president? Sources and effects of institutional reform

In recent years, the organization of the EU Presidency has once again become a topic of debate. In June 2004, the member states concluded the latest round of IGC negotiations with an agreement on the Constitutional Treaty. The IGC had been prepared through the European Convention, a constitutional forum composed of state representatives, national and European parliamentarians, and Commission officials, convened from February 2002 until June 2003. For the theme of this book, the most important features of the Constitutional Treaty are the provisions on the chairmanship of the European Council and the Council of Ministers, summarized in Table 8.1. Whereas the rotation model is scheduled to remain in place for almost the entire Council machinery, the Constitutional Treaty provides for two main modifications. First, and most importantly, it would establish a semi-permanent president of the European Council, elected by a qualified majority of the heads of state and government for a term of two and a half years, renewable once. Second, the Constitutional Treaty places the chairmanship of the Foreign Affairs Council in the hands of a new EU minister for foreign affairs, who would simultaneously serve as a member of the European Commission.

At the time of writing, it appears unlikely that the Constitutional Treaty will ever enter into force. Following negative referendum results in France and the Netherlands in 2005, the ratification process has been frozen. Yet it cannot be ruled out that the process will be restarted in response to changing political conditions, or that certain provisions in the Constitutional Treaty will be lifted into a less ambitious and more easily ratified document. In any case, the proposed modifications to the Presidency office raise a set of politically and theoretically interesting questions about the sources and effects of institutional reform. How can we explain that EU governments were considering abandoning the rotation of the chairmanship in two of the most central intergovernmental decision bodies? What would be the likely consequences of shifting from a rotation arrangement to an elected chairmanship in the European Council? Below, I explain how the theory of formal leadership sheds important light on the sources and effects of these proposed reforms, as well as on the process through which the suggestion for a European Council president made it into the Convention's draft treaty.

First, the kinds of problems that created a pressure for reform of the Presidency are consistent with theory's specified implications of the

Table 8.1. *EU Constitutional Treaty: provisions on the organization of the chairmanship*

Article I-22: The European Council President

1 The European Council shall elect its President, by a qualified majority, for a term of two and a half years, renewable once. In the event of an impediment or serious misconduct, the European Council can end his or her term of office in accordance with the same procedure.

2 The President of the European Council: (a) shall chair it and drive forward its work; (b) shall ensure the preparation and continuity of the work of the European Council in cooperation with the President of the Commission, and on the basis of the work of the General Affairs Council; (c) shall endeavour to facilitate cohesion and consensus within the European Council; (d) shall present a report to the European Parliament after each of the meetings of the European Council. The President of the European Council shall, at his or her level and in that capacity, ensure the external representation of the Union on issues concerning its common foreign and security policy, without prejudice to the powers of the Union Minister for Foreign Affairs.

3 The President of the European Council shall not hold a national office.

Article I-24: Configuration of the Council of Ministers

7. The Presidency of Council configurations, other than that of Foreign Affairs, shall be held by Member State representatives in the Council on the basis of equal rotation, in accordance with the conditions established by a European decision of the European Council. The European Council shall act by a qualified majority.

Article I-28: The Union Minister for Foreign Affairs

3. The Union Minister for Foreign Affairs shall preside over the Foreign Affairs Council.

---

rotation model. While ensuring a sharing of the benefits of the chairmanship, the rotation model gives rise to a continuity problem. Every six months, a new member state takes office in the midst of ongoing policy processes. Discontinuity in the execution of agenda management, brokerage, and representation is a natural result of this shift from one member state to another as the central coordinating force of the Council. This effect is further reinforced by the opportunities for distributional influence offered by the office, which lead to varying policy emphasis.

If we review the political debate in recent years about the pros and cons of the rotating Presidency, discontinuity problems appear to be the foremost concern of EU politicians, especially in relation to the European Council.[12] These concerns have been voiced more frequently and with greater weight than in the past. This is best explained by the

---

[12] See, especially, Blair 2002; Blair and Schröder 2002; Chirac 2002; Persson 2002.

expectation that existing problems of discontinuity will worsen as a result of the completed enlargement to ten new member states in 2004, and the planned accession of an additional two states in 2007. Whereas every enlargement round has given rise to a debate about the merits and demerits of the rotation model, the eastern enlargement of the EU is both qualitatively and quantitatively different, posing unprecedented challenges to the decision system. The new member states possess lower levels of economic and administrative resources, generating the fear that transitions from one Presidency to another will be less smooth and create more discontinuity than previously. At the same time, the accession of twelve new member states means that it becomes substantially longer between each government's periods at the helm, which reduces the national benefits of the office and challenges the principle of diffuse reciprocity.

Second, the theory of formal leadership can help us understand the process through which these concerns with the rotation model were translated into a treaty agreement on substantive reform, by highlighting the contribution of yet another influential chairman. From the moment it was aired, the proposal to introduce an elected European Council president was highly controversial. While promoted by France, the UK, Spain, and Sweden, the suggestion was met with intense dislike from almost all small and medium-sized member states, as well as the European Commission. The latter coalition feared that a shift to an elected chairmanship would be to their disadvantage, by creating an office that large states would come to dominate, and by strengthening the European Council at the expense of the Commission, thus leaving greater room for power-based bargaining in EU cooperation. Yet, despite this massive opposition and the requirement of consensus, the European Convention delivered a draft treaty that included the contentious new position and that was subject to a minimum of changes at the IGC.

Part of the explanation for this outcome rests with the skillful maneuvering of the chairman of the European Convention, Valéry Giscard d'Estaing, who played a pivotal role in shepherding the proposal for a European Council president through the negotiations.[13] As French president from 1974 to 1981, Giscard d'Estaing had taken the initiative to found the European Council and had unsuccessfully advocated the establishment of a European Council president, elected by popular

---

[13] Jonsson and Hegeland 2003; Norman 2003; Petersson et al. 2003; Gray 2004.

vote for a period of five years.[14] When the idea of a president, albeit not popularly elected, resurfaced in the political debate in 2002, and Giscard d'Estaing was appointed chairman of the Convention, a window of opportunity opened for the former French president.

In the Convention negotiations, Giscard d'Estaing personally pushed the proposal for a European Council president, making sure that no version of the draft treaty left his secretariat without the required provisions included. Whereas all members had been invited to present proposals at the early stages of the Convention's work, Giscard d'Estaing and his presidium established and maintained a virtual monopoly on the power of proposal during the spring of 2003, when the institutional architecture of the EU was negotiated. In late April, the Convention chairman presented his own blueprint for the EU institutions, which included a set of controversial components, among them the notion of a European Council president. While broadly criticized, Giscard d'Estaing's proposals functioned as a form of catharsis, paving the way for compromises between competing forces in the Convention. In its less extreme version, the chairman's institutional blueprint developed into a single negotiating text, around which the Convention's concluding negotiations converged. While sacrificing other pet ideas, such as a congress of European and national parliamentarians, Giscard d'Estaing did not let go of the opportunity to secure a reform he had sought for nearly three decades. The Convention chairman clearly would not have achieved the desired provisions in the absence of support from powerful EU governments. Yet it is equally true that France, the UK, and Spain would have experienced significant problems getting the unpopular proposal into the new treaty had not Giscard d'Estaing skillfully exploited his position to wield off attacks in the Convention and make sure that the suggestion stayed on the negotiating table.

Third, the theory of formal leadership generates specific expectations about the effects of the proposed changes to the office of the Presidency. Most importantly, we would expect this move from a rotating to an elected chairmanship to be associated with a shift from discontinuity to control as the central concern of the parties. Unless EU governments wish to grant one of the member states an extraordinary source of influence in the European Council, they will establish mechanisms of control that circumscribe the room for maneuver enjoyed by the new president. This prediction is further underlined by the experiences from international negotiation forums with chairmen drawn from the participating

---

[14] See, e.g., Giscard d'Estaing 1984.

states, such as the multilateral environmental conferences surveyed in Chapter 7.

Whereas this hypothesis cannot be evaluated until the new position becomes operational, if it ever does, we have already seen evidence of member states establishing measures of control through the institutional design of this chairmanship. EU governments engaged in *ex ante* control when opting for a less ambitious definition of the new president's prerogatives than Giscard d'Estaing initially proposed in his institutional blueprint. Furthermore, EU governments refrained from putting the new European Council president in hierarchical control of the chairmen of the Council's many decision-making bodies, where the office will continue to rotate. This is an important limitation compared to the existing system, where the prime minister in charge of the European Council can direct a legion of national chairmen at all levels of the Council machinery. It remains to be seen whether EU governments will use other forms of *ex ante* mechanisms as well. But the experiences from other multilateral negotiations would lead us to expect that the heads of state and government in the European Council would select a president with central and/or weak preferences in the most salient issues, thus limiting the risk of undesired agency.

In addition, EU governments established important instruments of *ex post* control through the institutional design of the new office. Whereas the presidents of both the Commission and the Parliament are appointed for a period of five years, the term of the European Council president was limited to two and a half years, renewable once. This rule reduces the likelihood that the president would seek to systematically favor certain distributional outcomes, since he or she could only be re-elected for another term if a qualified majority of the members are content with the performance and actively grant their consent. EU governments also made sure to include a provision enabling a qualified majority of the heads of state and government to end the president's term of office in the event of serious misconduct.

Implications for theories of international negotiation and cooperation

Whereas some students of European politics submit that the EU is sufficiently unique to prevent meaningful comparison with other political systems at the national or international level, I find this approach methodologically suspect and substantively unjustified. Instead, comparisons with negotiations in other multilateral forums speak to the generalizability of the theoretical argument and empirical results of this book. In addition, the book generates findings with bearing on the ongoing debate in IR theory on leadership, efficiency, and distribution in international cooperation.

Generalizing the European experience

Chapter 7 put the EU experience in a comparative perspective, for purposes of probing the generalizability of the theoretical claims and empirical results. I considered evidence on formal leadership in three institutional contexts: the CSCE/OSCE, the GATT/WTO, and the UN conferences on the law of the sea, the ozone layer, and climate change. The selection of cases ensured variation across alternative areas of international cooperation, as well as alternative ways of organizing the chairmanship. This allowed me to test the hypothesis that institutional design matters for the discretion and influence of negotiation chairs – a proposition I had been unable to assess in the EU context, where the design of the chairmanship had remained constant. More specifically, the theory of formal leadership generated the expectation that rotation would create dynamics of diffuse reciprocity with states offering each other latitude in the execution of the chairmanship, whereas the other two models would involve more pronounced concerns with control and less discretion for chairmen to influence the distributional dimension of negotiated agreements.

The comparison revealed that the European experience is not exceptional. The broader implication of this result is a strong suggestion for students of international negotiation to pay due attention to the power of the chair as a force in multilateral bargaining. In all three international contexts, formal leaders had been delegated central functions in the negotiations and influenced political outcomes. Yet the kind of powers the chairmanship had been equipped with and the form of influence formal leaders had exerted varied across the three institutional contexts. The theory of formal leadership helped us explain this variation.

First, the comparative evidence endorses the claim that functional demands drive the delegation of responsibilities to chairmanship institutions. The historical record shows that states empower formal leaders to address problems whose removal makes it easier for the parties to negotiate efficient agreements. Furthermore, the cases reveal important differences in the powers conferred on formal leaders, which can be tied to varying functional pressures in the three negotiation contexts and the varying presence of alternative leaders capable of performing similar functions. States have not adopted a standardized model for the responsibilities conferred to formal leaders in international cooperation, but tailored the office to match specific functional needs.

The development of cooperation in the CSCE/OSCE illustrates how functional demands may shift over time, with direct and observable consequences in the powers delegated to formal leaders. Between 1973 and 1989, the competing priorities of the United States and the Soviet Union granted the neutral members – the chairmen of the CSCE's informal negotiation system – a central role in defining negotiable agendas. The extreme level of distrust between the two camps similarly created a strong demand for third-party brokerage, which the neutral countries provided at the CSCE's ministerial conferences. By contrast, there was no identifiable need for representation *vis-à-vis* other bodies in this loosely institutionalized process of détente. The end of the Cold War fundamentally changed the preconditions for cooperation, the ambitions of the regime, and the demand for formal leadership. The annually rotating Chairman-in-Office was placed at the center of the OSCE, and subsequently delegated increasingly far-reaching responsibilities, in direct response to functional needs in the new organization. Even if brokerage remained important, the real growth areas were agenda management and representation, where the CiO nowadays enjoys powers that match or even surpass those of the EU Presidency.

Cooperation in the GATT/WTO demonstrates how the presence of alternative leaders, next to variation in functional needs, influences the delegation of process powers to the chairmanship. The large number of parties in global trade rounds, the high level of issue conflict, and the consensus rule have created a strong demand for third-party intervention. During the last four negotiation rounds, the parties have drawn on the brokerage services of the supranational chairman of the coordinating Trade Negotiations Committee – the director general of the GATT/WTO Secretariat. By contrast, the demand for an agenda manager that can help settle conflicts over priorities has traditionally been limited by the practice of the US and the EU to engage in pre-negotiations that establish the topics of a trade round and define the mandates of negotiating groups. The representation function of GATT/WTO chairmen has been even less pronounced, best explained by the absence of inter-institutional negotiations and the Secretariat's performance of certain external representation functions.

The three UN-sponsored negotiations on the law of the sea, the ozone regime, and the climate change convention provide a surprisingly similar picture of the demand for formal leadership at multilateral environmental conferences. The combination of broad conference mandates and equal agenda-setting rights produced overcrowded negotiation agendas, causing the participating states to endow the conference chairmanships with important agenda-management powers, especially the power to formulate single negotiating texts. Similarly, the large number of participants, the broad spectrum of preferences, and the requirement of consensus, made it exceedingly difficult for the parties to identify a zone of agreement on their own. The engagement of the conference chairman as broker constituted the negotiating parties' favored solution for escaping deadlock and producing progress. In all three negotiations, the conferral of agenda-management and brokerage powers to the chairmanship was gradual, reflecting the parties' increasing awareness of the collective-action problems involved in decentralized bargaining. By contrast, the organization of these multilateral conferences did not create a functional demand for internal or external representation.

Second, the comparative record on the supply of formal leadership underscores that negotiation chairs generally possess informational and procedural resources that enable them to influence outcomes, but are constrained by formal institutional rules. The negotiations offer ample evidence of formal leaders facilitating bargaining and interstate agreement through efficiency-enhancing interventions. The evidence on the influence over distributional outcomes is more mixed. The negotiations surveyed illustrate how demanding decision rules and divergent preferences often limit the capacity of negotiation chairs to shape distributional outcomes, by drastically reducing the zone of agreement. Yet the cases also point to interesting and important variation across the three institutional contexts, best explained by the institutional design of the chairmanship. Where states institute rotating chairmanships, they appear less concerned with issues of control and grant more extensive discretion to negotiation chairs, than in cases where they elect a chairman from one of the parties or empower a supranational official.

Whereas the chairmanship of both the CSCE and the OSCE facilitated regime cooperation, the evidence on distributional effects reveals compelling variation over time. The discretion of formal leaders in the CSCE was strongly limited by the diverging preferences of the two superpowers and the requirement of consensus. Yet equally important was the *ex ante* control exerted by the superpowers when selecting the neutral states as negotiation chairs. As opposed to members of the two competing blocs, the neutral states tended to hold preferences toward the middle of the spectrum, and therefore had few incentives to seek outcomes that would systematically favor either the East or the West, especially since their overarching interest was to keep the process of détente alive. In the OSCE, by contrast, independent executive powers grant the government at the helm extensive discretion in agenda management and representation. The CiO actively prioritizes among competing concerns in the formulation of the political program, and shapes the contents of OSCE policy through public statements and mission directives that do not necessarily reflect consensus among the organization's members.

Existing accounts of global trade negotiations accord an important role to the TNC chairman in the brokering of compromises, but do not offer systematic evidence of influence over the distributional dimension of these agreements. In the process of stitching together package agreements, the director general has made effective use of the privileged resources of the chairmanship, calling informal negotiation sessions in the Green Room, conducting bilateral talks to unveil bottom lines, and developing single negotiating texts around which bargaining can converge. The absence of a simultaneous influence over the division of gains is best explained by the combination of a demanding decision rule and a significant preference gap between the two main parties, which has reduced the zone of agreement and the discretion of the TNC chairman. But existing literature also indicates that the supranational chairman's overarching objective more often has concerned process – keeping the trade negotiations on track – than substance – the specific provisions in individual dossiers.

The three environmental negotiations generate similar observations on the influence of formal leaders. While testifying to positive effects on the efficiency of the negotiations, existing accounts offer little proof of a systematic impact on distributional outcomes. The elected chairmen of the conferences transformed the wealth of competing proposals into negotiable core texts, created structural negotiation conditions conducive for concessions, encouraged the parties to unveil their bottom lines in confidential talks, discovered issue-linkages, and engineered package agreements. The absence of influence over distributional outcomes may be explained by the requirement of consensus and the institutional design of the chairmanship. Merely identifying a zone of agreement posed a challenge, and the possibility to select one efficient outcome rather than another oftentimes did not exist. In addition, the principle of election offered an effective instrument of *ex ante* control that limited the likelihood of exploitation. Typically, the overall conference chairman was selected from a country with weak and/or central preferences in the negotiations, whereas the chairmanships of the subsidiary bodies were either distributed to ensure regional power balance or divided between co-chairs from competing interest constellations.

Expanding the scope of comparison further, Table 8.2 summarizes the design of the chairmanship in some of the most prominent international organizations and negotiation processes. It demonstrates that rotation of the chairmanship constitutes the dominant principle, and most often takes the shape of one state controlling all intergovernmental bodies during a specific time period. The table further shows that the election of state representatives tends to be coupled with time restrictions, as well as mechanisms of power division between various geographical group-ings. Finally, it points to a set of international organizations where supranational officials have been delegated the authority to chair the central executive decision forums.

This variation presents students of international cooperation with a set of important questions for future research. How can we explain that states in some cases choose rotation arrangements, while opting for supranational chairmen or elected state representatives in other cases? To what extent does the institutional design of the chairmanship shape the influence of formal leaders and explain variation across cases in distributional impact? Do these cases grant support to a rationalist perspective on formal leadership, emphasizing functional institutional evolution, informational and procedural power resources, and formal constraints on actor behavior, or the sociological alternative, underlining inefficient institutional development, legitimacy and moral authority as power resources, and the constraining effect of informal norms about appropriate behavior?

The exclusive concern of this book with formal leadership in European and international politics should not hide the fact that the chairmanship is a universal institutional feature in political life. Whereas comparisons with decision-making at local and national levels are beyond the parameters of this study, recent research on American poli-tics points to the general importance of the power of the chair, further expanding the research agenda. Addressing the question of how political parties secure legislative success, Gary Cox and Mathew McCubbins stress the ability of the majority party to control the agenda through access to the formal power positions in national parliaments, especially the speakership and committee chairmanships.[15] By exercising positive and negative agenda-shaping powers, the formal leaders of national legislatures seek to secure the passing of legislation that implements the majority party's political vision. The implication of privileged agenda control for power relationships in domestic politics is profound: "Across

---

[15] Cox and McCubbins 2004.

Table 8.2. *Chairmanship arrangements in international cooperation*

Organization	Rotation between states	Election of state representative	Appointment of supranational official
APEC	Economic Leaders, Ministerial Meetings, Senior Officials (one year)		
ASEAN	Summit, Ministerial Meetings, Standing Committee (one year)		
AU	Assembly[b], Executive Council[b], Perm. Rep. Committee[b] (one year)		
Council of Europe	Committee of Ministers Ministers' Deputies (six months)		
EFTA	Council (six months)		
EU	European Council, Council of Ministers, Committees and Groups (six months)		
G8	Summit (one year)		
IAEA		General Conference[b] (duration of meeting) Board of Governors (one year)	
IMF		Board of Governors (time unspecified)	Executive Board (managing director)
NATO	Ministerial Meetings (one year)		North Atlantic Council Defense Planning Committee (secretary general)
Nordic Council of Ministers	Council of Ministers (one year)		
OECD		Ministerial Meetings (one year)	Council (secretary general)

Table 8.2. (*cont.*)

Organization	Rotation between states	Election of state representative	Appointment of supranational official
OSCE	Ministerial Council, Permanent Council (one year)		
UN	Security Council (one month)	General Assembly[a][b], Main Committees[c] (one year)	
UNEP		Governing Council[a][b] (duration of meeting), Committee of Perm. Rep. (one–two years)	
UNFCCC		Conference of the Parties[a][b] (one year)	
World Bank		Board of Governors (time unspecified)	Board of Executive Directors (president)
WTO		Ministerial Conferences (duration of meeting), General Council[a], Committees and Bodies[c] (one year)	Trade Negotiations Committee (director general)

Notes:

[a] Geographical rotation of right to nominate candidate for election prescribed in treaty, rules of procedure, or equivalent document.

[b] Geographical balance in the composition of the bureau or presidium prescribed in treaty, rules of procedure, or equivalent document.

[c] Geographical division of chairmanships prescribed in treaty, rules of procedure, or equivalent document.

the world's democratic legislatures, voting power is everywhere equal but agenda power is everywhere unequal. Legislators all get one vote but only a few have a special say over what gets voted on."[16]

Leadership, efficiency, and distribution in international cooperation

If the argument about the power of the chair can be generalized to multilateral negotiations at large, then what are its implications for theories of international cooperation? We conclude by returning to the questions posed at the very beginning of this book. Why do some negotiations lead to agreements that exploit all possible joint gains, whereas others collapse or leave sub-optimal gains on the table? Why do some states gain more than others from multilateral agreements? While natural components in most research on international cooperation, these issues recently have become the topic of renewed debate among IR theorists disputing the role of political leadership. Existing research presents us with two competing approaches, which may be referred to as the "efficient negotiation perspective" and the "entrepreneurial leadership perspective." These alternative perspectives create counter-expectations about the efficiency of negotiations, the demand for entrepreneurial leadership, and the distribution of gains from international cooperation. The argument of this book carries distinct implications for this debate, challenging the efficient negotiation perspective, providing support for the entrepreneurial leadership perspective, and encouraging theoretical refinement.

According to the first perspective, most forcefully expressed by Andrew Moravcsik, multilateral negotiations are naturally efficient and interventions from political entrepreneurs are likely to be either futile or redundant.[17] This perspective is grounded in game-theoretical models of decentralized bargaining.[18] Bargaining and decision-making involve no or low transaction costs, and may be seen as taking place on a frictionless spot market. States possess sufficient information about each other's preferences to identify mutually beneficial agreements, and face no shortage of ideas or focal points around which specific agreements can be constructed. "The information and ideas required for efficient bargaining are plentiful and cheap. The range of potential agreements, national preferences, and institutional options can thus be assumed to be common knowledge among governments."[19] By

---

[16] Cox and McCubbins 2004, 371.
[17] See, especially, Moravcsik 1998, 1999a, 1999b.
[18] Nash 1950; Schelling 1960; Walton and McKersie 1965; Raiffa 1982; Scharpf 1997.
[19] Moravcsik 1998, 61.

consequence, states rarely fail to reap the full benefits of cooperation because of impediments in the bargaining process. Instead, the central analytical concern of this perspective is the distribution of gains between the parties. More specifically, it suggests that the distribution of gains in decentralized negotiations will reflect the relative bargaining power of the parties, as defined by the parties' best alternative to a negotiated agreement.

This perspective on the efficiency and distributional implications of multilateral bargaining translates into a skeptical position on the importance of leaders and entrepreneurs. If states are capable of identifying efficient agreements themselves and transaction costs are low, then there will be little demand for political leadership, which will prove redundant when offered. Alternatively, if the distribution of state preferences prevents a zone of agreement from materializing, then the efforts of leaders and entrepreneurs are bound to fail and are thus futile. Since political leadership in neither case will constitute a necessary or sufficient condition for agreement, there are few reasons to believe that leaders or entrepreneurs will gain a position to shape the distributional outcomes of international cooperation.

The propositions of the efficient negotiation perspective are challenged by the entrepreneurial leadership perspective, which takes bargaining impediments as its starting point and underlines the role of leaders and entrepreneurs in overcoming these problems.[20] This perspective is rooted in the rational choice tradition as well, but mainly draws on collective-action theory and transaction-cost theory.[21] It underlines that complex multilateral negotiations tend to be fraught with various forms of bargaining problems that prevent states from concluding mutually advantageous deals. The initiation of bargaining is typically burdened by conflicts over the agenda. The negotiations as such tend to suffer from the parties' recalcitrance to reveal their true preferences and unwillingness to offer concessions. When states indeed wish to communicate their honest preferences, this is made more difficult by the complexity of multilateral negotiations. If the parties eventually manage to identify a zone of agreement, they often run into the problem of having to agree on one among multiple equilibria.

This pessimistic perspective on the efficiency of multilateral negotiations translates into an optimistic position on the importance of political leadership. Whereas the parties on their own may be unable to

---

[20] See, especially, O. Young 1991, 1999a; but also Fiorina and Shepsle 1989; Underdal 1994; Malnes 1995.

[21] Coase 1937; Olson 1965; Frohlich, Oppenheimer, and Young 1971; Keohane 1984.

overcome bargaining impediments, leaders and entrepreneurs can dramatically improve the chances of success through measures that solve or circumvent these collective-action problems. More specifically, they can facilitate agreement by shaping the agenda of international negotiations, drawing attention to the issues at stake, devising innovative policy options, building viable coalitions, and brokering agreement. Proponents of this perspective generally conclude that leadership or entrepreneurship is a necessary, but not sufficient, condition for success in multilateral negotiations. In this vein, Oran Young asserts: "Leadership . . . is a critical determinant of success or failure in the processes of institutional bargaining that dominate efforts to form international regimes or, more generally, institutional arrangements in international society."[22] While paying relatively less attention to the distribution of gains from multilateral negotiations, this perspective suggests that leaders and entrepreneurs are self-interested and likely to be rewarded for their services. The collective benefits generated by their interventions ensure that the parties are in a position to compensate those who provide political leadership. Yet these rewards need not be material in nature, but can also take the shape of intangible currencies, such as prestige, reputation, political influence in other arenas, or progress toward the achievement of some larger personal goal.

This book generates three forms of implications for this theoretical debate on leadership, efficiency, and distribution in international cooperation. First, it grants support to the notion that bargaining impediments and transaction costs are normal and ever-present ingredients of the negotiation process, creating a demand for political leadership. The book suggests that the chairmanship as an institutional form is a product of those very bargaining impediments that the efficient negotiation perspective assumes do not exist. It claims that we cannot understand the delegation of agenda-management, brokerage, and representation functions to chairmanship institutions unless we recognize the collective-action problems that motivate states to empower formal leaders. It supports this theoretical argument with extensive empirical material, demonstrating how states, in the EU and elsewhere, turn to negotiation chairs for aid when confronted with overloaded agendas, deadlocked negotiations, and an absence of institutional formulas for external representation.

Second, this book suggests that the dominant conception of bargaining power must be revised if it is to properly explain the outcomes of

---

[22] O. Young 1991, 281.

multilateral negotiations. The study does not offer an alternative comprehensive theory of bargaining power, comparable to the notion of asymmetric interdependence or BATNA. But it demonstrates why the conventional wisdom must be supplemented with an understanding of the power wielded by formal leaders. More specifically, the book identifies the informational and procedural power resources of negotiation chairs, and explains when, why, and how these privileged resources permit formal leaders to shift outcomes away from the equilibria predicted by traditional bargaining theory. Multilateral agreements with distributional outcomes unusually conformant with the interests of formal leaders should not present a puzzle. Even where power asymmetries are strong (as in the OSCE) or cooperation highly institutionalized (as in the EU), formal leaders may enjoy sufficient discretion to shape the division of gains from multilateral negotiations.

Third, and finally, this book forces students of international cooperation to pay close attention to the sources of political leadership. While recognizing the demand and scope for political leadership in multilateral negotiations, the entrepreneurial leadership perspective is regrettably agnostic about the identity of leaders. Typically, entrepreneurial leaders are defined by their attempts to address collective-action problems, and may be state officials, supranational bureaucrats, representatives of non-governmental organizations, or private individuals. No category of actors in international bargaining is seen as having a monopoly on this function. This study points to the limits of this approach, by distinguishing between formal and informal sources of political leadership, and by demonstrating how access to the power platform of the chairmanship grants actors leadership resources they otherwise would not have possessed. In a comparative perspective, negotiation chairs enjoy a distinct institutional position, with particular procedural and informational resources, as well as a specific set of formal constraints, compared to alternative leaders and entrepreneurs. While it may be true that many types of actors can engage in political leadership, this book generates the expectation that negotiation chairs will feature particularly prominently in future analyses of successful international cooperation. Rather than leaving the provision of political leadership to the whim and goodwill of individual governments, secretariats, and NGOs, states in world politics have designed a potent institutional platform for this purpose – the chairmanship.

Appendix: EC/EU Presidencies 1958–2020*

Year	First six months	Second six months
1958	Belgium	Germany
1959	France	Italy
1960	Luxembourg	Netherlands
1961	Belgium	Germany
1962	France	Italy
1963	Luxembourg	Netherlands
1964	Belgium	Germany
1965	France	Italy
1966	Luxembourg	Netherlands
1967	Belgium	Germany
1968	France	Italy
1969	Luxembourg	Netherlands
1970	Belgium	Germany
1971	France	Italy
1972	Luxembourg	Netherlands
1973	Belgium	Denmark
1974	Germany	France
1975	Ireland	Italy
1976	Luxembourg	Netherlands
1977	United Kingdom	Belgium
1978	Denmark	Germany
1979	France	Ireland
1980	Italy	Luxembourg
1981	Netherlands	United Kingdom
1982	Belgium	Denmark
1983	Germany	Greece
1984	France	Ireland
1985	Italy	Luxembourg
1986	Netherlands	United Kingdom
1987	Belgium	Denmark
1988	Germany	Greece
1989	Spain	France
1990	Ireland	Italy

Table (*cont.*)

Year	First six months	Second six months
1991	Luxembourg	Netherlands
1992	Portugal	United Kingdom
1993	Denmark	Belgium
1994	Greece	Germany
1995	France	Spain
1996	Italy	Ireland
1997	Netherlands	Luxembourg
1998	United Kingdom	Austria
1999	Germany	Finland
2000	Portugal	France
2001	Sweden	Belgium
2002	Spain	Denmark
2003	Greece	Italy
2004	Ireland	Netherlands
2005	Luxembourg	United Kingdom
2006	Austria	Finland
2007	Germany	Portugal
2008	Slovenia	France
2009	Czech Republic	Sweden
2010	Spain	Belgium
2011	Hungary	Poland
2012	Denmark	Cyprus
2013	Ireland	Lithuania
2014	Greece	Italy
2015	Latvia	Luxembourg
2016	Netherlands	Slovakia
2017	Malta	United Kingdom
2018	Estonia	Bulgaria
2019	Austria	Romania
2020	Finland	

*The planned rotation order after 2006 is based on a Council decision from 2004, and may be subject to future alterations.

References

BOOKS AND ARTICLES

Ackrill, Robert W. (2000) CAP Reform 1999: A Crisis in the Making? *Journal of Common Market Studies* 38(2): 343–353.

Antrim, Lance N. and James K. Sebenius (1992) Formal Individual Mediation and the Negotiators' Dilemma: Tommy Koh at the Law of the Sea Conference, in *Mediation in International Relations: Multiple Approaches to Conflict Management*, Jacob Bercovitch and Jeffrey Z. Rubin (eds.), 97–130. Houndmills: Macmillan.

Arrow, Kenneth J. (1985) The Economics of Agency, in *Principals and Agents: The Structure of Business*, John W. Pratt and Richard J. Zeckhauser (eds.), 37–51. Boston, Mass.: Harvard Business School Press.

Arter, David (2000) Small State Influence Within the EU: The Case of Finland's "Northern Dimension Initiative." *Journal of Common Market Studies* 38(5): 677–697.

Aspinwall, Mark and Gerald Schneider (2000) Same Menu, Separate Tables: The Institutionalist Turn in Political Science and the Study of European Integration. *European Journal of Political Research* 38(1): 1–36.

Bachrach, Peter and Morton S. Baratz (1962) Two Faces of Power. *American Political Science Review* 56: 947–952.

Bachrach, Peter and Morton S. Baratz (1963) Decisions and Nondecisions: An Analytical Framework. *American Political Science Review* 57: 632–642.

Bakker, Edwin (2002) International Challenge for the Netherlands: The OSCE Chairmanship-in-Office in 2003. *Helsinki Monitor* 13(2): 216–220.

Baron, David P. (1994) A Sequential Choice Theory Perspective on Legislative Organization. *Legislative Studies Quarterly* 19(2): 267–296.

Bassompierre, Guy de (1988) *Changing the Guard in Brussels: An Insider's View of the Presidency*. New York, N.Y.: Praeger.

Beach, Derek (2004) The Unseen Hand in Treaty Reform Negotiations: The Role and Influence of the Council Secretariat. *Journal of European Public Policy* 11(3): 408–439.

(2005) *The Dynamics of European Integration: Why and When EU Institutions Matter*. Basingstoke: Palgrave Macmillan.

Benedick, Richard Elliot (1991) *Ozone Diplomacy. New Directions in Safeguarding the Planet*. Cambridge, Mass.: Harvard University Press.

(1993) Perspectives of a Negotiation Practitioner, in *International Environmental Negotiation*, Gunnar Sjöstedt (ed.), 219–243. Newbury Park, Calif.: Sage.

Bengtsson, Rikard (2004) *Historisk brytpunkt i Europa – EU:s utvidgning*. Stockholm: SNS Förlag.

Bengtsson, Rikard, Ole Elgström, and Jonas Tallberg (2004) Silencer or Amplifier? The European Union Presidency and the Nordic Countries. *Scandinavian Political Studies* 27(3): 311–334.

Bercovitch, Jacob (1992) The Structure and Diversity of Mediation in International Relations, in *Mediation in International Relations*, Jacob Bercovitch and Jeffrey Z. Rubin (eds.), 1–29. Houndmills: Macmillan.

Bercovitch, Jacob (ed.) (1996) *Resolving International Conflicts: The Theory and Practice of Mediation*. Boulder, Colo.: Lynne Rienner Publishers.

Bercovitch, Jacob and Jeffrey Z. Rubin (eds.) (1992) *Mediation in International Relations*. Houndmills: Macmillan.

Best, Edward, Mark Gray, and Alexander Stubb (2000) *Rethinking the European Union: IGC 2000 and Beyond*. Maastricht: European Institute of Public Administration.

Bjurulf, Bo (2001) Öppenheten – framgång bakom lyckta dörrar, in *När Europa kom till Sverige: Ordförandeskapet i EU 2001*, Jonas Tallberg (ed.), 119–134. Stockholm: SNS Förlag.

Bjurulf, Bo and Ole Elgström (2004) Negotiating Transparency: The Role of Institutions. *Journal of Common Market Studies* 42(2): 249–269.

Bloed, Arie (1997) The OSCE Main Political Bodies and Their Role in Conflict Prevention and Crisis Management, in *The OSCE in the Maintenance of Peace and Security: Conflict Prevention, Crisis Management, and Peaceful Settlement of Disputes*, Michael Bothe, Natalino Ronzitti, and Allan Rosas (eds.), 35–52. The Hague: Kluwer Law International.

(2001) Romania the New Chairman-in-Office of the OSCE. *Helsinki Monitor* 12(1): 48–54.

Bodansky, Daniel (1994) Prologue to the Climate Change Convention, in *Negotiating Climate Change: The Inside Story of the Rio Convention*, Irving M. Mintzer and J. A. Leonard (eds.), 45–74. Cambridge: Cambridge University Press.

(2001) The History of the Global Climate Change Regime, in *International Relations and Global Climate Change*, Urs Luterbacher and Detlef F. Spinz (eds.), 23–40. Cambridge, Mass.: MIT Press.

Bonvicini, Gianni (1988) Mechanisms and Procedures of EPC: More than Traditional Diplomacy? in *European Political Cooperation in the 1980s: A Common Foreign Policy for Western Europe?* Alfred Pijpers, Elfriede Regelsberger, and Wolfgang Wessels (eds.), 49–70. Dordrecht: Martinus Nijhoff Publishers.

Borione, Delphine and Jean Ripert (1994) Exercising Common but Differentiated Responsibility, in *Negotiating Climate Change: The Inside Story of the Rio Convention*, Irving M. Mintzer and J. A. Leonard (eds.), 77–96. Cambridge: Cambridge University Press.

Brunsson, Nils (1989) *The Organization of Hypocrisy: Talk, Decisions, and Actions in Organizations*. Chichester: Wiley.

Bulmer, Simon and Wolfgang Wessels (1987) *The European Council: Decision-Making in European Politics*. Houndmills: Macmillan.

Bunse, Simone (2000) The Presidency of the Council of Ministers as a Policy Entrepreneur? A Case Study of the "Northern Dimension" Initiative under the Finnish Presidency (1 July–31 December 1999). MPhil thesis, University of Oxford.

Carnevale, Peter J. and Sharon Arad (1996) Bias and Impartiality in International Mediation, in *Resolving International Conflicts: The Theory and Practice of Mediation*, Jacob Bercovitch (ed.), 39–53. Boulder, Colo.: Lynne Rienner Publishers.

Catellani, Nicola (2001) Short and Long-term Dynamics in the EU's Northern Dimension. COPRI Working Paper 41.

    (2003) *The EU's Northern Dimension: Testing a New Approach to Neighbourhood Relations*. Research report 35. Stockholm: Swedish Institute of International Affairs.

Checkel, Jeffrey T. (2001) Why Comply? Social Learning and European Identity Change. *International Organization* 55(3): 553–588.

Coase, Ronald H. (1937) The Nature of the Firm. *Economica* 4: 386–405.

Cockfield, Lord (1994) *The European Union: Creating the Single Market*. Chichester: Wiley.

Condorcet, Marquis de (1785) *Essai sur l'application de l'analyse à la probabilité des décisions rendues à la pluralité des voix*. Paris.

Cooperation and Conflict (2003) Symposium on the Danish EU Council Presidency. *Cooperation and Conflict* 38(3).

Corbett, Richard (1998) The Council Presidency as Seen from the European Parliament. Paper presented at the conference The Presidency of the European Union, Belfast, 15–16 October 1998.

Costa, Olivier, Anne Couvidat, and Jean-Pascal Daloz (2003) The French Presidency of 2000: An Arrogant Leader?, in *European Union Council Presidencies: A Comparative Analysis*, Ole Elgström (ed.), 120–137. London: Routledge.

Cox, Gary W. and Mathew D. McCubbins (2004) Setting the Agenda: Responsible Party Government in the US House of Representatives. Unpublished book manuscript.

Crombez, Christophe (1996) Legislative Procedures in the European Community. *British Journal of Political Science* 26: 119–228.

Crum, Ben (2006) The EU Presidency: Comparing the Italian and Irish Presidencies of the 2003–2004 Intergovernmental Conference, in *Leadership in the "Big Bangs" of European Integration*, Derek Beach and Colette Mazzucelli (eds.). Basingstoke: Palgrave.

Cutcher-Gershenfeld, Joel and Michael Watkins (1999) Toward a Theory of Representation in Negotiation, in *Negotiating on Behalf of Others: Advice to Lawyers, Business Executives, Sports Agents, Diplomats, Politicians, and Everybody Else*, Robert H. Mnookin and Lawrence E. Susskind (eds.), 23–51. Thousand Oaks, Calif.: Sage.

Danish Television (2003) Documentary about the Danish Presidency and the Enlargement Negotiations.

Davignon, Etienne (1986) Preface in *La Coopération Politique Européenne*, by Philippe de Schoutheete. 2nd edn. Brussels: Labor.

Dewost, Jean-Louis (1984) La Présidence dans le Cadre Institutionnel des Communautés Européennes. *Revue du Marché Commun* 273: 31–34.

DiMaggio, Paul J. and Walter W. Powell (1983) The Iron Cage Revisited: Institutional Isomorphism and Collective Rationality in Organizational Fields. *American Sociological Review* 48: 147–160.

Dinan, Desmond and Sophie Vanhoonacker (2000a) IGC 2000 Watch (Part 1): Origin and Preparation. *ECSA Review* 13(2).

(2000b) IGC 2000 Watch (Part 2): The Opening Round. *ECSA Review* 13(3).

(2000c) IGC 2000 Watch (Part 3): Pre- and Post-Nice. *ECSA Review* 13(4).

Djoghlaf, Ahmed (1994) The Beginnings of an International Climate Law, in *Negotiating Climate Change: The Inside Story of the Rio Convention*, Irving M. Mintzer and J. A. Leonard (eds.), 97–111. Cambridge: Cambridge University Press.

Dowdeswell, Elisabeth and Richard J. Kinley (1994) Constructive Damage to the Status Quo in *Negotiating Climate Change: The Inside Story of the Rio Convention*, Irving M. Mintzer and J. A. Leonard (eds.), 113–128. Cambridge: Cambridge University Press.

Dupont, Christophe (1994) Coalition Theory: Using Power to Build Cooperation, in *International Multilateral Negotiations*, I. William Zartman (ed.), 148–177. San Francisco, Calif.: Jossey-Bass.

Dür, Andreas and Gemma Mateo (2004) Treaty-Making in the European Union: Bargaining, Issue Linkages, and Efficiency. *European Integration Online Papers* 8: 18.

Edwards, Geoffrey and Alfred Pijpers (eds.) (1997) *The Politics of European Treaty Reform: The 1996 Intergovernmental Conference and Beyond*. London: Pinter.

Edwards, Geoffrey and Helen Wallace (1977) *The Council of Ministers of the European Community and the President in Office*. London: Federal Trust for Education and Research.

Elgström, Ole (2003a) "The Honest Broker"? The Council Presidency as a Mediator, in *European Union Council Presidencies: A Comparative Analysis*, Ole Elgström (ed.), 38–54. London: Routledge.

(ed.) (2003b) *European Union Council Presidencies: A Comparative Analysis*. London: Routledge.

Elgström, Ole and Jonas Tallberg (2003) Conclusion: Rationalist and Sociological Perspectives on the Council Presidency, in *European Union Council Presidencies: A Comparative Analysis*, Ole Elgström (ed.), 191–205. London: Routledge.

Eliasson, Nils (1993) The Future of the CSCE Secretariat, in *The CSCE in the 1990s: Constructing European Security and Cooperation*, Michael R. Lucas (ed.), 223–226. Baden-Baden: Nomos Verlagsgesellschaft.

Epstein, David and Sharyn O'Halloran (1999) *Delegating Powers: A Transaction Cost Politics Approach to Policy Making under Separate Powers*. Cambridge: Cambridge University Press.

Evans, Peter B., Harold K. Jacobson, and Robert D. Putnam (eds.) (1993) *Double-Edged Diplomacy: International Bargaining and Domestic Politics*. Berkeley, Calif.: University of California Press.

Farrell, Henry and Adrienne Héritier (2003a) *The Invisible Transformation of Codecision: Problems of Democratic Legitimacy.* Report 2003: 7. Stockholm: Swedish Institute for European Policy Studies.

(2003b) Formal and Informal Institutions under Codecision: Continuous Constitution-Building in Europe. *Governance* 16(4): 577–600.

Fearon, James D. (1991) Counterfactuals and Hypothesis Testing in Political Science. *World Politics* 43: 169–195.

Finnemore, Martha and Kathryn Sikkink (1998) International Norm Dynamics and Political Change. *International Organization* 52(4): 887–917.

Fiorina, Morris P. and Kenneth A. Shepsle (1989) Formal Theories of Leadership: Agents, Agenda Setters, and Entrepreneurs, in *Leadership and Politics: New Perspectives in Political Science*, Bryan D. Jones (ed.), 17–40. Lawrence, Kans.: University Press of Kansas.

Forsberg, Tuomas and Ojanen, Hanna (2000) Finland's New Policy: Using the EU for Stability in the North, in *The Northern EU: National Views on the Emerging Security Dimension*, Gianni Bonvicini, Tapani Vaahtoranta, and Wolfgang Wessels (eds.), 115–129. Helsinki: Finnish Institute of International Affairs.

Friis, Lykke (2003) An "Emperor Without Clothes"? *Cooperation and Conflict* 38(3): 283–290.

Frohlich, Norman, Joe A. Oppenheimer, and Oran R. Young (1971) *Political Leadership and Collective Goods.* Princeton, N.J.: Princeton University Press.

Galloway, David (1999a) Agenda 2000 – Packaging the Deal. *Journal of Common Market Studies* Annual Review 37: 9–35.

(1999b) Common Foreign and Security Policy: Intergovernmentalism Donning the Mantle of the Community Method, in *The Council of the European Union*, by Martin Westlake, 211–233. London: John Harper.

(2001) *The Treaty of Nice and Beyond: Realities and Illusions of Power in the EU.* Sheffield: Sheffield Academic Press.

Garrett, Geoffrey (1992) International Cooperation and Institutional Choice: The European Community's Internal Market. *International Organization* 46(2): 533–560.

Garrett, Geoffrey and Barry R. Weingast (1993) Ideas, Interests, and Institutions: Constructing the European Community's Internal Market, in *Ideas and Foreign Policy: Beliefs, Institutions, and Political Change*, Judith Goldstein and Robert O. Keohane (eds.), 173–206. Ithaca, N.Y.: Cornell University Press.

George, Alexander L. and Andrew Bennett (2005) *Case Studies and Theory Development in the Social Sciences.* Cambridge, Mass.: MIT Press.

George, Alexander L. and Timothy J. McKeown (1985) Case Studies and Theories of Organizational Decision Making. *Advances in Information Processing in Organizations* 2: 21–58.

Ghebali, Victor-Yves (1989) *La Diplomatie de la Détente: La CSCE, d'Helsinki à Vienne (1973–1989).* Bruxelles: Bruylant.

(2001) Is the OSCE Chairmanship Still a Relevant Institution? *Helsinki Monitor* 13(3): 201–203.

Golub, Jonathan (1999) In the Shadow of the Vote? Decision Making in the European Community. *International Organization* 53(4): 733–764.

Grant, Charles (1994) *Delors: Inside the House that Jacques Built*. London: Nicholas Brealey.

Gray, Mark (2004) The Convention's Internal Dynamic: Leadership, Alliances and Lessons to be Learned, in *The Political Dynamics of Constitutional Reform: Reflections on the Convention on the Future of Europe*, Anna Michalski (ed.), 39–59. The Hague: Netherlands Institute of International Relations Clingendael.

Gray, Mark and Alexander Stubb (2001) The Treaty of Nice – Negotiating a Poisoned Chalice? *Journal of Common Market Studies* Annual Review 39: 5–23.

Haglund, Anne (2002) Nordic Presidencies and the European Union's Northern Dimension Initiative. Paper presented at the annual meeting of the Swedish Political Science Association, Växjö, 6–8 October 2002.

Hall, Peter A. and Rosemary C. R. Taylor (1996) Political Science and the Three New Institutionalisms. *Political Studies* 44: 936–957.

Hall, Rodney Bruce (1997) Moral Authority as a Power Resource. *International Organization* 51(4): 591–622.

Hamlet, Lawrence (2002) Resolving Collective Action Problems and Preventing Agency Losses: How States Design the Secretariats of International Organizations. Paper prepared for the Workshop on World Politics, University of Michigan, 19 April 2002.

Hampson, Fen Osler with Michael Hart (1995) *Multilateral Negotiations. Lessons from Arms Control, Trade, and the Environment*. Baltimore, Md.: Johns Hopkins University Press.

Haukkala, Hiski (2001) Comment: National Interests Versus Solidarity Towards Common Policies, in *The Northern Dimension: Fuel for the EU?* Hanna Ojanen (ed.), 107–115. Helsinki: Finnish Institute of International Affairs.

Hayes-Renshaw, Fiona and Helen Wallace (1997) *The Council of Ministers*. Basingstoke: Macmillan.

(2006) *The Council of Ministers*. 2nd edn. Basingstoke: Palgrave Macmillan.

Hayes-Renshaw, Fiona, Wim van Aken, and Helen Wallace (2005) When and Why the Council of Ministers of the EU Votes Explicitly. Paper presented at the Ninth Biennial Conference of the European Union Studies Association, Austin, 31 March–2 April 2005.

Heininen, Lassi (2001) Ideas and Outcomes: Finding a Concrete Form for the Northern Dimension Initiative, in *The Northern Dimension: Fuel for the EU?* Hanna Ojanen (ed.), 20–53. Helsinki: Finnish Institute of International Affairs.

Heraclides, Alexis (1993a) *Security and Co-operation in Europe: The Human Dimension 1972–1992*. London: Frank Cass.

(1993b) *Helsinki-II and Its Aftermath: The Making of the CSCE into an International Organization*. London: Pinter.

Héritier, Adrienne (1995) "Leaders" and "Laggards" in European Clean Air Policy, in *Internationalization and Economic Policy: Convergence or Diversity?* Brigitte Unger and Frans Van Waarden (eds.), 278–305. Aldershot: Avebury.

Hermann, Margaret G., Thomas Preston, Baghat Korany, and Timothy M. Shaw (2001) Who Leads Matters: The Effects of Powerful Individuals. *International Studies Review* 3(2): 83–131.

Hoekman, Bernard M. and Michel M. Kostecki (2001) *The Political Economy of the World Trading System*. 2nd edn. Oxford: Oxford University Press.

Höll, Otmar (1987) The CSCE Process: Basic Facts, in *CSCE: N + N Perspectives. The Process of the Conference on Security and Co-operation in Europe from the Viewpoint of the Neutral and Non-Aligned Participating States*, Hanspeter Neuhold (ed.), 9–21, Laxenburg: Austrian Institute for International Affairs.

Holmström, Bengt (1979) Moral Hazard and Observability. *The Bell Journal of Economics* 10(1): 74–91.

Hopmann, P. Terrence (1996) *The Negotiation Process and the Resolution of International Conflicts*. Columbia, S.C.: University of South Carolina Press.

Immergut, Ellen M. (1996) The Theoretical Core of the New Institutionalisms. *Politics and Society* 26(1): 5–34.

Institut für Europäische Politik (ed.) (2003) *Enlargement/Agenda 2000–Watch No. 6/2003*. Berlin: Institut für Europäische Politik.

Jacobs, Francis B. (2001) Institutional Dynamics after Nice: Views from the European Parliament. Are the EU Institutions Becoming More Open and Transparent? Unpublished paper, May 2001.

Joenniemi, Pertti (2002) Racing to Regionalise? The EU's Northern Dimension Initiative. Paper presented at the International Studies Association conference, New Orleans, 24–27 March 2002.

Jönsson, Christer (2002) Diplomacy, Bargaining and Negotiation, in *Handbook of International Relations*, Walter Carlsnaes, Thomas Risse, and Beth A. Simmons (eds.), 212–234. London: Sage.

Jonsson, Håkan and Hans Hegeland (2003) *Konventet bakom kulisserna: om arbetsmetoden och förhandlingsspelet i Europeiska konventet*. SIEPSs utredningar 2003: 2u. Stockholm: Svenska institutet för europapolitiska studier.

Keohane, Robert O. (1984) *After Hegemony*. Princeton, N.Y.: Princeton University Press.

Kiewiet, D. Roderick and Mathew D. McCubbins (1991) *The Logic of Delegation: Congressional Parties and the Appropriations Process*. Chicago, Ill.: University of Chicago Press.

King, Gary, Robert O. Keohane, and Sidney Verba (1994) *Designing Social Inquiry: Scientific Interference in Qualitative Research*. Princeton, N.J.: Princeton University Press.

Kingdon, John W. (1984) *Agendas, Alternatives, and Public Policies*. Boston, Mass.: Little, Brown.

Kirchner, Emil (1992) *Decision-Making in the European Community: The Council Presidency and European Integration*. Manchester: Manchester University Press.

Kirchner, Emil J. and Anastassia Tsagkari (1993) *The EC Council Presidency: The Dutch and Luxembourg Presidencies*. London: UACES.

Kleiboer, Marieke (1998) *The Multiple Realities of International Mediation*. Boulder, Colo.: Lynne Rienner Publishers.

Koh, Tommy T. B. and Shanmugam Jayakumar (1985) The Negotiating Process of the Third United Nations Conference on the Law of the Sea, in *United Nations Convention on the Law of the Sea 1982: A Commentary. Vol. 1*, Myron H. Nordquist (ed.), 29–134. Dordrecht: Martinus Nijhoff Publishers.

Kollman, Ken (2003) The Rotating Presidency of the European Council as a Search for Good Policies. *European Union Politics* 4(1): 51–74.

Krasner, Stephen D. (1991) Global Communications and National Power: Life on the Pareto Frontier. *World Politics* 43(3): 336–366.

Kremenyuk, Victor A. (ed.) (2002) *International Negotiation: Analysis, Approaches, Issues*. 2nd edn. San Francisco, Calif.: Jossey-Bass.

Laffan, Brigid (1999) The Berlin Summit: Process and Outcome of the Agenda 2000 Budgetary Proposals. *ECSA Review* 12(4).

(2000) The Big Budgetary Bargains: From Negotiation to Authority. *Journal of European Public Policy* 7(5): 725–743.

Lang, Winfried (1989) Multilateral Negotiations: The Role of Presiding Officers, in *Processes of International Negotiations*, Frances Mautner-Markhof (ed.), 23–42. Boulder, Colo.: Westview Press.

Lankowski, Carl (1999) Germany's 1999 EU Council Presidency. *ECSA Review* 12(4).

Laursen, Finn (ed.) (2002) *The Amsterdam Treaty: National Preference Formation, Interstate Bargaining and Outcome*. Odense: Odense University Press.

Laursen, Finn and Sophie Vanhoonacker (eds.) (1992) *The Intergovernmental Conference on Political Union*. Maastricht: European Institute of Public Policy.

Lax, David A. and James K. Sebenius (1986) *The Manager as Negotiator*. New York, N.Y.: Free Press.

Lehne, Stefan (1991) *The Vienna Meeting of the Conference on Security and Cooperation in Europe, 1986–1989: A Turning Point in East-West Relations*. Boulder, Colo.: Westview Press.

Lequesne, Christian (2001) The French Presidency: The Half Success of Nice. *Journal of Common Market Studies* Annual Review 39: 47–50.

Liefferink, Duncan and Mikael Skou Andersen (1998) Strategies of the "Green" Member States in EU Environmental Policy. *Journal of European Public Policy* 5(2): 254–270.

Lindberg, Leon N. and Stuart A. Scheingold (1970) *Europe's Would-Be Polity: Patterns of Change in the European Community*. Englewood Cliffs, N.J.: Prentice-Hall.

Luce, R. Duncan and Howard Raiffa (1957) *Games and Decisions*. New York, N.Y.: Wiley.

Ludlow, Peter (1998) The 1998 UK Presidency: A View from Brussels. *Journal of Common Market Studies* 36(4): 573–583.

(2001) The Treaty of Nice: Neither Triumph nor Disaster. *ECSA Review* 14(2): 1–4.

(2002) *The Seville Council*. Brussels: EuroComment.

(2004) *The Making of the New Europe: The European Councils in Brussels and Copenhagen 2002*. Brussels: EuroComment.

Luif, Paul (2003) EU Cohesion in the UN General Assembly. Occasional Papers, No. 49. Paris: European Union Institute for Security Studies.

Malnes, Raino (1995) "Leader" and "Entrepreneur" in International Negotiations: A Conceptual Analysis. *European Journal of International Relations* 1(1): 87–112.

March, James G. and Johan P. Olsen (1989) *Rediscovering Institutions: The Organizational Basis of Politics*. New York, N.Y.: Free Press.

March, James G. and Johan P. Olsen (1998) The Institutional Dynamics of International Political Orders. *International Organization* 52(4): 943–969.

Martikainen, Tuomu and Tiilikainen, Teija (eds.) (2000) *Suomi EU:n Johdossa: Tutkimus Suomen Puheenjohtajuudesta 1999*. Helsinki: Helsingin Yliopisto, Yleisen Valtioopin Laitos, Acta Politica 13.

Martin, Lisa L. and Beth Simmons (1998) Theories and Empirical Studies of International Institutions. *International Organization* 52(4): 729–757.

Maurer, Andreas (2000) The German Presidency of the Council: Continuity or Change in Germany's European Policy? *Journal of Common Market Studies* Annual Review 38: 43–47.

McCubbins, Mathew D., Roger G. Noll, and Barry R. Weingast (1987) Administrative Procedures as Instruments of Political Control. *Journal of Law, Economics, and Organization* 3(2): 243–277.

McCubbins, Mathew D. and Thomas Schwartz (1984) Congressional Oversight Overlooked: Police Patrols versus Fire Alarms. *American Journal of Political Science* 28(1) 165–179.

McKelvey, Richard (1976) Intransitivities in Multidimensional Voting Models and Some Implications for Agenda Control. *Journal of Economic Theory* 12: 472–482.

McNamara, Kathleen R. (2002) Rational Fictions: Central Bank Independence and the Social Logic of Delegation. *West European Politics* 25(1): 47–76.

Mesquita, Bruce Bueno de (1990) Multilateral Negotiations: A Spatial Analysis of the Arab-Israeli Dispute. *International Organization* 44(3): 317–340.

Mesquita, Bruce Bueno de and Frans N. Stokman (eds.) (1994) *European Community Decision-Making: Models, Applications and Comparisons*. New Haven, Conn.: Yale University Press.

Metcalfe, David (1998) Leadership in European Union Negotiations: The Presidency of the Council. *International Negotiation* 3(3): 413–434.

Meunier, Sophie (2000) What Single Voice? European Institutions and EU–US Trade Negotiations. *International Organization* 54(1): 103–135.

Meunier, Sophie and Kalypso Nicolaïdis (2001) Trade Competence in the Nice Treaty. *ECSA Review* 14(2): 7–8.

Miles, Edward L., Arild Underdal, Steinar Andresen, Jørgen Wettestad, Jon Birger Skjærseth, and Elaine M. Carlin (2002) *Environmental Regime Effectiveness: Confronting Theory with Evidence*. Cambridge, Mass.: MIT Press.

Miller, Gary J. (1992) *Managerial Dilemmas: The Political Economy of Hierarchy*. Cambridge: Cambridge University Press.

Mintzer, Irving M. and J. Amber Leonard (eds.) (1994) *Negotiating Climate Change: The Inside Story of the Rio Convention*. Cambridge: Cambridge University Press.

Mnookin, Robert H. and Susskind, Lawrence E. (eds.) (1999) *Negotiating on Behalf of Others: Advice to Lawyers, Business Executives, Sports Agents, Diplomats, Politicians, and Everybody Else*. Thousand Oaks, Calif.: Sage.

Moe, Terry M. (1990) The Politics of Structural Choice: Toward a Theory of Public Bureaucracy, in *Organization Theory: From Chester Bernard to the*

Present and Beyond, Oliver E. Williamson (ed.), 116–153. New York, N.Y.: Oxford University Press.

Moore, Mike (2003) *A World Without Walls: Freedom, Development, Free Trade and Global Governance*. Cambridge: Cambridge University Press.

Moravcsik, Andrew (1998) *The Choice for Europe: Social Purpose and State Power from Messina to Maastricht*. Ithaca, N.Y.: Cornell University Press.

(1999a) A New Statecraft? Supranational Entrepreneurs and International Cooperation. *International Organization* 53(2): 267–306.

(1999b) Theory and Method in the Study of International Negotiation: A Rejoinder to Oran Young. *International Organization* 53(4): 811–814.

Moravcsik, Andrew and Kalypso Nicolaïdis (1999) Explaining the Amsterdam Treaty: Interests, Influence, Institutions. *Journal of Common Market Studies* 37(1): 59–85.

Nash, John F. (1950) The Bargaining Problem. *Econometrica* 18: 155–162.

Neligan, David (1998) Organising the Presidency: The Council Perspective. Paper presented at the conference The Presidency of the European Union, Belfast, 15–16 October 1998.

Neuhold, Hanspeter (1987) The Group of the N + N Countries Within the CSCE Process, in *CSCE: N + N Perspectives. The Process of the Conference on Security and Co-operation in Europe from the Viewpoint of the Neutral and Non-Aligned Participating States*, Hanspeter Neuhold (ed.), 23–35. Laxenburg: Austrian Institute for International Affairs.

Nicolaïdis, Kalypso (1999) Minimizing Agency Costs in Two-Level Games: Lessons from the Trade Authority Controversies in the United States and the European Union in *Negotiating on Behalf of Others: Advice to Lawyers, Business Executives, Sports Agents, Diplomats, Politicians, and Everybody Else*, Robert M. Mnookin and Lawrence E. Susskind (eds.), 87–126. Thousand Oaks, Calif.: Sage.

Nicoll, William (1998) The Evolution of the Office of the Presidency. Paper presented at the conference The Presidency of the European Union, Belfast, 15–16 October 1998.

(1999) The Budget Council, in *The Council of the European Union*, by Martin Westlake, 179–190. 2nd edn. London: John Harper.

Norman, Peter (2003) *The Accidental Constitution: The Story of the European Convention*. Brussels: EuroComment.

Nugent, Neill (1995) *The Government and Politics of the European Union*. 3rd edn. Houndmills: Macmillan.

Nuttall, Simon (1992) *European Political Co-operation*. Oxford: Clarendon.

(2000) *European Foreign Policy*. Oxford: Oxford University Press.

Oberthür, Sebastian and Thomas Gehring (2001) *Conceptualising Interaction Between International and EU Environmental Institutions*. Report, *Ecologic*, June 2001.

Odell, John (2003) Making and Breaking Impasses in International Regimes: The WTO, Seattle, and Doha. Unpublished paper.

(2005) Chairing a WTO Negotiation. *Journal of International Economic Law* 8(2): 425–448.

Ojanen, Hanna (1999) How to Customize Your Union: Finland and the "Northern Dimension of the EU", in *Northern Dimensions. The Yearbook of the*

Finnish Institute of International Affairs 1999, 13–26. Helsinki: Finnish Institute of International Affairs.

Olson, Mancur (1965) *The Logic of Collective Action: Public Goods and the Theory of Groups.* Cambridge, Mass.: Harvard University Press.

O Nuallain, Colm (ed.) (1985) *The Presidency of the European Council of Ministers.* London: Croom Helm.

Paemen, Hugo and Alexandra Bensch (1995) *From the GATT to the WTO: The European Community in the Uruguay Round.* Leuven: Leuven University Press.

Peters, B. Guy (1999) *Institutional Theory in Political Science.* London: Pinter.

Peterson, John and Helene Sjursen (eds.) (1998) *A Common Foreign Policy for Europe? Competing Visions of the CFSP.* London: Routledge.

Petersson, Olof, Ulrika Mörth, Johan P. Olsen and Jonas Tallberg (2003) *Demokrati i EU: Demokratirådets rapport 2003.* Stockholm: SNS Förlag.

Pierson, Paul (1996) The Path to European Integration: A Historical-Institutionalist Analysis. *Comparative Political Studies* 29(2): 251–267.

(2000) The Limits of Design: Explaining Institutional Origins and Change. *Governance* 13(4): 475–499.

(2004) *Politics in Time: History, Institutions, and Social Analysis.* Princeton: Princeton University Press.

Pollack, Mark A. (2003) *The Engines of European Integration: Delegation, Agency, and Agenda Setting in the EU.* Oxford: Oxford University Press.

Powell, Walter W. and Paul J. DiMaggio (eds.) (1991) *The New Institutionalism in Organizational Analysis.* Chicago, Ill.: University of Chicago Press.

Preeg, Ernest H. (1970) *Traders and Diplomats: An Analysis of the Kennedy Round of Negotiations under the General Agreement on Tariffs and Trade.* Washington D.C.: Brookings Institution.

Putnam, Robert D. (1988) Diplomacy and Domestic Politics: The Logic of Two-Level Games. *International Organization* 42: 427–460.

Raiffa, Howard (1982) *The Art and Science of Negotiation.* Cambridge, Mass.: Harvard University Press.

Riker, William (1980) Implications from the Disequilibrium of Majority Rule for the Study of Institutions. *American Political Science Review* 74: 432–446.

Risse, Thomas (2000) "Let's Argue!": Communicative Action in World Politics. *International Organization* 54(1): 1–39.

Ross, George (1995) *Jacques Delors and European Integration.* Cambridge: Polity Press.

(2001) France's European Tour of Duty, or Caution – One Presidency May Hide Another. *ECSA Review* 14(2): 4–6.

Rubin, Jeffrey Z. (1993) Third-Party Roles: Mediation in International Environmental Disputes, in *International Environmental Negotiation*, Gunnar Sjöstedt (ed.), 275–290. Newbury Park, Calif.: Sage.

Sanches da Costa Pereira, Pedro (1988) The Use of a Secretariat, in *European Political Cooperation in the 1980s: A Common Foreign Policy for Western Europe?* Alfred Pijpers, Elfriede Regelsberger, and Wolfgang Wessels (eds.), 85–103. Dordrecht: Martinus Nijhoff Publishers.

Sandholtz, Wayne and John Zysman (1989) 1992: Recasting the European Bargain. *World Politics* 42(1): 95–128.

Saunders, Harold K. (1985) We Need a Larger Theory of Negotiation: The Importance of Pre-Negotiating Phases. *Negotiation Journal* 1(3): 249–262.

Sbragia, Alberta (1996) Environmental Policy: The "Push-Pull" of Policy-Making in *Policy-Making in the European Union*, Helen Wallace and William Wallace (eds.), 235–255. Oxford: Oxford University Press.

Scharpf, Fritz W. (1988) The Joint-Decision Trap: Lessons from German Federalism and European Integration. *Public Administration* 66: 239–278.

(1997) *Games Real Actors Play*. Boulder, Colo.: Westview Press.

Schelling, Thomas C. (1960) *The Strategy of Conflict*. Cambridge: Harvard University Press.

Schmidt, Susanne K. (2001) A Constrained Commission: Informal Practices of Agenda-Setting in the Council in *The Rules of Integration: Institutionalist Approaches to the Study of Europe*, Gerald Schneider and Mark Aspinwall (eds.), 125–146. Manchester: Manchester University Press.

Schneider, Gerald and Mark Aspinwall (eds.) (2001) *The Rules of Integration: Institutionalist Approaches to the Study of Europe*. Manchester: Manchester University Press.

Schott, Jeffrey J. and Jayashree Watal (2000) Decision Making in the WTO, in *The WTO after Seattle*, Jeffrey J. Schott (ed.), 283–292. Washington D.C.: Institute for International Economics.

Schout, Adriaan (1998) The Presidency as Juggler: Managing Conflicting Expectations. *Eipascope* 1998(2): 2–10.

Schout, Adriaan and Sophie Vanhoonacker (2001) The Presidency as Broker? Lessons from Nice. Paper presented at the Fourth Pan-European International Relations Conference, Canterbury, 8–10 September 2001.

Schoutheete, Philippe de (1988) The Presidency and the Management of Political Cooperation, in *European Political Cooperation in the 1980s: A Common Foreign Policy for Western Europe?* Alfred Pijpers, Elfriede Regelsberger, and Wolfgang Wessels (eds.), 71–84. Dordrecht: Martinus Nijhoff Publishers.

Schwaag Serger, Sylvia (2001) *Negotiating CAP Reform in the European Union – Agenda 2000*. SLI Report 2001: 4. Lund: Swedish Institute for Food and Agricultural Economics.

Scott, W. Richard, John W. Meyer, and associates (1994) *Institutional Environments and Organizations: Structural Complexity and Individualism*. London: Sage.

Sebenius, James K. (1983) Negotiation Arithmetic: Adding and Subtracting Issues and Parties. *International Organization* 37: 281–316.

(1984) *Negotiating the Law of the Sea*. Cambridge, Mass.: Harvard University Press.

(1996) Sequencing to Build Coalitions: With Whom Should I Talk First?, in *Wise Choices: Decisions, Games, and Negotiations*, Richard J. Zeckhauser, Ralph L. Keeney, and James K. Sebenius (eds.), 324–328. Boston: Harvard Business School Press.

Shackleton, Michael (2000) The Politics of Codecision. *Journal of Common Market Studies* 38(2): 325–342.

Shackleton, Michael and Tapio Raunio (2003) Codecision since Amsterdam: A Laboratory for Institutional Innovation and Change. *Journal of European Public Policy* 10(2): 171–187.

Shepsle, Kenneth A. (1979) Institutional Arrangements and Equilibrium in Multi-Dimensional Voting Models. *American Journal of Political Science* 23: 27–60.

Shepsle, Kenneth A. and Barry R. Weingast (1984) Uncovered Sets and Sophisticated Voting Outcomes with Implications for Agenda Institutions. *American Journal of Political Science* 28: 49–74.

(1995) Positive Theories of Congressional Institutions, in *Positive Theories of Congressional Institutions*, Kenneth A. Shepsle and Barry R. Weingast (eds.), 5–35. Ann Arbor, Mich.: University of Michigan Press.

Sherrington, Philippa (1998) The Presidency in Context. Paper presented at the conference The Presidency of the European Union, Dublin, 15–16 October 1998.

(2000) *The Council of Ministers: Political Authority in the European Union.* London: Pinter.

Sizoo, Jan and Jurrjens, Rudolf (1984) *CSCE Decision-Making: The Madrid Experience.* The Hague: Martinus Nijhoff Publishers.

Sjöstedt, Gunnar (1994) Negotiating the Uruguay Round of the General Agreement on Tariffs and Trade in *International Multilateral Negotiations. Approaches to the Management of Complexity*, I. William Zartman (ed.), 44–69. San Francisco, Calif.: Jossey-Bass.

(1999) Leadership in Multilateral Negotiations: Crisis or Transition?, in *International Negotiation*, Peter Berton, Hiroshi Kimura, and I. William Zartman (eds.), 223–253. New York, N.Y.: St Martin's Press.

(2002) WTO som förhandlingsorganisation – ett försummat perspektiv, in *Handelspolitik i förändring: Organisation och förhandling i Sverige, EU och WTO*, Joakim Reiter and Christer Jönsson (eds.), 140–165. Stockholm: SNS Förlag.

Smith, Michael E. (2001) The Quest for Coherence: Institutional Dilemmas of External Action from Maastricht to Amsterdam, in *The Institutionalization of Europe*, Alec Stone Sweet, Wayne Sandholtz, and Neil Fligstein (eds.), 171–193. Oxford: Oxford University Press.

(2004) *Europe's Foreign and Security Policy: The Institutionalization of Cooperation.* Cambridge: Cambridge University Press.

Starkey, Brigid, Mark A. Boyer, and Jonathan Wilkenfeld (1999) *Negotiating a Complex World: An Introduction to International Negotiation.* Lanham, Md.: Rowman & Littlefield.

Stefan-Bastl, Jutta (2001) The Austrian OSCE Chairmanship. Assessment and Outlook. *Helsinki Monitor* 12(4): 257–271.

Stein, Caroline (2000) What Is a Good Presidency and How Is It Achieved? Comparing and Evaluating the Austrian, German and Finnish Presidencies. Master's thesis, College of Europe, Natolin.

Stein, Janice Gross (ed.) (1989) *Getting to the Table: The Processes of International Prenegotiation.* Baltimore, Md.: Johns Hopkins University Press.

Stenelo, Lars-Göran (1972) *Mediation in International Negotiations.* Lund: Studentlitteratur.

Steunenberg, Bernard (1994) Decision Making under Different Institutional Arrangements: Legislation by the European Community. *Journal of Theoretical and Institutional Economics* 150: 642–669.

Stirk, Peter M. R. and David Weigall (1999) *The Origins and Development of European Integration: A Reader and Commentary*. Pinter: London.

Stokke, Olav Schram (2001a) *The Interplay of International Regimes: Putting Effectiveness Theory to Work*. FNI Report 14/2001. Oslo: Fridtjof Nansen Institute.

(ed.) (2001b) *Governing High Seas Fisheries: The Interplay of Global and Regional Regimes*. Oxford: Oxford University Press.

Stone Sweet, Alec and Wayne Sandholtz (1997) European Integration and Supranational Governance. *Journal of European Public Policy* 4(3): 297–317.

Strömvik, Maria (1998) Fifteen Votes and One Voice? The CFSP and Changing Voting Alignments in the UN. *Statsvetenskaplig Tidskrift* 101(2): 181–196.

(2005) To Act as a Union: Explaining the Development of the EU's Collective Foreign Policy. Ph.D. dissertation, Lund University.

Stubb, Alexander (2000) The Finnish Presidency. *Journal of Common Market Studies* Annual Review 38: 49–53.

(2002) *Negotiating Flexibility in the European Union: Amsterdam, Nice and Beyond*. Houndmills: Palgrave.

Svensson, Anna-Carin (2000) In the Service of the European Union: The Role of the Presidency in Negotiating the Amsterdam Treaty 1995–1997. Ph.D. dissertation, Uppsala University.

Széll, Patrick (1993) Negotiations on the Ozone Layer in *International Environmental Negotiation*, Gunnar Sjöstedt (ed.), 31–48. Newbury Park, Calif.: Sage.

Tallberg, Jonas (ed.) (2001) *När Europa kom till Sverige: Ordförandeskapet i EU 2001*. Stockholm: SNS Förlag.

(2002) Delegation to Supranational Institutions: Why, How, and with What Consequences? *West European Politics* 25(1): 23–46.

(2003a) The Agenda-Shaping Powers of the EU Council Presidency. *Journal of European Public Policy* 10(1): 1–19.

(2003b) *European Governance and Supranational Institutions: Making States Comply*. London: Routledge.

(2004) The Power of the Presidency: Brokerage, Efficiency, and Distribution in EU Negotiations. *Journal of Common Market Studies* 42(5): 999–1022.

Taulègne, Béatrice (1993) *Le Conseil européen*. Paris: Presses Universitaires de France.

Tetlock, Philip E. and Aaron Belkin (eds.) (1996) *Counterfactual Thought Experiments in World Politics: Logical, Methodological, and Psychological Perspectives*. Princeton, N.J.: Princeton University Press.

Thomson, Robert, Frans N. Stokman, Christopher H. Achen, and Thomas König (eds.) (2006) *The European Union Decides*. Cambridge: Cambridge University Press.

Tiilikainen, Teija (2003) The Finnish Presidency of 1999: Pragmatism and the Promotion of Finland's Position in Europe, in *European Union Council Presidencies: A Comparative Analysis*, Ole Elgström (ed.), 104–119. London: Routledge.

Tolba, Mostafa K. (1998) *Global Environmental Diplomacy. Negotiating Environmental Agreements for the World 1973–1992*. Cambridge, Mass.: MIT Press.

Touval, Saadia (1989) Multilateral Negotiation: An Analytical Approach. *Negotiation Journal* 5(2): 159–173.

Touval, Saadia and I. William Zartman (eds.) (1985) *International Mediation in Theory and Practice*. Boulder, Colo.: Westview Press.

Troy Johnston, Mary (1994) *The European Council: Gatekeeper of the European Community*. Boulder, Colo.: Westview Press.

Tsebelis, George (1990) *Nested Games*. Berkeley, Calif.: University of California Press.

(2002) *Veto Players: How Political Institutions Work*. Princeton, N.J.: Princeton University Press.

Tsebelis, George and Geoffrey Garrett (2000) Legislative Politics in the European Union. *European Union Politics* 1(1): 9–36.

Underdal, Arild (1994) Leadership Theory: Rediscovering the Arts of Management, in *International Multilateral Negotiations*, I. William Zartman (ed.), 178–197. San Francisco, Calif.: Jossey-Bass.

Vandamme, Jacques (1987) The Tindemans Report (1975–76), in *The Dynamics of European Union*, Roy Pryce (ed.), 149–173. London: Croom Helm.

Wall, James A. and Ann Lynn (1993) Mediation: A Current Overview. *Journal of Conflict Resolution* 37(1): 160–194.

Wallace, Helen (1985) The Presidency of the Council of Ministers of the European Community: Tasks and Evolution, in *The Presidency of the European Council of Ministers: Impacts and Implications for National Governments*, Colm O Nuallain (ed.), 1–22. London: Croom Helm.

(2002) The Council: An Institutional Chameleon? *Governance* 15(3): 325–344.

Walton, Richard E. and Robert B. McKersie (1965) *A Behavioral Theory of Labor Negotiations*. New York, N.Y.: McGraw-Hill.

Weingast, Barry R. (2002) Rational Choice Institutionalism, in *The State of the Discipline*, Ira Katznelson and Helen Milner (eds.), 660–692. New York, N.Y.: W. W. Norton.

Weingast, Barry R. and William J. Marshall (1988) The Industrial Organization of Congress: Or Why Legislatures, like Firms, are not Organized as Markets. *Journal of Political Economy* 96: 132–163.

Werts, Jan (1992) *The European Council*. Amsterdam: North-Holland.

West European Politics (2002) The Politics of Delegation: Non-Majoritarian Institutions in Europe. Special issue of *West European Politics* 25(1).

Westlake, Martin (1999) *The Council of the European Union*. 2nd edn. London: John Harper.

Westlake, Martin and David Galloway with Toon Digneffe (2004) *The Council of the European Union*. 3rd edn. London: John Harper.

Wettestad, Jørgen (2002) The Vienna Convention and Montreal Protocol on Ozone-Layer Depletion, in *Environmental Regime Effectiveness: Confronting Theory with Evidence*, Edward L. Miles, Arild Underdal, Steinar, Andresen, Jørgen Wettestad, Jon Birger Skjærseth, and Elaine M. Carlin (eds.), 149–170. Cambridge, Mass.: MIT Press.

Whitman, Richard (1998) The Role of the Presidency in Promoting a CFSP. Paper presented at the conference The Presidency of the European Union, Belfast, 15–16 October 1998.

Williamson, Oliver E. (1995) Transaction Cost Economics and Organizational Theory, in *Organization Theory: From Chester Bernard to the Present and Beyond*, Oliver E. Williamson (ed.), 207–256. New York, N.Y.: Oxford University Press.

Winham, Gilbert R. (1977) Negotiation as a Management Process. *World Politics* 30(1): 87–114.

(1979) The Mediation of Multilateral Negotiations. *Journal of World Trade Law* 13(3): 193–208.

(1986) *International Trade and the Tokyo Round Negotiation*. Princeton, N.Y.: Princeton University Press.

(1992) *The Evolution of International Trade Agreements*. Toronto: University of Toronto Press.

Wurzel, Rüdiger K. W. (1996) The Role of the Presidency in the Environmental Field: Does It Make a Difference Which Member State Runs the Presidency? *Journal of European Public Policy* 3(2): 272–291.

(2000) Flying into Unexpected Turbulence: The German EU Presidency in the Environmental Field. *German Politics* 9(3): 23–42.

(2001) The EU Presidency and the Integration Principle: An Anglo-German Comparison. *European Environmental Law Review*, January 2001: 8–15.

Young, H. Peyton (ed.) (1991) *Negotiation Analysis*. Ann Arbor, Mich.: The University of Michigan Press.

Young, Oran R. (1967) *Intermediaries: Third Parties in International Crises*. Princeton N.J.: Princeton University Press.

(1991) Political Leadership and Regime Formation: On the Development of Institutions, in International Society. *International Organization* 45(3): 281–308.

(1999a) Comment on Andrew Moravcsik, 'A New Statecraft? Supranational Entrepreneurs and International Cooperation'. *International Organization* 53(4): 805–809.

(1999b) *Governance in World Affairs*. Ithaca, N.Y.: Cornell University Press.

(2002) *The Institutional Dimensions of Environmental Change: Fit, Interplay, and Scale*. Cambridge, Mass.: MIT Press.

Zartman, I. William (1994a) Two's Company and More's a Crowd: The Complexities of Multilateral Negotiation in *International Multilateral Negotiations*, I. William Zartman (ed.), 1–10. San Francisco, Calif.: Jossey-Bass.

(ed.) (1994b) *International Multilateral Negotiations*. San Francisco, Calif.: Jossey-Bass.

Zellner, Wolfgang (2002) The Ninth OSCE Ministerial in Bucharest 2001. *Helsinki Monitor* 13(1): 62–71.

Zielonka, Jan (ed.) (1998) *Paradoxes of European Foreign Policy*. The Hague: Kluwer.

OFFICIAL DOCUMENTS AND SPEECHES

Blair, Tony (2002) A Clear Course for Europe. Speech in Cardiff, 28 November 2002.

Blair, Tony and Gerhard Schröder (2002) Reform of the European Council. Letter to Prime Minister Aznar of Spain. 25 February 2002.

Chirac, Jacques (2002) Speech in Strasbourg, 6 March 2002.

Council of the European Union (1993) Rules of Procedure. Reproduced in *The Council of the European Union*, by Martin Westlake, 137–144. London: John Harper.

Council of the European Union (1999a) Press Release 6546/99, Environment Council 11/03/1999.

Council of the European Union (1999b) Press Release 9406/99, Environment Council 24/06/1999.

Council of the European Union (1999c) Common Position No. 39/1999 adopted by the Council on 29 July 1999 with a view to adopting Directive 1999/. . ./EC of the European Parliament and of the Council of . . . on end-of-life vehicles. *Official Journal* C 317, 4/11/1999: 19–33.

Council of the European Union (1999d) Press Release 10390/99, General Affairs Council 29/07/1999.

Council of the European Union (1999e) An Effective Council for an Enlarged Union. Guidelines for Reform and Operational Recommendations. 13863/99, 8 December 1999.

Council of the European Union (2000a) Action Plan for the Northern Dimension in the External and Cross-Border Policies of the European Union 2000–2003. 9401/00 Limite, Brussels, 14 June 2000.

Council of the European Union (2000b) Presidency Note: Proposal for a Regulation of the European Parliament and of the Council Regarding Public Access to European Parliament, Council and Commission Documents. 14938/00 Limite. 22 December 2000.

Council of the European Union (2000c) Press Release 8828/00, Green Light for End-of-Life Vehicles Directive, Parliament-Council Conciliation Committee 23/05/2000.

Council of the European Union (2002a) Measures to Prepare the Council for Enlargement. Report by the Presidency to the European Council. 9939/02, 13 June 2002.

Council of the European Union (2002b) Council Decision of 22 July 2002 Adopting the Council's Rules of Procedure. *Official Journal of the European Communities* L 230, 28/8/2002: 7.

Council of Ministers of the European Community (1979) Rules of Procedure. Reproduced in *The Council of the European Union*, by Martin Westlake, 133–136. London: John Harper.

Council of Ministers of the European Economic Community (1958) The Rules of Procedure. Reproduced in *The Council of the European Union*, by Martin Westlake, 130–133. London: John Harper.

Council Secretariat (1997) Council Guide. 1. Presidency Handbook. Luxembourg: Office for Official Publications of the European Communities.

Council Secretariat (1999) Rådets arbetssätt inför utvidgningen av unionen. SN 2139/99, 19 March 1999.

Council Secretariat (2002) Preparing the Council for Enlargement. Report by the Secretary-General. SN 1636/2/02 REV 2, 11 March 2002.

Danish Presidency (2002a) One Europe. Programme of the Danish Presidency of the EU. July to December 2002. Copenhagen: Royal Danish Ministry of Foreign Affairs.

Danish Presidency (2002b) Results of the Danish EU Presidency. One Europe from Copenhagen to Copenhagen. Copenhagen: Royal Danish Ministry of Foreign Affairs.

Danish Presidency (2002c) The European Council in Copenhagen. Letter of 11 December from Prime Minister Anders Fogh Rasmussen to his colleagues. Internet: www.eu2002dk, accessed 11 August 2003.

Dutch Government (2003) The Netherlands OSCE Chairmanship. Ten Questions and Answers. Internet: www.osce.org/cio/Netherlands/documents/files/cio-priorities.pdf, accessed 30 May 2003.

European Commission (1997a) Proposal for a Council Directive on End of Life Vehicles. COM (97) 358 Final. *Official Journal* C 337, 07/11/1997: 3.

European Commission (1997b) Agenda 2000: For a Stronger and Wider Union. COM (97) 2000, 16 July 1997.

European Commission (2000) Proposal for a Regulation of the European Parliament and of the Council Regarding Public Access to European Parliament, Council and Commission Documents. COM (2000) 30 final/2.

European Commission (2003) Commission Working Document. The Second Northern Dimension Action Plan, 2004–2006. COM (2003) 343 Final, 10 June 2003.

European Council (1974) Communiqué from Meeting of the Heads of Government of the Community, Paris 9–10 December 2004 (Paris communiqué).

European Council (1977) Organizational Rules for European Council Meetings (London declaration).

European Council (1983) Solemn Declaration on European Union. Stuttgart European Council, 19 June 1983.

European Council (1997) Presidency Conclusions, Luxembourg European Council, 12–13 December 1997. SN 400/97.

European Council (1998) Presidency Conclusions, Vienna European Council, 11–12 December 1998. SN 300/98.

European Council (1999a) Presidency Conclusions, Cologne European Council, 3–4 June 1999. SN 150/99.

European Council (1999b) Presidency Conclusions, Helsinki European Council, 10–11 December 1999. SN 300/99.

European Council (2001) Presidency Conclusions, Göteborg European Council, 15–16 June 2001. SN 200/01.

European Council (2002a) Presidency Conclusions, Seville European Council, 21–22 June 2002. SN 200/02.

European Council (2002b) Presidency Conclusions. Brussels European Council, 24–25 October 2002. 14702/02.

European Council (2002c) Presidency Conclusions. Copenhagen European Council, 12–13 December 2002. SN 400/02.

European Parliament (2000) European Parliament legislative resolution on the common position adopted by the Council with a view to the adoption of a

European Parliament and Council Directive on end-of-life vehicles. *Official Journal* C 309, 27/10/2000: 62–70.

European Parliament and Council of the European Union (2000) Directive 2000/53/EC of the European Parliament and of the Council of 18 September 2000 on End-of-Life Vehicles. *Official Journal* L 269, 21/10/2000: 34–42.

European Parliament and Council of the European Union (2001) Regulation of the European Parliament and of the Council Regarding Public Access to European Parliament, Council and Commission Documents. No. 1049/2001. 30 May 2001. *Official Journal* L 145/43.

Finnish Presidency (1999) Programme for the Finnish Presidency of the European Union. SN 2940/2/99 Rev 2.

Foreign Ministers of the European Community (1970) Report by the Foreign Ministers of the Member States on the Problems of Political Unification (Luxembourg report).

Foreign Ministers of the European Community (1973) Second Report on European Political Cooperation on Foreign Policy (Copenhagen report).

Foreign Ministers of the European Community (1981) Report on European Political Cooperation (London report).

French Presidency (2000) Priorities of the French Presidency of the European Union. Paris 2000.

German Presidency (1999) Objectives and Priorities of the German Presidency in the Council of the European Union. Internet: www.eupresidency.de/ausland/English/01/frameset.html.

Giscard d'Estaing, Valéry (1984) *Deux Français sur trios*. Paris: Flammarion.

Lipponen, Paavo (1997) The European Union Needs a Northern Dimension. Speech at the conference The Barents Region Today, Rovaniemi, 15 September 1997.

OSCE (2000) OSCE Handbook. Vienna: Secretariat of the Organization for Security and Co-operation in Europe.

OSCE (2003) Chairmanship: Tasks. Internet: www.osce.org/pc/chairmanship, accessed 23 April 2003.

OSCE Newsletter (2002) Porto Ministerial Council Sets Course for OSCE in Twenty-First Century. *OSCE Newsletter* 9(11): 1–4.

Patten, Chris (1999) A Northern Dimension for the Policies of the Union: Current and Future Activities. Speech at the Foreign Ministers' Conference on the Northern Dimension, Helsinki, 12 November 1999.

Persson, Göran (2002) Speech by Prime Minister Göran Persson at the seminar "The Future of the European Union and the Role of the Council," 25 April 2002.

Rasmussen, Anders Fogh (2003) Danish Foreign Policy after the Presidency. Speech at the Danish Institute of International Studies, 15 January 2003.

Reflection Group (1995) Reflection Group's Report. Brussels, 5 December 1995.

Swedish EU Committee (2001) Minutes from the Swedish EU Committee 2000/2001: 22, 15 March 2001.

Swedish Presidency (2001) Programme of the Swedish EU Presidency. 1 January to 30 June 2001. Stockholm: Ministry for Foreign Affairs.

Three Wise Men (1979) Report on European Institutions. Report presented by the Committee of the Three to the European Council, Brussels, October 1979.

Tindemans, Leo (1976) European Union. Report by Mr. Leo Tindemans to the European Council. Bulletin of the European Communities, Supplement 1/1976.

Vollebæk, Knut (1998) The 1999 Norwegian OSCE Chairmanship. Oslo: The Norwegian Atlantic Committee, Security Policy Library No. 10/1998.

Index